D0594272

professional dissent

public affairs and administration
editor: James S. Bowman
(vol. 2)

Garland reference library
of social science
(vol. 128)

the public affairs and administration series

James S. Bowman, editor
Florida State University

professional dissent
an annotated bibliography and resource guide

James S. Bowman
Frederick A. Elliston
Paula Lockhart

Z
7164
.C81
B763
1984

Indiana University
Library
Northwest

Garland Publishing, Inc. • New York & London
1984

© 1984 James S. Bowman
All rights reserved

Library of Congress Cataloging in Publication Data

Bowman, James S., 1945–
  Professional dissent.

  (Public affairs and administration series ; 2)
  (Garland reference library of social science, v. 128)
  Includes index.
  1. Whistle blowing—Bibliography. 2. Professional
ethics—Bibliography. I. Elliston, Frederick.
II. Lockhart, Paula. III. Title. IV. Series.
V. Series: Garland reference library of social science ;
v. 128.
Z7164.C81B763 1984 [HD60]   016.174   82-48768
ISBN 0-8240-9217-1

Cover design by Laurence Walczak

Printed on acid-free, 250-year-life paper
Manufactured in the United States of America

. . . The men who create power make an indispensable contribution to the nation's greatness, but the men who question power make a contribution just as indispensable . . . for they determine whether we use power or power uses us.

John F. Kennedy

I don't want any yesmen around me. I want people who tell me the truth even though it costs them their jobs.

Samuel Goldwyn

The large organization wants its people to be ferocious competitors outside and docile followers inside.

Anon.

contents

series foreword

The twentieth century has seen public administration come of age as a field and practice. This decade, in fact, marks the one hundredth anniversary of the profession. As a result of the dramatic growth in government, and the accompanying information explosion, many individuals—managers, academicians and their students, researchers—in organizations feel that they do not have ready access to important information. In an increasingly complex world, more and more people need published material to help solve problems.

The scope of the field and the lack of a comprehensive information system has frustrated users, disseminators, and generators of knowledge in public administration. While there have been some initiatives in recent years, the documentation and control of the literature have been generally neglected. Indeed, major gaps in the development of the literature, the bibliographic structure of the discipline, have evolved.

Garland Publishing, Inc., has inaugurated the present series as an authoritative guide to information sources in public administration. It seeks to consolidate the gains made in the growth and maturation of the profession.

The Series consists of three tiers:
1. core volumes keyed to the major subfields in public administration such as personnel management, public budgeting, and intergovernmental relations;
2. bibliographies focusing on substantive areas of administration such as community health; and
3. titles on topical issues in the profession.

Each book will be compiled by one or more specialists in the area. The authors—practitioners and scholars—are selected in open competition from across the country. They design their work to include an introductory essay, a wide variety of bibliographic materials, and, where appropriate, an information resource section. Thus each contribution in the collection provides a systematic basis for managers and researchers to make informed judgments in the course of their work. Since no single volume can adequately encompass such a broad, interdisciplinary subject, the Series is intended as a continuous project that will incorporate new bodies of literature as needed. The titles in preparation represent the initial building blocks in an operating information system for public affairs and administration. As an open-ended endeavor, it is hoped that not only will the Series serve to summarize knowledge in the field but also will contribute to its advancement.

This collection of book-length bibliographies is the product of considerable collaboration on the part of many people. Special appreciation is extended to the editors and staff of Garland Publishing, Inc., to the individual contributors in the Public Affairs and Administration Series, and to the anonymous reviewers of each of the volumes. Inquiries should be made to the Series Editor:

James S. Bowman
Tallahassee

foreword

One sign that an important new issue of social policy has arrived is that even well-informed students of the topic find they need a guide to the proliferating literature in the field. Such is the case with the topic of ethical standards and professional dissent for individuals working in organizations. From an episodic phenomenon largely linked to cycles of social policy conflict (e.g., McCarthyism in the early 50's, the anti-Vietnam war movement of the 60's), issues involving the ethical conduct of individual employees have moved today to matters of sustained importance for many employees, managers, interest groups, policymakers, the media and American society at large.

Reflecting this trend, this bibliographical guide documents the fact that "classic" whistle-blowing literature of the past few decades is now being supplemented by three main types of additional writings:

1. more richly detailed, in-depth accounts of specific incidents and their outcomes. Both "one-perspective" and "Rashomon-type" or multi-actor accounts have begun to appear recently that give readers detailed reconstructions of ethical conflict and whistle-blowing situations.

2. serious intra-disciplinary and inter-disciplinary debates, in which social and natural scientists, philosophers, lawyers, and others are beginning to construct more powerful analytical categories than generally used before, and to subject these categories to careful methodological examination.

3. descriptions of real changes taking place in organizational treatment of professional dissent, not just enactments of legal commands, or declarations of management intentions. As new social priorities generate these policies and practices, the literature of the early 80's is producing materials that

assess how meaningful those changes are in concrete situations, measured in terms of the social problem to which they are supposed to respond.

We are all in debt to Professor Bowman and his colleagues for the fine job they have done in assembling this guide. In the spirit of our television game culture, I would award them each a solid silver whistle, and the guarantee of a grant to update this work in three years when we will clearly need to have that done.

Alan F. Westin
Columbia University

to Chris and Andy

professional dissent

Section I

Introduction*

*The authors would like to express their appreciation to the
W. K. Kellogg Foundation (Bowman) and the National Science
Foundation EVIST Program (Grant No. 055-8006-553) (Elliston,
Lockhart) for assistance on this project.

The last decade was a period of time characterized not only by repeated national scandals revealing high level corruption but also by studies documenting widespread improprieties in daily management. If the list of headline allegations is long and familiar, so is the variety of questionable conduct in routine activities of the professions. The cumulative effect of disreputable incidents and dubious mundane behavior has been to erode public faith in societal institutions. Responsible commentators now believe that corruption is ubiquitous and systematic in American life, and cannot be simply dismissed as a part of "post-Watergate morality." Indeed, in an era of massively complex organizations which provide substantial opportunities and incentives for disreputable action, deviance is likely to become an increasingly vexatious social problem in the years ahead.

The point has long ago been reached when to say that there is a crisis of confidence in America is simply to repeat a well-worn cliché. Yet, there is still no certain method of channeling this concern into the social system. Given the pervasive group norms in organizations and the professions, it is perhaps surprising that the public has learned as much as it has about corruption in society. In fact it has been largely because of dissenting employees that it has come to light: Ernest A. Fitzgerald (defense cost overruns); Frank Serpico (New York City police corruption); Daniel Ellsberg (the Vietnam War); Deep Throat (Watergate); and Karen Silkwood (nuclear power). As subsequent events have shown (see below), these dramatic examples were not merely a series of isolated incidents, but instead were indicative and symbolic of problems frequently encountered in professional life and contemporary management.

It is for this reason that the issue of professional dissent is an important one. There is no morality without action; ethics cannot survive unless people speak their conscience when it really matters. If one distinguishing mark of professionals is the ability to recognize ethical problems, to act as moral custodians of the organization in which they work, it should not be unexpected that a large number of cases of protest have involved professionals. While survey evidence demonstrates that the American people have lost faith in the way the system is operated, it also shows that they have not lost confidence in the system itself. Perhaps one reason for this continued faith is that dissenting professionals--whistle-blowers--have kept the bond of trust between American institutions and the public alive.[1]

Indeed, the late 1960's and 1970's witnessed the initiation of the Age of the Whistle-blower.[2] Not only did many individuals become a national cause célèbre, but also whistle-blowing began to be institutionalized by the activities of interest groups, professional associations, and Congress. This suggests how far society has come in its quest for truth and justice in organizations.

The more sensational examples of impropriety have brought into focus latent concerns about the freedom of expression in society. People today are more receptive to these concerns than ever before as (1) organizations grow larger; (2) expectations of work rise; (3) more females, with fresh perspectives on work, enter the labor force; (4) America increasingly becomes a nation of professional employees; (5) corruption persists in bureaucracy; and (6) the mass media continue to report these issues. Alan F. Westin writes that "many observers believe that demands for new individual rights in the workplace will reach their mature status in the 1980's."[3]

Presidents, senators, professional associations, public interest groups, ethicists, and journalists all have attempted to define whistle-blowing. A useful definition was offered by Alan Campbell, Director of the Office of Personnel Management, during the 1980 Congressional oversight hearings on the subject:

> Quite simply, I view whistle-blowing as a popular shorthand label for any disclosure of a legal violation, mismanagement, a gross waste of funds, an abuse of authority, or a danger to public health or safety, whether the disclosure is made within or outside the chain of command.[4]

Thus, a whistle-blower is an employee who reveals information about illegal, inefficient, or wasteful action that endangers the health, safety, or freedom of the public.

There are at least two significant societal issues related to whistle-blowing. The first is responsibility and accountability in a democratic society. In light of pervasive citizen distrust of social institutions, this is hardly an academic problem. Ways need to be found to introduce democratic rights into private and public bureaucracies. The second issue is fair practices: in order to assure responsibility and accountability, due process procedures are necessary to protect employees who care about the general interest. Effective methods need to be discovered to balance an individual's duty to their employer with their duty to the public. In fact, "many of the rights and privileges ...so important to a free society that they are constitutionally protected...are vulnerable to abuse through an employer's power."[5] The people have a right, in a word, to learn about significant problems in American society without having those who expose them destroy their careers in the process.

It is critical that the "I win, you lose," zero-sum approach to dissent in organizations change. Responsible protest should be treated fairly to the benefit of both the employee and the employer. Directing corrective efforts to dissenters themselves instead of the policy or practice they protest will not alter the conditions that make whistleblowing necessary. Disclosure of waste, illegal activity, and abuse of power should be seen as a commitment to make business and government more worthy of public trust. Open discussion strengthens, not weakens, a democratic society. Despite the attention that dissent in organizations has received in recent years, whistle-blowing alone will never establish standards of public accountability and credibility that the citizenry deserves and expects. Yet, if the measures discussed by the authors in this compilation were instituted, blowing the whistle would be less necessary than it is today.

The body of literature on professional dissent prior to the turn of the last decade is relatively small. Although dissent at the workplace is as old as humankind, it has only recently crystallized into a movement comparable in content, if not scope, to earlier civil rights and liberation movements.[6] Accordingly, numerous analysts have begun to explore the historical, economic, political, scientific, legal, and philosophical facets of the subject, as this volume testifies.

As might be anticipated, this literature varies from sensational cases histories and emotional polemics to scholarly analyses and legal reports. Therefore, basic works, particularly useful in beginning an inquiry into the subject, have been identified by asterisks (*) in appropriate places in the sections of this volume.

Following the introduction, Sections II and III contain books and articles on dissent and corruption based on place of employment: business and government. The next two sections focus on these issues in specific professions. Since many problems in professional dissent are most sharply posed in science and engineering, these fields are explored in Section IV. Section V records parallel concerns in law and other selected professions. Given the fact that many professionals work in a variety of organizational settings during their careers, the citations in these four sections are cross-referenced.

Important contextual literature providing relevant background information appears in Sections VI and VII, which examine philosophical and theoretical materials. Newspapers and magazine articles on professional dissent are compiled in Section VIII.

Section IX consists of Congressional documents, court cases and legal analyses, and employee protection sections of state and federal laws. Reference sources--a bibliography of bibliographies and a listing of journals, periodical guides, directories, and audio-visual resources--comprise Sections X and XI. The penultimate section contains personal guidance books and articles as well as individual accounts by or about whistle-blowers. The volume concludes with a list of key organizations, their addresses, and telephone numbers. Included are telephone "hotlines" established by major federal agencies that may be used by employees and private citizens to report waste, mismanagement, and fraud.

Throughout this guide to the literature, citations and entries are listed in alphabetical order. This reference work, like nearly all others, does not pretend to be exhaustive. It does offer, however, a comprehensive indication of the types of information available to the student, scholar, professional, and employees and managers concerned about dissent in organizations.

* * *

Compiling a thorough bibliography is never an easy task. While this volume is no exception, it benefited from an uncommon form of teamwork that deserves a brief comment. The genesis of the project was a bibliography and resource guide prepared by the first author in early 1980 for the annual meeting of the American Society for Public Administration. It focused on whistle-blowing in business and government in addition to reference material relevant to organizational and government ethics.

In the process of expanding this effort for publication in book form, he had the good fortune to learn that Frederick Elliston (then located in Albany, New York) was engaged in a comparable project. Dr. Elliston not only had ready access to excellent research facilities and secretarial services, but also to professional colleagues in related fields, including Albert Flores and Deborah Johnson of Rensselear Polytechnic Institute. For the next two years, the New York team and the series editor compiled, reviewed, and edited all entries, and completely reconstructed the initial work to bring it up to the end of 1982.

At least two features of this working relationship appear noteworthy. First, the collective effort was accomplished through a unique and genuine collaboration between professionals, friends and family. We are particularly indebted to Jane and Kate Van Schaick of the Criminal Justice Research Center in Albany, New York for their bibliographic assistance, and to Deborah and David Elliston for their typing and editorial help. Second, most of the work was performed without a face to face meeting with collaborators. Despite (or perhaps because of) this, we are exceptionally pleased to present this reference tool to its users.

Notes

1. The seemingly frivolous nature of the term "whistle-blower" is recognized but not necessarily regretted, as it has become fully imbedded in the popular culture and professional literature. The etymology of the word is discussed in William Safire, Safire's Political Dictionary (3rd ed.; New York: Random House, 1978), p. 790.

   The authors share the view that the flippant connotation of whistle-blowing is useful since it avoids an association with treason. See Lea P. Stewart, "'Whistle Blowing': Implications for Organizational Communication," Journal of Communication, 80 (Autumn 1980), p. 90.

2. The best known case of blowing the whistle was Department of Defense employee Ernest A. Fitzgerald's 1968 testimony before Congress that revealed cost overruns on the C-5A military air transport. However, two earlier

incidents in contemporary history may also be noted. In 1965, State Department Analyst Otto Otepka gave documents to Congress claiming that the Kennedy administration harbored communists. James Boyd, a legislative aide to Senator Thomas Dodd, revealed unethical use of campaign monies in 1966.

3. "Introduction." Alan F. Westin and Stephan Salisbury, Individual Rights in Corporations (New York: Pantheon Books, 1980), p. xi.

4. U.S. Congress, House of Representatives, Committee on Post Office and Civil Service. Civil Service Reform Oversight 1980--Whistleblower. 96th Cong., 2nd Sess., 1980, pp. 196-197.

5. Lawrence Blades, "Employment at Will vs. Individual Freedom: On Limiting the Abusive Exercise of Employer Power," Columbia Law Review, 67 (December 1967), p. 1407.

6. For a comparison of the arguments surrounding the two movements, see Frederick Elliston, "Civil Disobedience and Whistleblowing: A Comparative Appraisal of Two Forms of Dissent," Journal of Business Ethics, 1 (Spring 1982), 23-28.

Section II

Business

A. Whistle-Blowing and Dissent

1. "Armor for Whistle-blowers." _Business Week_, 6 July 1981, pp. 97-98.

    Reports that whistle-blowing is gaining firm legal ground and predicts it will become more common. Several state Supreme Courts have ruled that employees can recover damages if fired for refusing to break a law. Discusses the recent Michigan "Whistleblowers' Protection Act" which makes it illegal to dismiss, threaten, or discriminate against employees because they report a violation of law or regulation.

2. "As I See It: To Tell or Not to Tell." _Forbes_, 1 February 1976, pp. 41-43.

    A discussion between David James, a partner of Arthur Young and Company, and Securities and Exchange Commission chief accountant, John Burton, about the crackdown on companies for failing to tell stockholders about payments to foreign governments. James explains the problems the new morality poses for accountants, and Burton offers a rebuttal.

3. Beauchamp, Tom L. and Norman E. Bowie, eds. _Ethical Theory and Business_. Englewood Cliffs, NJ: Prentice-Hall, 1979. See item 729.

4. Blades, Lawrence. "Employment at Will vs. Individual Freedom: On Limiting the Abusive Exercise of Employer Power." _Columbia Law Review_, 67 (December 1967), 1404-1435. See item 1226.

5. Blumberg, Phillip I. "Commentary on 'Professional Freedom and Responsibility: The Role of the Professional Society.'" _Newsletter on Science, Technology, and Human Values_, No. 22 (January 1978), 43-46.

6. Blumberg, Phillip I. "Corporate Responsibility and the Employee's Duty of Loyalty and Obedience: A Preliminary Inquiry." _Oklahoma Law Review_, 24 (August 1971), 279-318. See item 1227.

7. Bogen, Kenneth T. "Managing Technical Dissent in Private Industry: Societal and Corporate Strategies for Dealing with the Whistle-blowing Professional." _Industrial and Labor Relations Forum_, 13 (1979), 3-32. See item 448.

8. "Britain: Dividends From Blowing the Whistle on Oil-gate." Business Week, 23 October 1978, p. 64.

   Discusses Roland W. "Tiny" Rowland, Deep Throat of Britain's OILGATE scandal, who blew the whistle on British Petroleum, Shell and other companies for illegal sales to Rhodesia.

9. "Can Your Employees 'Blow the Whistle' on Internal Wrongdoing?" ABA Banking Journal, 72 (November 1980), 26.

   Discusses the Bank of America's program which allows employees to call or write an administrative unit to comment on work-related matters. All communications are handled in confidence. Citibank has established a mechanism for the internal disclosure and investigation of allegations of questionable practices.

10. Clutterbuck, David. "Blowing the Whistle on Corporate Misconduct." International Management, 35 (January 1980), 14-18.

   Analyzes cases and suggests organizational mechanisms to prevent whistle-blowing such as internal ombudsmen and open door policies. Employee complaints are seen as beneficial because they provide an opportunity to correct problems.

11. Cook, Daniel D. "Whistle-Blowers--Friend or Foe." Industry Week, 5 October 1981, pp. 50-54, 56.

   After many efforts to make Ford Motor Company officials aware of an alleged safety problem with the Pinto, a Ford employee "blew the whistle." Recent court rulings and a Michigan law are beginning to support such actions which could force corporations to address internal allegations of wrongdoing in a more straight-forward manner.

12. Donaldson, Thomas, "Employee Rights." Corporations and Morality. Englewood Cliffs, NJ: Prentice-Hall, 1981, Chapter Seven, pp. 129-157. See item 709.

13. Ewing, David W. "The Employee's Right to Speak Out: The Management Perspective." Civil Liberties Review, 5 (September/October 1978), 10-15.

Discusses cases where employees spoke out against their firms and were suppressed for it. In doing so, however, the companies failed in their efforts to silence the employee, resulting in both lost money and reputation.

14. Ewing, David W. "Employees' Rights." Society, 15 (November/December 1977), 104-111.

After arguing that management fears freedom of speech as a threat to the hierarchy of power, the status of employee speech in the United States is described. While the lack of rights continues to be the rule, exceptions and in-roads are occurring in the area of employee privacy. Ewing presents guidelines to balance employee interests and employer needs.

15. Ewing, David. "What Business Thinks About Employee Rights." Harvard Business Review, 77 (September/October 1977), 81-93.

A survey of subscribers shows that (a) most support wider employee rights, including whistle-blowing; (b) many think the emphasis on individual rights may pose a threat to business stability; and (c) the stereotype of the business executive as conservative and oppressive is inaccurate.

16. Fernandez, Joseph A. "Employee Rights: Radical Propaganda or Reality?" ABA Banking Journal, 73 (September 1981), 152-158.

Argues that banks must come to grips with such emerging employee rights as privacy, freedom to dissent, and job security. The employment-at-will doctrine is slowly being worn away. There are four rights that employees should enjoy: (1) privacy, (2) dissent and expression, (3) whistleblowing, and (4) due process.

17. Hacker, Andrew. "Loyalty and the Whistle Blower." Across the Board, 15 (November 1979), 4-9, 67.

Suggests sociological reasons why loyalty to organization had been considered so important. Then describes several cases of whistle-blowing, indicating a dilution of loyalties of employees. Concludes by speculating on the effect of lessened loyalty.

18. "The High Cost of Whistling." *Newsweek*, 14 February 1977, pp. 75-77.

19. Hirschman, Albert L. *Exit, Voice, and Loyalty*. Cambridge: Harvard University Press, 1970.

   Organizations provide only to viable options for those who disagree with official policy: exit (leaving the organization) or loyalty (remaining quietly with the organization). Hirschman suggests that organizations would be substantially improved by providing a "voice" option so that people could express their concerns in a constructive manner. Also see his "Exit, Voice, and Loyalty: Further Reflections and a Survey of Recent Contributions," *Social Science Information*, 13, 1 (1974), 7-26.

20. von Hoffman, Nicholas. "Alone at High Noon." *Nation*, 27 December 1980, pp. 709-710.

   Review of Alan Westin's *Whistle-Blowing!* (item 1392) that is skeptical of his juridico-administrative solutions as not cost-beneficial. Instead, von Hoffman recommends rejuvenated labor unions, consumer co-ops, and other mass-based voluntary organizations as more direct and effective.

21. Ingram, Timothy M. "On Muckrackers and Whistle Blowers." *Business and Society Review*, 1 (August 1972), 21-30.

   Describes and illustrates both whistle-blowers and in-house critics or muckrakers who expose company information via employee underground newspapers. Muckrackers are seen as internal agents of change while whistle-blowers are seen as external forces to alter organizations.

22. Jackson, Dudley. *Unfair Dismissal*. London and New York: Cambridge University Press, 1975. See item 1240.

23. Jacobs, Bruce A. "Blowing the Whistle on Company Misdeeds." *Industry Week*, 31 March 1980, pp. 23-24.

   In 1979, 28 top executives were convicted or implicated in corporate crime; most were reinstated. Jacobs focuses on proposed American Bar Association code of ethics revision and the role of corporate attorneys in business.

24. Johnson, Douglas A. and Kurt Pany. "Exposed or Covered Up: Will An Employee Blow the Whistle?" Management Accounting, 63 (July 1981), 32-36.

Study conducted to determine the impact of procedures available for reporting corporate irregularities and methods for dealing with suspected or known misconduct and offenders. Forty-five auditors were surveyed to analyze a set of cases describing an irregularity. Results showed that the probability of reporting embezzlement and conflict-of-interest is higher than the probability of reporting a bribe.

25. Kenny, T. P. "The Asbestos Situation or Whose Safety First?" Journal of the Institute of Personnel Management, 58 (June 1976), 46.

Examines the dilemma that personnel managers faced in the years after 1931 (the year in which asbestos legislation was first enacted) concerning the hazards of working with asbestos. Kenny explains why no one spoke out on the possible dangers and proposes that a professional code of behavior may have aided the personnel managers.

26. McAdams, Tony. "Dismissal: A Decline in Employer Autonomy?" Business Horizons, 21 (February 1978), 67-72.

Analyzes three recent cases which suggest that courts are "cautiously building a list of conditions under which [business] employees may not be lawfully discharged" (p. 72).

27. Miller, Richard A. "Price Fixing and Whistleblowing: A 'Bounty' for a Mutiny on the Good Ship Co-lusion (sic)." Antitrust Law and Economics Review, 10 (1978), 87-96.

Suggest a bounty for violations of antitrust laws. A percent of the violator's fine would go to the whistle-blower.

28. Mitchell, Greg. Truth...And Consequences: Seven Who Would Not Be Silenced. New York: Dembner Books, 1982. See item 1381.

29. Molander, Earl A. "Case Five: Whistle Blowing at the Trojan Nuclear Plant." Responsive Capitalism: Case Studies in Corporate Social Conduct. New York: McGraw-Hill, 1980, pp. 51-55.

30. Nader, Ralph, Peter J. Petkas, and Kate Blackwell, eds. Whistle-Blowing: The Report of the Conference on Professional Responsibility. New York: Grossman, 1972. See item 1382.

31. Raven-Hansen, Peter. "Dos and Don'ts for Whistle-blowers: Planning for Trouble." Technology Review, 82 (May 1980), 34-44. See item 470.

32. Reeves, Richard. "The Last Angry Men." Esquire, 1 March 1978, pp. 41-48.

     A review of whistle-blowers in business and government who stood up against the system, their reasons, and the results.

33. Robbins, Albert. "Dissent in the Corporate World: When Does an Employee Have the Right to Speak Out?" Civil Liberties Review, 5 (September/October 1978), 6-10, 15-17.

     Provides a special report in this issue of the Review which discusses current trends and the First National Seminar on Individual Rights in the Corporation.

34. Sheler, Jeffrey L. "When Employees Squeal on Fellow Workers." U.S. News and World Report, 16 November 1981, p. 81.

     Discusses the fact that some employees risk dismissal for reporting real or imagined abuses by fellow workers. Employers claim good reasons for dealing harshly with their whistle-blowers, especially when complaints are taken outside the workplace to the media. Many states have banned retaliatory firings, but employers have contested such laws in court as unwarranted government interference.

35. Solomon, Lewis and Terry Garcia. "Protecting the Corporate Whistle Blower Under Federal Anti-Retaliation Statutes." The Journal of Corporation Law, 5 (Winter 1980), 275-297. See item 1251.

36. Stanley, John D. "Dissent in Organizations." Academy of Management Review, 6 (January 1981), 13-19.

  "Dissent in organizations is not always tolerated and is rarely encouraged. Lack of dissent can lead to managerial miscalculations and major strategic and tactical errors . . . [Examines] the use of countervailing views in religious, government, and business organizations, and across cultural lines, as a means of improving decision making" (p. 13).

37. Stevens, George E. "The Legality of Discharging Employees for Insubordination." American Business Law Journal, 18 (Fall 1980), 371-389. See item 1252.

38. Stewart, Lea P. "'Whistle Blowing': Implications for Organizational Communication." Journal of Communication, 80 (Autumn 1980), 90-101. See item 834.

*39. Summers, Clyde W. "Protecting All Employees Against Unjust Dismissal." Harvard Business Review, 58 (January-February 1980), 132-139.

  A shortened version of Summers' article "Individual Protection Against Unjust Dismissal: Time for a Statute" (see item 40). Some 70 percent of the work force in the private sector has no contractual protection from arbitrary or unjust discharge; common law permits an employer to fire an employee "at will." Summers argues that a system similar to that set up through union agreements should be put into law. The body of law created through arbitration under collective agreements has demonstrated the feasibility and benefits of such legislation.

40. Summers, Clyde W. "Individual Protection Against Unjust Dismissal: Time for a Statute." Virginia Law Review, 62 (April 1976), 481-532. See item 1254.

41. Thackray, John. "The Corporate Individual." Management Today, November 1980, 74-77.

According to many, the issue of employee rights will
be central to corporate management in the 1980's,
since a significant number of employees view actions
entered into by their companies as threatening their
rights. Attention is being focused on such issues as
privacy of employee records, sexual harassment on the
job, and protection for "whistle-blowers."

42. Treatster, Joseph. "The Hushing of America." Gal-
    lery, August 1979, 40-43, 100-104.

    Whistle-blowers are seen as earnest, conscientious,
    dedicated, traditional, politically inept and middle-
    of-the-road people with strong principles who do not
    seek publicity. Discusses dissenters and describes
    the organizations that support them.

43. Vogel, A. "Why Don't Employees Speak Up?" Personnel
    Administration, 30 (1967), 18-24.

44. Wade, Nicholas. "Protection Sought for Satirists and
    Whistle Blowers." Science, 7 December 1973, pp.
    1002-1003.

*45. Walters, Kenneth D. "Your Employees' Right to Blow
     the Whistle." Harvard Business Review, 53
     (July/August 1975), 26-34, 161-162.

    Examines the growing legal support of whistleblo-
    wers in organizations as shown by recent court cases.
    Walters considers four factors in deciding if whistle-
    blowers should be protected against sanctions: their
    motive, the availability and use of internal channels,
    organizational friction, and individual discretion.
    He emphasizes the importance of individuals' carefully
    weighing all factors in each case. Collective action,
    employee rights and regulatory provisions are legal
    trends which may legitimize whistleblowing. Walters
    concludes with some recommendations: insure employee's
    free speech rights, improve grievance procedures, exa-
    mine concepts of social responsibility, respect employ-
    ee's conscience, and recognize the adverse public re-
    action to dealing harshly with dissenters.

*46. Waters, James A. "Catch 20.5: Corporate Morality as
     an Organizational Phenomenon." Organizational
     Dynamics, 6 (Spring 1978), 3-19.

An account of the unintended consequences of effective organizational operation and control systems which can block whistle-blowing. Waters identifies seven barriers: socialization, task group cohesiveness, chain of command, ambiguity in goals and priorities, separation of decisions, division of work, and protection from outside intervention. He goes on to identify questions useful in locating potentially illegal or unethical behavior and to outline programs to promote ethical standards.

47. Weinstein, Deena. "Opposition to Abuse Within Organizations: Heroism and Legalism." ALSA Forum, 4 (Fall 1979), 5-21. See item 294.

48. Weinstein, Deena. "Bureaucratic Opposition: The Challenge to Authoritarian Abuses at the Workplace." Canadian Journal of Political and Social Theory, 1 (Spring/Summer 1977), 31-46. Also see item 294.

*49. Westin, Alan F. and Stephan Salisbury, eds. Individual Rights in the Corporation: A Reader on Employee Rights. New York: Pantheon Books, 1980.

A collection on the potential extension of the Bill of Rights to corporate employment. Over fifty contributions deal with topics such as liberty and work, limiting employer prerogatives, the debate over an employee Bill of Rights, freedom of expression on the job, privacy in the workplace, and the rights of fair procedure and participation. Westin's Introduction outlines current trends and argues that demands for new individual rights in corporations will reach their mature status in the 1980's.

50. "The Whistleblowers." Time, 17 April 1972, pp. 85-86.

Takes organizations as political rather than rational systems, and appraises two opposition strategies: (1) informing, which naively assumes common goals, higher level administrators or lateral and external organizations; and (2) direct action such as withholding information and slow downs. Warns of administrative reprisals with limited protections.

51. "Whistle Blowing: The Role of Management." Effective Manager, 4 (February 1981), 1-3.

A variety of laws, such as the equal employment opportunity legislation and occupational safety and health statutes, contain provisions prohibiting retributive action against employees who blow the whistle. The courts have not yet made whistle-blowers completely safe, but they will do so if employers do not formulate their own in-house policies. Argues that monetary awards should be given to dissenters.

Section II

Business

B. Ethics, Corruption, and Social Responsibility

52. Abbott, Walter F. and R. Joseph Monsen. "Measurement of Corporate Social Responsibility: Self Reported Disclosures as a Method of Measuring Corporate Social Involvement." Academy of Management Journal, 22 (September 1979), 501-515.

Develops a corporate social involvement disclosure scale based on a content analysis of the annual reports of the Fortune 500 companies. Abbott discovers: (1) the change over time of the social involvement of these corporations; (2) the direction and scope of their activity; and (3) the effect that corporate social involvement has on profitability.

53. Abouzeid, Kamal M. and Charles N. Weaver. "Social Responsibility in the Corporate Goal Hierarchy." Business Horizons, 21 (June 1978), 29-35.

Despite the increasing emphasis in recent years on the social responsibility of business, this study shows that financial goals remain the primary objective of corporate enterprise.

54. Ackerman, Robert and Raymond Bauer. Corporate Social Responsiveness. Reston, VA: Reston Publishing, 1976.

Treats corporate responsiveness as a management issue rather than a social or ethical problem. The authors discuss how to assess organizational performance empirically; the roles of staff and line officers in handling social issues; and the stages in implementing social policies. Twenty-nine cases are integrated within the seven chapters to illustrate the main points.

55. Adams, Randolph K. An Analysis of Existing Ethical Guidelines and the Development of a Proposed Code of Ethics for Managers. Springfield, VA: National Technical Information Service, 1976.

A thorough investigation of codes based on a mail questionnaire of business, government and professional organizations. Author develops a universal code of conduct for managers.

56. Allen, Fred T. "Corporate Morality: Executive Responsibility." Atlanta Economic Review, 26 (May/June 1976), 8-11.

Calls upon chief executives to set and enforce corporate moral and ethical standards. Allen asserts
that no price is too high because in the long run
there is no alternative to ethical business behavior.

57. Allen, Robert F. "The IK in the Office."
    Organizational Dynamics, 8 (Winter 1980), 26-41.

    Draws an unattractive analogy between the behavior
    of many individuals in organization and that of mem-
    bers of the IK, a tribe in Africa who exhibit a loss
    of humanity as a result of their desperate struggle
    for survival. The analogy is supported by a survey in-
    dicating that people feel organizations tend to encour-
    age their members to behave unethically, dishonestly
    and inhumanely. Alen suggests strategies for change.

58. Alpern, Kenneth. "Moral Dimensions of the Foreign
    Corrupt Practices Act: Comments on Hooker and
    Pastin." Presented at Conference on Business and
    Professional Ethics, 15 May 1981, University of
    Illinois at Chicago Circle. Mimeographed.

    Examines the Foreign Corrupt Practices Act using the
    rule-based or deontological arguments suggested by Pas-
    tin and Hooker. Alpern concludes that FCPA is indeed
    supported by morality.

59. Anshen, Melvin, ed. Managing the Socially Respon-
    sible Corporation. New York: Macmillan, 1974.

    An anthology examining different aspects of the no-
    tion "socially responsible organization." Includes
    several conceptual pieces stressing the need and the
    profit in socially responsible behavior, followed by
    chapters on the social audit in corporations and on
    specialized social responsibilities.

60. Bacot, Eugene. "All's Fair?" Business Admini-
    stration, 3 December 1970, 15-19.

    Surveys reveal that business people want guidance in
    dealing with ethical dilemmas. Data are discussed and
    a code of ethics is presented.

61. Barry, Vincent. Moral Issues in Business. 2nd Ed-
    ition. Belmont, CA: Wadsworth, 1983.

A textbook for business ethics courses, each chapter of which considers a set of business issues such as economic justice, personnel actions, ecology, consumer relations, industrialization, employee responsibilities, and the environment. Short readings are provided at the end of each chapter.

62. Baumhart, Raymond. An Honest Profit: What Businessmen Say About Ethics in Business. London: Holt, Rinehart, and Winston, 1968.

A classic work that points out the influence of the businessperson in modern society and considers its ethical implications. Baumhart undertakes an empirical study with data compiled from research projects involving over 1800 executives. Most respondents believe that good ethics is good business in the long run. The author identifies three significant trends: (1) progress in knowledge about business behavior and the application of ethical principles to industrial situations; (2) clear signs of increased interest in ethics; and (3) a gradual improvement in managerial behavior.

63. Bauniol, William, Rensis Likert, Henry C. Wallach, and John J. McGorvan. A New Rationale for Corporate Social Policy. Lexington, MA: Lexington Books, 1970.

Three essays on corporate responsibility and social policy, written for the Committee on Economic Development, which reflect different approaches to developing a rationale for a "defense of corporate social involvement." The authors cover notions of "public goods", the corporate role in their production, and corporate views on therapy, human resource accounting, and the changing interest of stockholders in corporate social activity.

64. Behrman, Jack N. Discourses on Ethics and Business. Cambridge, MA: Oelgeschlager, Gunn, and Hain, 1981.

An examination of social changes affecting business in society and the fundamental ethical content of commercial activity. See especially the chapters entitled "Truth, Information, Disclosure, and the Right to Lie" and "Codes of Conduct."

65. Berg, Ivar. "Employee Discontent in a Business Society." Society, 14 (March/April 1977), 51-56.

Presents a model for understanding management options in relation to worker dissatisfaction. Also discusses the reasons why managers, who have the capacity to influence workers and hence their efficiency, do not avail themselves of these opportunities.

66. Berenbeim, Ronald. Nonunion Complaint Systems: A Corporate Appraisal. New York: The Conference Board, 1980.

Survey results reveal that (1) employee complaints are widespread; (2) most executives have found complaint systems to be successful; and (3) employee use of these systems is not widespread and is almost nonexistent in some companies.

67. Bequai, August. White Collar Crime: A 20th Century Crisis. Lexington, MA: Lexington Books, 1978.

Although white-collar crime costs society more than $40 billion annually, this entire area of criminal activity has been neglected. Bequai defines white-collar crime, giving specific examples, and deals with the problems of investigation and prosecution. He closes with speculations on future developments and the changing dimensions of crime as a result of technological innovation.

68. Blumenthal, William M. "Business Ethics: A Call for a Moral Approach." Financial Executive, 44 (January 1976), 32-34.

Proposes the formation of an organization that will promote business responsibility. Such an organization would establish benchmarks for the determination of what is right or wrong. These in turn may become a basis for public confidence in private enterprise. Blumenthal suggests that business take seriously criticisms of its integrity and he proposes a moral approach to ethical and social responsibility.

69. Boling, T. Edwin. "Organizational Ethics: Rules, Creativity and Idealism." Management Handbook for Public Administration. John W. Sutherland. New York: Van Nostrand Reinhold Co., 1978, chapter three, pp. 221-253.

    A thorough exploration of ethical dilemmas that individuals face as members of organizations. Boling offers useful background material for understanding the context within which whistle-blowing occurs.

70. Boling, T. Edwin. "The Management Ethics Crisis: An Organizational Perspective." Academy of Management Review, 3 (April 1978), 360-365.

    Discusses the conflict between the classical business ideology and managerial ideology, suggesting that the cause may be the inadequacy of old ethical systems. Boling offers theoretical and practical suggestions for solving management's ethical dilemma. Noting that business has an ethical lag, he identifies three principles designed to overcome it: (1) organizations must establish ethical premises; (2) individual moral judgments should reflect the norms of social groups; and (3) moral action should be a matter of cooperative social relations. Boling concludes by stressing that cooperative codes of ethics will serve as vehicles for shaping organizational morality.

71. Bowman, James S. "The Management of Ethics: Codes of Conduct in Organizations." Public Personnel Management, 10 (1981), 59-66.

    Discusses the role of the individual and the organization in the management of ethics. Codes of ethics are analyzed by reporting the attitudes and actions of managers in business and government.

72. Bowman, James S. "Managerial Ethics in Business and Government." Business Horizons, 19 (October 1976), 48-54.

    Survey data reveal that business people and government officials are very concerned about management ethics, and are ready to translate that concern into action.

73. Bradshaw, Thornton and David Vogel, eds. Corporations and their Critics: Issues and Answers to

Problems of Corporate Social Responsibility. New York: McGraw-Hill, 1981, part IV.

Five essays explore the organizational implications of corporate responsibility.

74. Brenner, Steven N. and Earl A. Molander. "Is the Ethics of Business Changing?" Harvard Business Review, 55 (January/February 1977), 57-71.

A comparison of the opinions of executives today to those of 15 years ago suggests that business principles now are higher than before. Highlights areas such as common dilemmas, accepted practices, economic pressures, societal forces, cynicism, guidelines and codes, and social responsibility.

75. Burck, Gilbert. "Hazards of Corporate Responsibility." Fortune, 87 (June 1973), 114.

Argues that corporate executives are being held responsible for activities "beyond business." Burck defends the thesis that private enterprise would provide more benefits to the community if it concerned itself solely with business.

76. Carmichael, D. R. "Corporate Accountability and Illegal Acts." Journal of Accountancy, 143 (January 1977), 77-81.

77. Carney, Thomas, False Profits. Notre Dame, IN: University of Notre Dame Press, 1982.

Contends that government over-regulation and management emphasis on quick profits have stifled the imagination, entrepreneurship and inventiveness of American technologists. Carney offers proposals for cooperation between industry and academic research, including that government establish a venture capital company to provide money for independent inventors.

78. Carroll, Archie B. "Business Ethics and the Management Hierarchy." National Forum, 58 (Summer 19-78), 37-40.

Argues that ethical or unethical conduct in business is mostly influenced by the superior-subordinate relationship, rather than by standards external to the organization. Carroll cites data from several corporations suggesting that the pressures to compromise personal standards are mostly felt in subordinate positions and that top executives may exert pressure for unethical conduct without realizing it. He offers three steps by which top executives may reduce some of these pressures.

79. Carroll, Archie B. "Linking Ethics to Behavior in Organizations." Advanced Management Journal, 43 (Summer 1978), 4-11.

Offers a conceptual framework and some strategies for administrators to improve organizational behavior.

80. Carroll, Archie B. "Managerial Ethics: A Post Watergate View." Business Horizons, 18 (April 1975), 75-80.

A poll shows that executives may not know that subordinates commit unethical acts out of loyalty to the organization. Carroll discusses the results of questions on current issues in business and social responsibility.

81. Chamberlain, Neil W. The Limits of Corporate Responsibility. New York: Basic Books, 1973.

Explores the corporation's role in ameliorating social problems. Chamberlain views the business-society interface in light of changing social environments, and discusses the constraints placed from within and without on corporate social responsibility. He describes the many relationships of corporations to society and outlines the limits of corporate responsibility.

82. Chatov, Robert. "What Corporate Ethics Statements Say." California Management Review, 22 (Summer 1980), 20-29.

83. Churchill, Neil C. and Arthur B. Toan. "Reporting on Corporate Social Responsibility: Progress Report." Journal of Contemporary Business, 7 (Winter 1978), 5-17

Examines the status of corporate social measurement and reporting today, and makes projections about the nature and degree of corporate accountability in the future.

84. Clausen, A. W. "Voluntary Disclosure: Someone Has to Jump Into the Icy Water First." Arthur Anderson Chronicle, 36 (April 1976), 4-12.

   The president of the Bank of America discusses the importance of ethical codes for corporations, noting the massive erosion of public confidence in the integrity of business. He argues that corporate enterprise must go beyond a code of conduct, and proposes developing a model voluntary disclosure code such as the one under study by the Bank of America.

85. Clinard, Marshall B., et al. Illegal Corporate Behavior. Washington, DC: National Institute of Law Enforcement and Criminal Justice, 1979.

   An examination of corporate crime, enforcement actions, predictions of violations, criminal liability of executives, and methods of control. The authors find that "approximately two-thirds of large corporations violated the law, some of them many times" (p. xxv).

86. Conard, Alfred F. "Response: The Meaning of Corporate Responsibilities: Variations on a Theme of Edwin M. Epstein." Hastings Law Journal, 30 (May 1975), 1329-1352.

   Takes Epstein's comprehensive analysis of corporate responsibility one step further and examines what the term means to those who use it. Conrad offers four interpretations or levels of corporate responsibility and concludes that, although raising corporate consciousness may aid in balancing investors' interests against other interests, it cannot be expected to solve problems associated with personnel, pollution and prices. This limitation is evident in industries where the gap between the current situation and the ideal is large.

87. Cooper, Michael R., et al. "Changing Employee Values: Deepening Discontent." Harvard Business Review, 57 (January-February 1979), 117-125.

   Survey data over a 25-year period confirm speculation that employees are discontent and that they expect more from their work than in the past. "Most worrisome . . ., however, is that these trends are continuing and that the gap in satisfaction between managers and hourly employees is growing" (p. 117). The demands of the 60's for self expression and personal growth are just beginning to be voiced in industry. Corporations must adjust to the new realities.

88. Cooper, Terry L. "Ethics, Values and Systems." Journal of Systems Management, 30 (September 1979), 6-12 (see item 740).

89. D'Aprix, Roger M. In Search of a Corporate Soul, New York: AMACOM, 1976.

Develops three theses: (1) organizations have not kept pace with changing attitudes and values; (2) organizations must become more in tune with society; and (3) change will only be accomplished from within. Corporations need a new reward system, matched to contemporary values, that gives individuals who are agents of change guidelines to humanize organizations.

90. Dagher, Samir P. and Peter H. Spader. "Poll of Top Managers Stresses Education and Leadership by Example as Strong Forces for Higher Standards." Management Review, 69 (March 1980), 54-57.

This survey demonstrates that executives are interested in ethics, and see education and enforceable codes of conduct as ways to improve business morality.

91. Dam, Cees Van and Lund M. Stallaert, eds. Trends in Business Ethics. Kluwer, Holland: Nijhoff Social Sciences Division, 1978.

Essays on corporate decision-making and social responsibility.

92. Davis, Keith and Robert L. Blomstrom. Business and Society: Environment and Responsibility. New York: McGraw-Hill, 1975.

Offers a system's approach to relate business to ecology, pluralism, and social power. This text is designed for college students or business managers in the hope that they will better understand the social role and the relationships of business to the public, the community, and the international world. The concluding section provides nine cases as a medium for testing and applying ideas and issues discussed in the book.

93. DeGeorge, Richard T. and Joseph A. Pichler, eds. Ethics, Free Enterprise, and Public Policy. New York: Oxford University Press, 1978. See item 741.

94. Dierkes, M. and R. A. Bauer eds. Corporate Social Accounting. New York: Praeger, 1973.

A collection of original papers concerned with various aspects of corporate responsiveness, and the accounting of their social and societal (rather than internal and economic) resources and expenditures. A useful reference for scholars concerned with problems in making corporations attentive to the social good and to a social rather than an economic ethic.

95. Donaldson, John and Mike Waller. "Ethics and Organization." Journal of Management Studies, 17 (February 1980), 34-55.

A review, written for managers that considers the paucity of ethical arguments and observance of codes in industry. The authors present arguments for the Golden Rule as the ethical criterion for moral evaluation of behavior in organizations. Particularly relevant is the explanation of why management theory, while ethical in its implications, is always stated in prudential terms, and why moral behavior is infrequently found in non-democratic organizations.

96. Donaldson, Thomas and Patricia H. Werhand, eds. Ethical Issues in Business: A Philosophical Approach. Englewood Cliffs, N.J.: Prentice-Hall, 1979. See item 743.

97. Donaldson, Thomas. "Ethics in the Business Schools: A Proposal." National Forum, 58, (Summer 1978), 11-14.

Argues that a course in applied ethical reasoning should be part of the education of business students. Donaldson believes the omission of ethics courses may constitute an overt invitation to omit the consideration of ethical issues in the context of business. Without such courses, the risk increases that our economic system will not remain healthy.

98. Edelhertz, Herbert and Charles Rogorin, eds. A National Strategy for Containing White Collar Crime. Lexington, MA: Lexington Books, 1980.

Suggests new legislation and alternative law enforcement procedures to control the growing rate of middle-class crime.

99. Elliot, Robert K. and John J. Willingham. Management Fraud: Detection and Deterrence. Princeton, N.J.: Petrocelli Books, 1980.

Contains a general assessment of management fraud and the auditing profession's deterrence role, followed by nine contributions on selected issues from a symposium.

100. Ellin, Joseph, Michael S. Pritchard, and Wade L. Robinson, eds. Ethics in Business and the Professions. New York: Humana Press, forthcoming.

101. "The Embattled Businessman." Newsweek, 16 February 1976, pp. 56-60.

"Business has never been the best loved of American institutions, but its standing these days is the lowest in memory . . ." (p. 56).

102. England, George W. The Manager and His Values: An International Perspective from the United States, Japan, Korea, India, and Australia. Cambridge, MA: Ballinger, 1975.

Reports the result of ten years of cross-national research on the personal values of 2,500 managers in five countries. Findings include (1) there are large individual differences in personal values within each population group; (2) personal value systems are relatively stable; (3) value systems influence managerial behavior and career success; and (4) values are both measurable and important to measure.

103. England, George W. "Personal Value Systems of Managers--So What?" Personnel Administrator, 20 (April 1975), 20-23.

Finds large individual differences in personal values within every group studied in Japan, Korea,

India, Australia and the United States. Such values
are relatively stable over time and influence the way
managers behave on the job.

*104. Ermann, M. David and Richard J. Lundman, eds. Corpor-
ate and Governmental Deviance: Problems of Organizational Behavior in Contemporary Society. 2nd
Edition. New York: Oxford University Press, 1982.

Four readings in the first section emphasize that organizations, not just individuals, commit deviant
acts. Seven essays in sections two and three deal
with organized abuses of institutionalized power. The
readings in the final section focus on the problem of
controlling corporate and governmental deviance.

105. "Ethics Rules: An Empty Exercise." Industry Week,
21 (June 1976), 7-8.

A majority of business people believe the solution
to ethical dilemmas should come from the business community rather than government. For example, the Business Roundtable, a prestigious organization of 158
large companies, urges its members to write codes of
conduct. Others argue for a Council on Business Ethics, a "watchdog" group similar to the bar associations of lawyers', consisting of professionals, acad-
emics, and business persons.

106. "Ethics (Symposium)." Public Interest, 63 (Spring
1981), 3-94.

Includes essays on public service, business management, economics, and education. See item 383.

107. Evans, William. Management Ethics: An Inter-Cultur-
al Perspective. Boston: Martinus Nijhoff Publishing, 1981.

Intended for use in courses that deal with ethical
and moral behavior in management. Covers responsibility in business; political and ethical contrasts; philosophical antecedents to modern thought; ethical problems in decision-making; power, authority, and accountability; management ethics; and individual action in
business. Evans analyzes management behavior from the
standpoint of the individual.

34

108. Ewing, David W. "Due Process Trends for Scientists
and Engineers." Conflicting Loyalties in the workplace (item 717), ed. F. A. Elliston (Notre Dame,
IN: University of Notre Dame Press, forthcoming).

Describes four different procedures for resolving
professional differences of opinion in large technical
corporations: (1) the 'white hats' approach where personnel managers investigate complaints; (2) the 'Open
Door' policy of corporations like IBM, where members
of the Chief Executive's Office deal with grievances;
(3) the Employee Assistance Department, a due process
system used at the Bank of America, where members of
the executive committee investigate allegations of
wrongdoing; and (4) the employee tribunal at Polaroid,
whose members are elected by employees.

109. Ewing, David W. Do It My Way Or You're Fired! New
York: John Wiley and Sons, 1983.

Through more than thirty-five case studies, Ewing
shows how "corporations have trampled on the rights of
employees . . . how employees have learned to 'blow
the whistle' . . . and how managers must learn to
modify their styles to provide a more humane working
environment".

110. Ewing, David W. "A Bill of Rights for Employees:
Constitutionalizing the Corporation." Across the
Board, 18 (March 1981), 42-49.

A few pioneering companies have experimented with
genuine employee rights, but "far too many have rested
on . . . flimsy alternatives . . ." (p. 49).

111. Ewing, David W. "Business and the Bill of Rights:
Free Speech From Nine to Five." Nation, 15 (June
1974), 755-756.

Identifies a trend toward greater freedom of speech
in organizations evidenced by the courts, administrative proceedings, the press, professional associations, business community and National Labor Relations
Board activities.

*112. Ewing, David W. Freedom Inside the Organization.
New York: E. P. Dutton, 1977.

Traces the history of civil liberties in this country, describing the forces that have kept them out of
the workplace. Ewing contends that the time is ripe
for recognizing the civil liberties of those who work
in organizations. "We have assumed that rights are
not as important for employees as for political citizens. Our assumption is in error" (p. 16). He suggests ways in which a new balance between employee
rights and managerial prerogatives can be achieved.
See Staughton Lynd's review of this book for a critical appraisal (item 163).

113. Ewing, David W. "Winning Freedom on the Job." Civil
Liberties Review, 4 (July/August 1977), 8-22.

Based on his book, Freedom Inside The Organization (item 112), this article reviews the employee
rights movement through the various state court decisions and proposes a bill of rights for employees
which would balance the needs of management and employees.

114. Ewing, David W. "Who Wants Employee Rights?"
Harvard Business Review, 49 (November/December
1971) 22-35, 155-160.

The second part of a report surveying Harvard Business Review subscribers, focusing on the rights of employees in relation to superiors. While it is not illegal to dismiss employees without allowing them to defend themselves or to punish them for refusing on ethical grounds to follow orders, business people now view
such supervisory behavior with disfavor. Findings suggest that this is an area ripe for increased legal regulation. See item 115.

115. Ewing, David W. "Who Wants Corporate Democracy?"
Harvard Business Review, 49 (September/October
1971), 12-21, 24-28, 146-149.

Operating on the belief that there is a persistent
movement toward increasing employee participation and
influence in corporate governance, Ewing interprets
management's feelings about different forms of participation (based largely on a survey of subscribers to
the Harvard Business Review). Ewing reports attitudes toward dissent, employee balloting on policy

issues, and giving workers more voice in the selection of the officers who run the company. The first of two articles (see item 114).

116. Fitch, H. Gordon and Charles B. Saunders. "Obedience in Organizations." Business and Society, 17 (Fall 1976), 5-14.

Describes three cases that illustrate obedience at socially destructive levels: Vandivier's aircraft brake scandal, Samuel Levitt's "The Andersonville Trial," and Richard Smith's "The Incredible Electrical Conspiracy." Milgram's electric shock experiments, which show that most of his subjects were obedient to authority even if the innocent were harmed, suggest the danger that organizational due-process mechanisms are insufficient. To be effective, appeal policies must be impartial, speedy, and without fear of reprisals.

117. Foundation of the Southwestern Graduate School of Banking. A Study of Corporate Ethical Policy Statements. Dallas, TX: Foundation of the Graduate School of Banking, Southern Methodist University, 1980.

Analyzes the policy statements of 174 American corporations on such matters as standards, international relationships, and interactions with government, customers, suppliers, and employees.

118. Frederick, William C. "Embedded Values: Prelude to Ethical Analysis." Paper presented at Conference on Business and Professional Ethics, 15 May 1981, University of Illinois at Chicago Circle. Mimeographed.

Discusses the fundamentals of value formation in individuals and organizations from two differing perspectives: philosophy (particularly applied ethics) and social science. Frederick argues for merging the best of both for the sake of a greater understanding of business's ethics.

119. Fulmer, Robert M. "Ethics and the Executive." The New Management. 2nd edition. New York: Macmillan, 1978, chapter 20, pp. 433-460.

A general overview, using survey data, of definitions, theories, historical development, approaches,
and problems in business ethics. Fulmer concludes
that one of the most far-reaching company activities
designed to improve business ethics is the adoption of
a code of ethics and standards of practice.

120. Gardiner, John A. and David J. Olson. Theft of the
     City: Readings on Corruption in Urban America.
     Bloomington, IN: Indiana University Press, 1974.

     Over forty selections analyze the definition of cor-
     ruption, its history, manifestations, and prescrip-
     tions for reform.

121. Garson, G. David and Michael P. Smith, eds.
     Organizational Democracy: Participation and
     Self-Management. Beverly Hills, CA: Sage, 1976.

     Seven contributors examine the theoretical founda-
     tions of self-management, foreign country case stud-
     ies, and trends in the United States.

122. Gavin, James F. and William S. Maynard. "Perceptions
     of Corporate Social Responsibility." Personnel
     Psychology, 28 (Autumn 1975), 377-387.

     A study of corporate executives' conflicts between
     social responsibilities and profit. Employees of a
     medium-size bank were given an attitude survey that
     showed their satisfaction may be influenced by the
     degree to which the organization fulfills its societal
     obligations.

123. Geis, Gilbert and Ezra Stotland, eds. White Collar
     Crimes: Theory and Research. Beverly Hills, CA:
     Sage, 1980.

     Examines a wide range of white collar crimes includ-
     ing computer fraud, collusion between business and
     government and organizational exploitation of people.

124. Glass, H. Bently. "Value Conflict Between Profes-
     sional and Social Responsibility." Management Sci-
     ence, 24 (November 1977), 360-361.

125. Gillespie, Norman C. "The Business of Ethics." Michi-
     gan Business Review, 27 (November 1975), 1-4.

Identifies standard arguments advanced by executives to justify their behavior: (1) what they are doing is generally done; (2) if they do not do it, someone else will; and (3) in private enterprise, it is necessary to compete on the same level as everyone else. Gillespie shows that while each is relevant in assessing business and decisions, none is sufficient to exempt corporate practices from moral review.

126. Goldman, Ian H. "Business Ethics: Profits, Utilities, and Moral Rights." Philosophy and Public Affairs, 9 (Spring 1980), 260-286. See item 758.

127. Goodman, Charles S. and C. Merle Crawford. "Young Executives: A Source of New Ethics?" Personnel Journal, 53 (March 1974), 180-187.

The authors try to determine the effect of the younger generation's "new ethics" on potentially unethical practices and find that business students do not reflect new ethical standards. Instead they hold values similar to those of current executives.

128. Gordon, Max. "Can Businesses Fire At Will?" Nation, 14 (July 1979), 42.

129. Granrose, John T. Business Values. Columbus, OH: Charles E. Merrill Publishing, 1982.

130. Green, Mark. The Other Government. New York: Grossman, 1975.

131. Greenwood, William T., ed. Issues in Business and Society. 3rd edition. Boston: Houghton Mifflin, 1977.

A collection of 40 readings on relationships and conflicts between business and society. These relationships lead inevitably to problems of ethics and the need to develop a philosophy of management. Both sides of controversial topics are covered, with 15 case studies to supplement the readings.

132. Hass, John J., ed. Beyond Management. New York: Theo Gaus' Son, 1974.

Seven short readings that discuss economic, social and ethical trends.

133. Haddox, John H. "Twin Plant and Corporate Responsibil-
     ities." Paper presented at Conference on Business
     and Professional Ethics, 15 May 1981, University of
     Illinois at Chicago Circle. Mimeographed.

     Addresses questions of corporate responsibilities
     involving multinational operations, specifically the
     "twin-plants" in Mexican cities bordering on the Unit-
     ed States. Haddox identifies some ethical assumptions
     and examines the history and present status of multi-
     national corporations.

134. Harris, Charles E. "Structuring a Workable Business
     Code of Ethics." University of Florida Law Re-
     view, 30 (Winter 1978), 310-382.

     An exhaustive analysis of the general approach of
     codes and their content, followed by a detailed model
     code.

135. Harvard Business Review. Guides to Corporate Respon-
     sibility Series. Reprint No. 21220. Cambridge,
     MA: Harvard University Press, 1972.

     A collection of 16 articles that address issues
     broadly subdivided into three main categories: a defin-
     ition of the role of business in society and govern-
     ment; the approaches and involvement of business in so-
     cial issues; and the role of the manager or executive
     as a community leader.

136. Harvard Business Review. Philosophy Business Ser-
     ies: Part II. Reprint No. 21151. Cambridge,
     MA: Harvard University Press, 1970.

     A compilation of 16 articles that appeared in the
     Harvard Business Review from 1969-1970. They pre-
     sent several different perspectives on the internal
     and external functions of business amid a changing so-
     cial environment.

137. Hatano, Daryl G. "Employee Rights and Corporate Re-
     strictions." California Management Review, 24
     (Winter, 1981), 5-13.

     "Two criteria, the employee's degree of public con-
     tact and the degree to which an issue is company re-

lated are standards that will help to find the point of balance between employees' liberties and individuals' combination [corporate] rights" (p. 12).

138. Heilbroner, Robert L., et al. In the Name of Profit. New York: Doubleday, 1972.

Six cases of corporate irresponsibility, intended to expose the kinds of executives involved in contemporary organizations. The concluding chapter calls for more corporate responsibility, acknowledging it is a complex and difficult task.

139. Held, Virginia. Property, Profits, and Economic Justice. Belmont, CA: Wadsworth Publishing Co., 1980.

140. Hill, Ivan, ed. The Ethical Basis of Economic Freedom. Chapel Hill, NC: American Viewpoint, 1976.

Twenty-one essays from various disciplines, including a major section on codes of ethics with commentaries by professional and trade association leaders.

141. Hoffman, W. Michael, ed. Proceedings of the Second National Conference on Business Ethics: Power and Responsibility in the American Business System. See item 766.

142. Hoffman, Michael and Thomas J. Wyly, eds. The Work Ethic in Business. Cambridge, MA: Oelgeschlager, Gunn, and Hain, 1982.

Contains the proceedings of the Third National Conference on Business Ethics. Representatives from higher education, business, labor, government, and public interest groups discuss topics including the changing attitudes toward the work ethic, the quality of work life, affirmative action and equal opportunity employment, government regulation and intervention, and worker dignity.

143. Holt, Robert N. "A Sampling of Twenty-Five Codes of Corporate Conduct: Call for Renascence." Directors and Boards, 5 (Summer 1980), 7-13.

Concludes that the corporate community is letting government dictate its ethical concerns.

144. Houck, John and William J. Heisler, eds. <u>A Matter of Dignity: Inquiries into the Humanization of Work.</u> Notre Dame, IN: University of Notre Dame Press, 1982.

Includes eleven essays by experts in business, research, labor, and education. Discusses the sources and possible solutions for the "blue-collar blues" which exist at all occupational levels, and examines the design and redesign of work practices not only as organizational objectives but as goals for personal growth.

145. Hunnius, Gerry, G. David Garson, and John Case, eds. <u>Worker's Control: A Reader on Labor and Social Change.</u> New York: Random House, 1973. See item 820.

146. Jacoby, Neil H. <u>Corporate Power and Social Responsibility.</u> New York: Macmillan, 1973.

Evaluates the effect on society and political life of corporate performance. The model developed resembles the classical theory of the firm, on the basis of which the author defends social responsibility as consistent with enlightened self-interest. Each chapter begins with a statement of the issues and concludes with suggestions aimed at reforming private and public policy. Jacoby suggests that a new "social contract" between society and business is evolving to better govern corporate power.

147. Johnson, Elmer W. "Corporate Leadership and the Judeo Christian Vision." Paper presented at Conference on the Judeo-Christian Vision and the Modern Business Corporation. University of Notre Dame, Notre Dame, IN, 15 April 1980. Mimeographed. See item 770.

148. Johnson, Harold L. "Ethics and the Executive: Profitable Business Is, By and Large, Ethical Business." <u>Business Horizons,</u> 24 (May/June 1981), 53-59.

Argues that "responsible practices cannot be wished into place . . ." (p. 56).

149. Johnson, M. Bruce, ed. The Attack on Corporate America. New York: McGraw-Hill, 1978.

Addresses the challenges raised by critics of business in 61 essays that analyze the pros and cons of the issues.

150. Jones, Donald G., ed. Business, Religion, and Ethics. Cambridge, MA.: Oelgeschlager, Gunn and Hain, 1982. See item 771.

*151. Jones, Donald G., ed. Doing Ethics In Business: New Ventures in Management Development. Cambridge, MA: Oelgeschlager, Gunn and Hain, 1982.

Designed for human resource managers, teachers and students of ethics and business critics, the book strikes a balance between practice and theory. The contributors describe ethics training programs for management and discusses various means for introducing ethics into business education and practice.

152. Krishnan, Rama. "Business Philosophy and Executive Responsibility." Academy of Management Journal, 16 (December 1973), 658-659.

Survey data reveal that business people believe corporations should be more responsible to society.

153. Krogstad, Jack L. and Jack C. Robertson. "Moral Principles for Ethical Conduct." Management Horizons, 10 (Fall 1979), 1-7.

Presents three moral principles--the categorical imperative, utilitarian greatest happiness principle, and universal generalization--that can give practical guidance in resolving ethical conflicts.

154. Kugel, Yerachmiel and Gladys W. Gruenberg, eds. Ethical Perspectives on Business and Society. Lexington, MA: Lexington Books, 1977.

Statements by contemporary political figures who argue that government regulations will not control corporate misconduct, which depends instead on the conscience of business people. Eight chapters in three parts cover government and society (e.g., foreign pay-offs by multinational firms), business and society (e.g., public trust and corporate reform), and the individual and society (e.g., professional ethics).

155. La Croix, W. L. <u>Principles for Ethics in Business</u>. Washington, DC: University Press of America, 1976.

An historical review of the ethical heritage of businesses today. Each has rules for its operations as an enterprise and also for its relations to society. Both relations have ethical principles, but a lack of conformity exists between the two, giving rise to "gray areas" in industry ethics. La Croix examines these areas, touching on ethics and competition, ethics and power, social responsibility, whistle-blowing, and advertising.

156. Ladd, Dwight R. "The Limits of Liability." <u>Business and Professional Ethics</u>, 2 (December 1979), <u>5-6</u>.

Argues that producer liability is not appropriate when assigning responsibility in cases of harmful consequences of technology. Since society supports and encourages the spread of technology, responsibility for its effects should be assessed in collective terms.

157. Laurendeau, Norman M. "The Case for Corporate Ombudsmen." Paper presented at Second National Conference on Ethics in Engineering, 5-6 March 1982, Bismark Hotel, Chicago, Illinois. Forthcoming in <u>Beyond Whistleblowing</u>, (item 722b).

158. Lerner, Max. "Business Ethics at Home and Abroad." <u>Personnel Administrator</u>, 22 (August 1977), 13-16, <u>24</u>.

Asserts the possibility of resolving our problems because, as Alexis de Tocqueville noted "the American people have a great capacity for self-correction" (p. 13).

159. Levy, Robert. "Business' Big Morality Play." <u>Dun's Review</u>, 116 (August 1980), 56-68.

A review of recent codes of ethics developed by American companies.

160. Linowes, David F. <u>The Corporate Conscience</u>. New York: Hawthorne Books, 1974.

Suggests the main motive for corporate responsibility is profit --that organizations be properly credited for the resources they expend in producing social goods. Those organizations most socially active would benefit rather than be at a competitive disadvantage with corporations that ignore responsibility.

161. Lodge, George Cabot. "Ethics and the New Ideology: Can Business Adjust?" <u>Management Review</u>, 66 (July 1977), 10-19.

Contrasts the old, but still resilient ideology of individualism, property, competition, limited state and scientific specialization with the new ideology of communitarianism, rights and duties of membership, community need, the active state, and holistic interdependence. Many business activities appear illegitimate under the old ideology, but are necessary given the present reality. Lodge calls for conscious development of the new ideology and the ethics it implies, before the socio-economic structure and ideology are so far apart that chaos results.

162. Luthans, Fred and Richard M. Hodgetts, eds. <u>Social Issues in Business</u>. New York: Macmillan, 1976.

Divided into five parts, Part I establishes the historical foundation for social responsibility. Parts II, III, and IV are devoted to the social issues of poverty and equal rights, ecology, and consumerism. Part V deals with developing a management strategy for social responsibility in the future. Each of the ten chapters is followed by cases. The authors have chosen twenty-nine readings to supplement each part.

163. Lynd, Staughton. "Company Constitutionalism?" <u>Yale Law Journal</u>, 87 (July 1978), 885-893.

Argues that David Ewing's <u>Freedom Inside the Organization</u> (see item 112) sacrifices workplace civil liberties when they threaten to cut too sharply into managerial efficiency. Lynd maintains that Ewing fails to realize that the logical conclusion of his reasoning is a workplace democracy where employees make all significant decisions.

164. McAdams, Tony and C. Burk Tower. "Personal Accountability in the Corporate Sector." American Business Law Journal, 16 (Spring 1978), 67-82.

165. McAdams, Tony and Robert Miljas. "Growing Criminal Liability of Executives." Harvard Business Review, 55 (March/April 1977), 36-40, 164-166.

Illustrates the consequences when management does not listen to problems, and therefore suggests an independent watchdog or ombudsman for organizations.

166. McGuire, Joseph W. "The Business of Business Ethics." National Forum, 58 (Summer 1978), 32-36.

Discusses problems involved in establishing standards for ethical business behavior based on three principles: (1) business is assigned by society the fiduciary responsibility for producing goods and services efficiently; (2) corporate executives most frequently have a stewardship obligation to absentee owners; (3) executives are not trained to make--and therefore often should not make--decisions about products and activities based upon grounds other than economic or legal. McGuire concludes that there are few firm ethical guidelines for executive action and decision.

167. McKie, James W., ed. The Social Responsibility and Business Predicament. Washington, DC: The Brookings Institute, 1974.

A collection of 12 essays by academicians drawn from economics, law and management that discuss the nature of business's social responsibility--its source, forms, limits as well as the role of government and employees in formulating business policies. Also included are bibliographies for each of the five sections.

168. Matlin, Gerald L. "Let's Make Ethical Codes Meaningful." Business and Professional Ethics, 1 (September 1977), 7-8.

Contends that past efforts to improve business's ethics have been unsuccessful because codes of conduct do not relate to people's daily activities. To formulate realistic codes, Matlin proposes establishing a Society for Business Ethics.

169. Mautz, Robert K., Raymond R. Reilly, and Michael W. Maher. "Personnel Failure: The Weak Link in Internal Control." Financial Executive, 47 (December 1979), 22-25.

Examines the powers of corporations and the ways they erode the rule of law and ethical precepts. Presents the case for the federal chartering of corporations.

170. Monsen, R. Joseph. "Social Responsibility and the Corporation: Alternatives for the Future of Capitalism." Journal of Economic Issues, vol. 6, (Spring 1972), 125-141.

Asserts that if society is to remain pluralistic, institutions other than the government must begin to play larger roles. Business is central to any such development because of its size and scope. The three major alternatives for corporate social responsibility are: (1) traditional profit maximization (as expressed by Milton Friedman); (2) profitable social concerns; and (3) direct allocation of corporate resources to public needs. Each has vastly different effects upon capitalism. A brief review of some of the major arguments for and against social responsibility by business is included.

171. "A Moral Philosophy of Business Symposium." Journal of Contemporary Business, 4 (Summer 1975), 1-87.

Five essays on business, ethics, and society.

172. Nader, Ralph, Mark Green, and Joel Seligman. Taming the Giant Corporation. New York: Norton, 1976.

173. Nash, Laura. "Business Ethics Without a Sermon." Harvard Business Review, 59 (December 1981), 78-90.

Discusses 12 questions for examining the ethics of a business decision.

174. Newstrom, John W. and William A. Ruch. "The Ethics of Business Students: Preparation for a Career." AACSB Bulletin, 12 (April 1976), 21-29.

175. Newstrom, John W. and William A. Ruch. "The Ethics of Management and the Management of Ethics." MSU Business Topics, 23 (Winter 1975), 29-37.

Nationally publicized scandals suggest that more pervasive ethical problems arise in daily management. Survey findings and cross-perceptional data from respondents suggest: (1) ethics is personal; (2) ethical beliefs of employees are similar to perceptions of top management; (3) managers capitalize on opportunities to be unethical; and (4) employees believe that their colleagues are more unethical than they are. Practical proposals to deal with this situation are presented.

176. Pastin, Mark and Michael Hooker. "Ethics and the Foreign Corrupt Practices Act." Paper presented at Conference on Business and Professional Ethics, 15 May 1981, University of Illinois at Chicago Circle. Mimeographed.

Focuses on one aspect of recent attention to corporate morality—the controversy surrounding payments made by American corporations to foreign officials for the purpose of securing business abroad. The authors discuss the Foreign Corrupt Practices Act and the question whether it should be repealed, and conclude that dominant theories of morality do not provide a sound moral basis for the law.

177. Powers, Charles W. and David Vogel. Ethics in the Education of Business Managers. Hastings-on-Hudson, NY: The Hastings Center, 1980.

Examines the recent growth of interest in business ethics, summarizes survey data, and discusses curricular concerns and pedagogical problems. Part of the Hastings Center Series (see item 670).

178. Preston, Lee, ed. Research in Corporate Social Performance and Policy, Vol. 1. Greenwich, CT: JAI Press, 1973.

Original essays provide a comprehensive overview of the problems in business social responsibility.

179. Purcell, Theodore V., S. J. "Institutionalizing Ethics into Top Management Decisions." Public Relations Quarterly, 22 (Summer 1977), 15-20.

Discusses a possible solution for introducing ethics at the top management level. Practical, three-fold procedure includes: (1) examination of general ethical principles; (2) analysis of middle-level ethical principles; and (3) in-depth study of cases. Examples of each are provided. Although the process is workable for corporation management, it calls for a certain degree of expertise. Purcell proposes that an ethical advocate be appointed to identify generic questions that should be asked routinely along with the usual legal, financial, and marketing questions. The concluding section discusses four objections to ethical advocacy by management executives.

180. Regan, Tom. Just Business: Essays in Business Ethics. New York: Random House, 1982.

181. Rein, Lowell G. "Is Your Ethical Slippage Showing?" Personnel Journal, 59 (September 1980), 740-743.

Suggestions for personnel managers to improve ethics in organizations are presented, including an ethics test.

182. Ruch, William A. and John W. Newstrom. "How Unethical Are We?" Supervisory Management, 20 (November 1975), 16-21.

An abbreviated version of the authors' "The Ethics of Management and the Management of Ethics" (see item 175).

183. Saul, George K. "Business Ethics: Where Are We Going?" Academy of Management Review, 6 (April 1981), 269-176.

Discusses public perceptions, definitions, societal expectations, education, and the business community.

184. Sawhill, John C. "A Question of Ethics." Newsweek, 29 October 1979, p. 27.

"American higher education is in a state of crisis... [W]e must learn to be better people in order to realize the full potential of science and technology."

185. Sawyer, George C. Business and Society: Managing Corporate Social Impact. Boston: Houghton Mifflin, 1979.

Analyzes corporate social impact in terms of the to-
tal sphere of corporate management, corporate self-interest and the management process. After a brief summary of relevant elements of economics, industrial development and management history, Sawyer focuses on a
framework for the management of corporate social impact. A tentative set of guidelines is advanced for
use by management in dealing with social issues. The
text contains 4 case studies and 22 chapters.

186. Sawyer, Lawrence B., Albert A. Murphy, and M.
Crossley. "Management Fraud--The Insidious
Specter." Assets Protection, 4 (May/June 1979),
13-20.

Discusses the forms, reasons, and solutions for
management fraud.

187. Sethi, S. Prakash. Crime in the Executive Suites:
Executive Criminal Liability for Corporate Law
Violations. Cambridge, MA: Oelgeschlager, Gunn,
and Hain, 1981.

Analyzes current and foreseeable trends to holding
corporate executives personally liable in corporate
criminal actions.

188. Sethi, S. Prakash. Corporate Free Speech:
Advocacy Issue Advertising by Business. Cambridge,
MA: Oelgeschlager, Gunn and Hain, 1982.

Addresses a topic of increasing importance to government officials, business people, and the general
public: the growing use by corporations of the mass
media to publicly defend their activities, decry
public intrusion into their activities, and urge the
public to consider the business viewpoint in a more
sympathetic light. Gives an indepth analysis, in
nonlegal terms, of the five major Supreme Court cases
between 1975 and 1979 that have greatly expanded the
scope of a corporation's right to engage in advocacy
and advertising.

189. Sethi, S. Prakash. Up Against the Corporate Wall.
4th edition. Englewood Cliffs, NJ: Prentice-Hall,
1981.

Major areas of discussion include business and quality of life; corporations and social institutions; the

individual; the military-industrial complex; and the variety of problems that are increasingly becoming the prime concern of business and society. Designed for executives, this book is aimed at developing a sensitivity to the issues, and a familiarity with the success and failure of industry strategies.

190. Sethi, S. Prakash. Allied Chemical and the Kepone Controversy. Richardson, TX: School of Management and Administration, The University of Texas at Dallas, 1980.

   Discusses the responsibility of Allied Chemical and Life Science Products in the Kepone contamination of the Hopewell, Virginia, area between July 1, 1971 and March 15, 1974. Sethi poses questions about the causes (negligence vs. design); the role of government agencies and the media; and regulatory vs. punitive solutions.

191. Silk, Leonard and David Vogel. Ethics and Profits: The Crisis of Confidence in American Business. New York: Simon and Schuster, 1976.

   Results of eight three-day meetings among small groups of 360 top corporate executives. The authors discuss the beliefs, values and concerns of the conference participants and highlight the need for a transcendent ideology and personal morality. Within the American business community, there is a wide spectrum of social and moral attitudes as shown by the comments of executives.

192. Smigel, Erwin O. and Lawrence H. Ross, eds. Crimes Against Bureaucracy. New York: Van Nostrand Reinhold, 1970. See item 412.

193. Sobel, Lester A., ed. Corruption in Business. New York: Facts on File, 1977.

   Designed as a record of the problem described in the title from the end of the 60's to the mid-70's. Materials consist largely of those which Facts on File compiled in its weekly report (see item 414).

194. Southard, Samuel. Ethics for Executives. New York: Thomas Nelson, 1975.

Examines the problems and potential of executive morality as it affects decision-making at all levels. Adapted from group studies in seminars attended by top executives. Each of the seven chapters includes a casestudy.

195. "Special Report." Civil Liberties Review, 5 (September/October 1978), 6-49.

196. "Special Section: Honesty/Ethical Standards." Gallup Opinion Index, 150 (January 1980), 7-29.

Survey findings rating the honesty and ethics of 20 occupations are presented.

197. Steiner, George A. Business and Society. New York: Random House, 1975.

An introductory chapter on the nature and scope of business-society relationships, followed by short chapters examining background historical developments. The next three parts (20 chapters) cover a broad range of current subjects such as business and labor unions, educational institutions, and consumers. Part V explores the major forces likely to have the greatest impact on future relationships-- such as population growth, social problems and worldwide influences.

198. Stevens, Edward. Business Ethics. Ramsey, NJ: Paulist Press, 1980.

Can business and ethics mix? Stevens suggests more specific questions for individuals: "How am I expressing my values in the decisions I make?" And "What are those values?" Each chapter begins with a statement of objectives followed by a series of theory-directed questions designed to measure the extent of the reader's prior inclinations toward the particular theory in question.

199. Stevenson, Russell B., Jr. "Corporations and Social Responsibility: In Search of Corporate Soul." George Washington Law Review, 42 (May 1974), 709-736.

Views the problems of corporate responsibility from the perspective of a corporation acting as if it were an individual with a soul. Stevenson describes ways in which companies have acted irresponsibly and then attempts to develop remedies. He sees defects in corporate actions as due to institutional problems and proposes that solutions may be found through an understanding of the mechanisms which can be used to influence corporate behavior. He concludes that by injecting a small amount of soul into businesses, they could be made more socially responsible.

200. Stewart, James B., ed. Regulation Values and the Public Interest. Notre Dame, IN: University of Notre Dame Press, 1980.

201. Stone, Christopher D. "Law and the Culture of the Corporation." Business and Society Review, 15 (Fall 1975), 5-17.

Suggests several proposals to insure that companies are more responsible to society, e.g., requiring practical configurations of information nets and management structures, and appointing special officers in charge of particular problem areas. Some problems generated by changing corporate attitudes are addressed. Stone recommends esteem of the design engineers to insure product safety, and suggests reward for excellence and better communication between the organization and government and the public.

202. Stone, Christopher D. Where the Law Ends. New York: Harper and Row, 1975.

Examines attempts to control corporate behavior since the Industrial Revolution through the marketplace and the law. Stone identifies both conceptual and ethical difficulties in these traditional efforts. Instead he advocates direct legal involvement in the decision-making process; reforming the executive offices (e.g., requiring a vice president for environmental affairs); introducing representatives of the public interest onto the boards of directors; instituting more public directorships and disqualifying executives from similar jobs; requiring a restructuring of management systems; controlling the information flow; and developing a new corporate culture.

203. Sufrin, Sidney C. Management of Business Ethics. Port Washington, NY: Kennikat Press, 1980.

"Not a manual or cookbook, but an effort to talk about. . . ethics and morality, and try to expose how social actions may be morally viewed" (p. ix).

204. Taylor, Lynda King. Can You Succeed in Business and Still Get to Heaven: Management, Motivation and Ethics in a Changing World. London: Association Business Programme, 1978.

Argues it should be possible to be successful in business and go to 'heaven'--an unencumbered state of contentment, and satisfaction that comes from successfully completing a difficult task rather than from winning a prize in a lottery. The connection between values and performance should play a dominant role in working life. If this connection determines business objectives, business success need not be incompatible with a genuine improvement in the quality of life.

205. Tullock, Henry W. and W. Scott Bauman. The Management of Business Conduct. Charlottesville, VA: University Press of Virginia, 1981.

Reports the findings from a study of the implementation of codes of ethics, and offers recommendations for executives.

206 U.S. Chamber of Commerce. White Collar Crime. Washington, DC: The Chamber, n.d.

207. Valasquez, Manuel G. Business Ethics: Concepts and Cases. Englewood Cliffs, NJ: Prentice-Hall, 1982.

208. Valone, James J. "A Guide for the Perplexed: An Ethical Matrix for the Modern Manager." Paper presented at Conference on Business and Professional Ethics, 15 May 1981, University of Illinois at Chicago Circle. Mimeographed.

Managers are often confronted with difficulties in preparing guidelines and principles which can aid in ethical decision-making. Therefore, Valone attempts to identify "some essential factors which must be considered and which are operating in any moral decision irrespective of one's ethical system and position" (p. 1).

209. Wallick, Franklin. The American Worker: An Endangered Species. New York: Ballantine Books, 1972.

    Popularized overview of occupational health and safety issues that documents the need to blow the whistle.

210. Walton, Clarence C., ed. The Ethics of Corporate Conduct. Englewood Cliffs, NJ: Prentice-Hall, 1977.

    Seven essays describing the environment in which business has operated in this century and tracing shifts in ideology that have brought about changes in ethical outlook. Discussion includes the moral environment, corporate behavior and the allied professions, and practical problems with specific solutions.

211. Wheatley, Edward W. Values in Conflict. Miami: Banyon Books, 1976.

    Designed to stimulate the reader to think about current pressures facing business and individuals in a changing society. Many of these pressures are based on the conflict between the value systems, the motivation for acquisition, growth, and profit. Ten chapters offer problem situations and current issues for discussion.

212. White, Bernard J. and B. Ruth Montgomery. "Corporate Codes of Conduct." California Management Review, 23 (Winter 1980), 80-87.

    Survey report and content analysis of 30 codes.

213. White, Stephen W., ed. Special Issue on Business and Professional Ethics. National Forum, 58 (Summer 1978), entire.

    See esp. McGuire, Joseph W., "The Business of Business Ethics" (pp. 31-36; item 166), and Carroll, Archie B., "Business Ethics and the Management Hierarchy" (pp. 37-40; item 78).

214. Williams, Oliver F., and John W. Houck. Full Value: Cases in Christian Business Ethics. New York: Harper and Row, 1978.

Provides an opportunity for Christians to become more aware of the implied effect of religious convictions in the business world. Includes interpretive materials.

215. Williams, Oliver and John Houck, eds. The Judeo-Christian Vision and the Modern Corporation. Notre Dame, IN: University of Notre Dame Press, 1982.

Twelve businessmen, scholars, attorneys and ethicists discuss the dilemma of choosing between profits and social needs. Includes discussions of capitalism, the Protestant work ethic, the legal responsibilities of modern corporations, and the secularization of present-day economic activities.

216. "Workplace Democracy and Employee Rights." Perspectives on the Professions, 1 (June 1981), entire.
A paper by David Schweikart followed by two commentaries.

217. Zemke, Ron. "Ethics Training: Can we Really Teach People Right From Wrong?" Training, 14 (May 1977), 37-41.

Overview of the recent interest in ethics with its implications for training.

Section III

Government

A. Whistle-Blowing and Dissent

218. Abourezk, James. Untitled Speech delivered at the Institute for Policy Studies Seminar on National Security Whistleblowers. Washington, DC, May 20, 1978. Mimeograph.

    Criticizes the Carter Administration's attempts to protect whistle-blowers and calls for appropriate provisions in the Civil Service Reform bill.

219. American Society for Public Administration. "Position Statement on Whistle Blowing: A Time to Listen.. A Time to Hear." Washington, DC: The Society, 1979.

    Recommends actions that federal, state, and local governments can take to improve accountability and describes the Society's interest in accountability and the obligations of public employees.

220. Anderson, Stanley V. The Role of Inspectors General in Federal Agencies. Preliminary Outline for the Administrative Conference of the United States, 14 December 1978.

221. Ban, Carolyn, Edie Goldenberg, and Toni Marzotto. "Firing the Unproductive Employee: Will the Civil Service Reform Act Make a Difference?" Paper presented at the Annual Meeting of the Midwest Political Science Association. 24-26 April 1980, Pick-Congress Hotel, Chicago, IL.

    Examines the Civil Service Reform Act, intended to promote efficiency by giving management more authority to deal with employees, while simultaneously protecting employee rights from arbitrary personnel action. In promoting both goals, agencies implementing the new law face a formidable challenge. The authors examine the objectives of the legislation and documents changes mandated by it. They conclude that it will be some time before new patterns become clear, and ask whether or not "the community of interests surrounding the CSRA [Civil Service Reform Act] has the patience to wait" (p. 35). A revised version of this paper was subsequently published in the Review of Public Personnel Administration 2 (Spring 1982), 87-100.

222. Baran, Andrew. "Federal Employment--The Civil Service Reform Act of 1978--Removing Incompetents and Pro-

tecting Whistle Blowers." <u>Wayne Law Review</u>, 26 (November 1979), 97-118.

Examines procedures of the Civil Service Reform Act designed to simplify the procedure for firing incompetent employees and to protect whistle-blowers from retribution. Baran explores the likelihood of these procedures succeeding. He chronicles legislation leading to the Act and concludes that it is at best only the beginning of real change.

223. Blades, Lawrence. "Employment at Will vs. Individual Freedom: On Limiting the Abusive Exercise of Employer Power.: <u>Columbia Law Review</u>, 67 (December 1967), 1404-1435. See item 1226.

*224. Bok, Sissela. "Whistleblowing and Professional Responsibility." <u>New York University Education Quarterly</u>, 11 (Summer 1980), 2-10.

"Given the indispensible service performed by so many whistle-blowers, strong public support is often merited. But . . . it [is] easy to overlook the dangers of whistle-blowing. . ." (p. 3). Bok probes ways to differentiate between cases of dissent, since clearcut instances are rare, and considers mechanisms for reducing its likelihood: eliminate legitimate causes for alarm; take dissent seriously within the organization; adopt an open door policy; introduce an independent review board; establish ombudsmen; prepare an employee bill of rights that states conditions under which one must blow the whistle. She recommends using cases to teach applied ethics and clarifying the notion of responsibility.

225. Bok, Sissela. "Whistleblowing and Professional Responsibilities." <u>Ethics Teaching in Higher Education</u>. Edited by Daniel Callahan and Sissela Bok. New York: Plenum Press, 1970, chapter 11, 277-295. See item 224.

226. Bollens, John and Henry Schmandt. "ABSCAM: Special Report." Pacific Palisades, CA: Palisades Publishers, 1981.

A monograph available to purchasers of the authors' text (see item 315) describing the Federal Bureau of Investigation's "sting" of members of Congress and other public officials.

60

227. Boyan, A. Stephen, Jr. "Whistleblowers: 'Auxiliary Precautions' Against Government Abuse." Ethical Society, 2 (Spring 1979), 5-8.

Argues that Ethical Society members should become involved in supporting whistle-blowers. Offering assistance helps to legitimize whistle-blowing, to make it acceptable behavior among government employees, and to increase government accountability.

*228. Bowman, James S. "Whistle-blowing in the Public Service: An Overview of the Issues." Review of Public Personnel Administration, 1 (Fall 1980), 15-28.

Examines the significance of corruption in American government today. Traces the emergence and institutionalization of whistle-blowing, the relationship between dissenting individuals and bureaucratic organizations, and reforms to encourage ethical behavior and reduce the need for whistle-blowing.

229. Branch, Taylor. "Courage without Esteem: Profile Whistle-Blowing." The Culture of Bureaucracy. Charles Peters and Michael Nelson. New York: Holt, Rinehart, and Winston, 1979, pp. 217-237.

Consists of brief case studies.

230. Burnett, Arthur L. "Management's Positive Interest in Accountability Through Whistleblowing." The Bureaucrat, 9 (Summer 1980), 5-10.

Argues for encouraging responsible whistle-blowing in order to promote efficiency, productivity, and quality performance of public servants. Management officials must change employee and public attitudes toward whistle-blowing. Even more than this, they have an obligation under the Civil Service Reform Act of 1978 to develop procedures to encourage employees to disclose alleged violations of law, mismanagement, and waste of funds.

231. Burnham, David. "Whistle Blowing in the Plutonium (sic)." Washingtonian, 14 (December 1978), 69.

*232. Chalk, Rosemary and Frank Von Hippel. "Due Process for Dissenting Whistle-Blowers." Technology Review, 81 (June/July 1979), 49-55.

In the interests of both organizations and individuals, due process procedures should be developed in order to deal with dissenters --including balanced review groups and opportunity for cross-examination. The authors discuss current trends in professional associations, business, and government and warn that whatever due process protections are provided "will have little value unless they are imbedded in a process which deals effectively with the substance of the dissent" (p. 55, original emphasis).

*233.   Clark, Louis. "Blowing the Whistle on Corruption: How to Kill a Career in Washington." Barrister, 5 (Summer 1978), 10-19.

Defines the term "whistle-blower," discusses recent cases and outlines retaliatory actions that organizations take against dissenters. Clark describes the activities of the Government Accountability Project, a Washington, public interest group that counsels government employees contemplating whistleblowing.

234.   Comptroller General. First Year Activities of The Merit Systems Protection Board and The Office of Special Counsel. Washington, DC: General Accounting Office, 1980.

Reviews first year activities of the Merit Systems Protection Board and the Office of Special Counsel, established in January 1979 to hear and decide Federal employees' appeals. They investigate and prosecute violations of prohibited personnel practices based on a review of records and interviews with officials at the Board, Special Counsel Headquarters or one of five field offices.

235.   Comptroller General. The Office of the Special Counsel Can Improve Its Management of Whistleblower Cases. Washington, DC: General Accounting Office, 1980.

The Special Counsel's effectiveness is jeopardized by serious start-up problems, delays in case processing, poor communications with whistle-blowers, and inadequate follow-up of agencies' responses to complaints.

236. Coven, Mark. "The First Amendment Rights of Policymaking Public Employees." Harvard Civil Rights--Civil Liberties Law Review, 12 (Summer 1977), 559-584.

Examines first amendment rights of middle- and upper-level employees of federal, state, and local government. Using a recent case as the basis of discussion, it is argued that increased protection for a policymaking employee's freedom of speech is necessary and constitutional.

*237. D. M. R. "The Right of Government Employees to Furnish Information to Congress: Statutory and Constitutional Aspects." Virginia Law Review, 57 (June 1971), 885-919.

Examines statutory and constitutional rights of employees, and considerations that should determine their scope and application. Concludes that new legislation is required and proposes a model statute that attempts to balance competing interests. Maintains that employees do not relinquish their constitutional rights when they accept government employment, and that public servants are a critical source of information about bureaucratic activities.

238. Ewing, David W. "Canning Directions: How the Government Rids Itself of Trouble-makers." Harper's, August 1979, pp. 16, 18, 22.

Discusses "suppressive techniques that agency administrators may use without jeopardy" to quell dissent. Reviews cases, illuminating personal characteristics and career problems of whistle-blowers. Comments on the difficulties faced by the Civil Service Commission in handling these cases.

239. Ewing, David. W. Freedom Inside the Organization. New York: E. P. Dutton, 1977. See item 112.

240. Feinstein, Andrew A. "Whistleblowers Get Protection Under New Civil Service Bill." The Public Citizen, Winter 1978, p. 2.

241. Frome, Michael. "Blowing the Whistle." Center Magazine, 11 (November/December 1978), 50-58.

Concerned about the government's response to whistle-blowers, the author suggests the Carter Administration has a policy of retaliation, intimidation, and suppression of whistle-blowers. Discusses seven cases.

242. Gest, Ted. "Blowing the Whistle on Waste: A Thankless Job." U.S. News and World Report, 29 June 1981, pp. 50-51.

Examines the new federal law enacted to protect civil servants who expose dishonest or negligent colleagues. Gest concludes it has not done the job and many informants still suffer reprisals from their bosses. He provides profiles of several whistleblowers and discusses their fate.

243. Government Accountability Project. "Analysis of the Inspector General Act of 1978." Unpublished paper. Washington, DC: The Institute for Policy Studies, 1979.

244. Government Accountability Project. "Civil Service Reform Act: Whistleblower Provisions." Unpublished paper. Washington, DC: The Institute for Policy Studies, 1979.

245. Government Accountability Project. A Whistleblower's Guide to the Federal Bureaucracy. Washington, DC: Institute for Policy Studies, 1977. See item 1353.

246. Greenfield, Meg. "Blowing the Whistle." Newsweek, 25 September 1978, p. 112.

Deals with the regulation of whistle-blowing, noting a directive to U.S. attorneys not to bring prosecutions for "theft of government information" against people who meet a variety of standards outlined for whistle-blowers. Argues that there is a basic mismatch between the steps intended to protect the dissenter and the nature of whistle-blowers themselves. With details not yet in place, a more temperate approach to the issue is suggested.

247. Hayes, John P. "The Men Who Blow the Whistle." Saga Magazine, May 1979, pp. 28-29.

Highlights government whistle-blowing cases. Hayes discusses the Civil Service Reform Act, which is designed to protect federal employees who report unlawful activity within the bureaucracy as well as the Government Accountability Project, a public interest group formed to help make officials accountable for their actions.

248. Hentoff, Nat. "Putting the Gag on CIA Whistle Blowers." Civil Liberties Review, 5 (July/August 1978), 37-40.

Discusses former Central Intelligence Agency agents who breached their secrecy agreements. The Fourth Circuit Court of Appeals placed a "lifetime gag order" on one of them, which Hentoff sees as an incredible assault on the First Amendment.

249. "The High Cost of Whistling." Newsweek, 14 February 1977, pp. 75-77.

Describes the fate of four whistle-blowers in the public and private sectors, each of whom lost his job and/or incurred heavy financial loss. As the outlook for legislation to protect whistle-blowers is dim, those who choose to blow the whistle can expect little thanks.

249a. Graham, Jill W. Principled Organizational Dissent. Ph.D Thesis, Department of Organizational Behavior, Northwestern University, 1983.

A psychological model of the antecedents and consequences of principled organizational dissent is proposed and tested using data from the 1980 Merit Systems Protection Board survey of federal employees. Six chapters cover: (1) definition of principled organizational dissent; (2) an interdisciplinary literature review; (3) development of a theoretical model; (4) description of methods used in this study; (5) results of data analysis; and (6) discussion of implications for future research and practice.

250. Hirschman, Albert L. Exit, Voice, and Loyalty. Cambridge: Harvard University Press, 1970. See item 19.

251. "Inspectors Blow the Whistle on Federal Waste." U.S. News and World Report, 14 December 1981, p. 6.

252. Kaufman, Richard F. "Whistleblowing and Full Disclosure." The Bureaucrat, 6 (Winter 1977), pp. 35-40.

Reviews tactics for punishing and silencing government whistle-blowers. Warns against these methods and urges legal protection of employees who tell the truth because whistle-blowing is an indispensable public service. Also see item 229.

253. Kaus, Robert. "How the Supreme Court Sabotaged Civil Service Reform." Washington Monthly, 10 (December 1978), 38-44.

Expresses concern about the court, declaring the 1978 Civil Service Reform Act unconstitutional and thereby weakening its provisions on firing civil servants.

254. Kendall, Lynn. "A Whistleblower Comes to Chicago." Ethical Society, 2 (Spring 1979), 12-14.

Describes the fate of one whistle-blower. Kendall argues for the development of a nationwide support network to aid and defend whistle-blowers, noting that the Ethical Action Committee of the American Ethical Union has begun to plan and develop such a program.

255. Kennedy, Carol S. "Whistleblowing: Contribution or Catastrophe?" Paper presented at the American Association for the Advancement of Science, 15 February 1978, Washington, DC.

Discusses expert testimony provided by 14 Food and Drug Administration (FDA) witnesses before Congress concerning alleged harassment and transfers. Kennedy describes experiences which finally led to her resignation, and offers recommendations for effective change: (1) the shroud of secrecy must be removed from FDA decisionmaking; (2) FDA officials must be held publicly accountable for their decisions; (3) the quality of scientific research needs upgrading; (4) meetings between industry and FDA officials that exclude professional staff should not occur; and (5) procedures should be established to protect professionals from unwarranted harassment and punitive measures.

256. Kieffer, Jarold A. "The Case for an Inspector General of the United States." The Bureaucrat, 9 (Summer 1980), 11-20.

   Points out deficiencies in present arrangements designed to expose wrongdoing. The public learns of official deviance primarily through random and bizarre events. Systematic procedures should be installed to correct this problem, beginning with the establishment of an independent Office of Inspector General of the United States.

257. Kohn, Howard. "The Government's Quiet War on Scientists Who Know Too Much." Rolling Stone, 28 March 1978, pp. 42-44.

258. Kovler, Peter. "Blowing the Whistle: Can Conscientious Federal Employees be Protected?" Commonwealth, 15 (September 1978), 591-593.

   Discusses legislation to protect whistle-blowers and the present status of selected cases. Kovler doubts that meaningful legislation will be passed.

259. Lammi, Elmer W. "Workers Afraid to Blow Whistle on Government." Moneysworth, 8 March 1978, p. 3.

260. "Laws Protect Whistle Blowers." Bioscience, 29 (June 1979), 388.

261. Light, Larry. "Agency to Protect Federal Whistle-blowers From Abuses, Struggles with Money Woes." Congressional Quarterly Weekly Report, 37 (June 1979), 1037-1038.

   Merit Systems Protection Board Chair, Ruth Prokop, claims that the inability of the agency to do its job is the result of loss of government funds.

262. Lindauer, Mitchell J. "Government Employee Disclosures of Agency Wrongdoing: Protecting the Right to Blow the Whistle." University of Chicago Law Review, 42 (Spring 1975), 530-561. See item 1241.

263. Lowy, Joan Bertin. "Constitutional Limitations on the Dismissal of Public Employees." Brooklyn Law Review, 43 (Summer 1976), 1-30.

"In the abstract, public employees enjoy substantial protections against wrongful termination of their employment. However the vindication of these rights ...presents equally substantial practical hurdles" (p. 28). Dismissal is subject to constitutional attack in cases involving deprivation of property, liberty, freedom of speech, arbitrary and irrational governmental action, unequal treatment, or presumption.

264. Luehrs, John E. and Toni Marzotto. "Whistleblowing: Protection Under the Civil Service Reform Act." Paper presented at the Annual Meeting of the Western Political Science Association, 27-29 March 1980 at the San Francisco Hilton, San Francisco, CA.

Analyzes the purpose and implementation of the whistle-blowing provisions of the Act. Luehrs contends that "a review of the initial, and therefore precedent setting, cases reveals a strong tendency on the part of management to justify its personnel actions...on the basis of government efficiency...." (p. 12).

265. Marks, Laurence. "Silencing the Whistleblowers." Atlas, 25 (September 1978), 48.

Reviews the Whistle-blower's Conference in Washington, DC, including case summaries.

266. Miller, James Nathan. "What Happens When Bureaucrats Blow Whistles?" Reader's Digest, 113 (July 1978), 197-204.

Refutes two myths about the federal bureaucracy: (1) that the average government worker is incompetent, concerned only with his own job security; and (2) that the Civil Service Commission (CSC) is a vigilant watchdog of employees' rights. Miller discusses cases to illustrate CSC's lack of support. He considers Senator Proxmire's proposal to institutionalize whistleblowing a promising approach.

267. Mitchell, Greg. Truth...And Consequences: Seven Who Would Not Be Silenced. New York: Dembner Books, 1982, pp. 87-126. See item 1381.

268. Mitchell, Greg. "Blowing the Whistle: For People Who Whistle While They Work, The Government Is Playing a New Tune." Washington Post Magazine, 12 August 1979, pp. 12-19.

68

Whistle-blowing is now institutionalized and part of government, although recent reforms have not eliminated the need for blowing the whistle.

269. Nader, Ralph, Peter J. Petkas, and Kate Blackwell, eds. <u>Whistle-Blowing: The Report of the Conference on Professional Responsibility.</u> New York: Grossman, 1972. See item 1382.

270. Nathan, Raymond. "Whistleblowers: Tattletales or Heroes?" <u>Ethical Society,</u> 2 (Spring 1979), 9-11.

Explores why tattletaling is seen as wrong but treats whistle-blowers as people acting on higher principles. Nathan encourages dissent as an institutional safety-valve, but one that is inoperative when whistle-blowers lose their jobs. Legislation will bring democracy and ethics to the workplace.

271. Nocera, Joseph. "Inspectors General: The Fraud of Fighting Fraud." <u>The Washington Monthly,</u> 10 (February 1979), 31-39

Argues that the Inspectors General are career government investigators known primarily for their ability to survive, to compromise, and keep their jobs.

272. Parmerlee, Marcia A., et al. "Correlates of Whistle-Blowers' Perception of Organizational Retaliation." <u>Administrative Science Quarterly,</u> 27 (March 1982), 17-34.

A survey of whistle-blowers reveals that organizations are more likely to retaliate against dissenters who were valued by their organization, and whose cases lacked public support.

273. Parris, Judith H. "Whistle Blowers' in the Executive Branch." Issue Brief No. IB78006. Washington, DC: Congressional Research Service, 1979.

Includes definition, background, policy analysis, bibliography, and chronology of events.

*274. Peters, Charles and Taylor Branch, eds. <u>Blowing the Whistle: Dissent in the Public Interest.</u> New York: Praeger Publishers, 1972.

Contains eleven articles that appeared in the Washington Monthly. Branch introduces these pieces and has written an introductory and concluding chapter.

275. Proxmire, William. The Fleecing of America. Boston: Houghton Mifflin, 1980.

Tells of the "Golden Fleece of the Month Award" established by Senator Proxmire to expose the most outrageous examples of federal waste. Proxmire analyzes the pressures on Congress to spend public funds, and suggests a program to eliminate them.

276. Raven-Hansen, Peter. "Dos and Don'ts for Whistleblowers: Planning for Trouble." Technology Review, 82 (May 1980), 34-44. See item 470.

277. Reeves, Richard. "The Last Angry Men." Esquire, 1 (March 1978), 41-48. See item 32.

278. Salter, Kenneth. Pentagon Papers Trial. Berkeley: Editorial Justa, 1975.

279. "Schweitzer the Whistleblower." National Review, 33 (November 1981), 1324.

280. Siedman, Eileen. "Professional Societies and Whistleblowing: An Ethical Challenge." Paper presented at the American Society for Public Administration National Conference, 13-15 April 1980, at the San Francisco Hilton, San Francisco, CA.

Professional associations have shied away from direct involvement in the employment problems of their members until recently. Siedman describes the activities of the American Society for Public Administration's Task Force on Whistle-blowing.

281. "Silencing Whistle-blowers." Progressive, 42 (September 1978), 10.

282. Stewart, Lea P. "'Whistle Blowing': Implications for Organizational Communication." Journal of Communication, 80 (Autumn 1980), 90-101. See item 834.

283. Treatster, Joseph. "The Hushing of America." Gallery, August 1979, pp. 40-43, 100-104. See item 42.

284. Uhl, Michael and Ted Ensign. "Blowing the Whistle on Agent Orange." Progressive, 42 (June 1978), 28.

285. "Uncle Sam's Fraud Hotline." U.S. News and World Report, 20 August 1979, p. 38.

286. U.S. Congress, Senate Committee on Governmental Affairs. The Whistleblowers: A Report on Federal Employees Who Disclose Acts of Governmental Waste, Abuse, and Corruption. 95th Congress, 2d Session, 1978. See item 1183.

*287. U.S. Merit Systems Protection Board. Whistleblowing and the Federal Employee: Blowing the Whistle on Fraud, Waste, and Mismanagement--Who Does it and What Happens. Washington, DC: The Board, 1981.

Report of a survey of federal employees which found that (1) they have substantial knowledge of fraud, waste, and abuse; (2) many wasteful or illegal activities go unreported; (3) the belief that "nothing could be done" is the major reason for not reporting; (4) a substantial percentage of employees who report illegal or wasteful activities suffer reprisals; (5) there is a widespread lack of knowledge concerning the existence of various channels to receive whistle-blower complaints; and (6) employees feel that agencies do not encourage dissent.

288. U.S. Merit Systems Protection Board. Decisions of the United States Merit Systems Protection Board. Vol. 1. Washington, DC: U.S. Government Printing Office, 1980.

Contains the text of Board decisions from January 11, 1979 through March 19, 1980.

289. U.S. Merit Systems Protection Board. Decisions of the United States Merit Systems Protection Board. Vol. 2. Washington, DC: U.S. Government Printing Office, 1980.

Contains the text of Board decisions from March 20, 1980 through July 22, 1980.

290. U.S. Merit Systems Protection Board. Index to Decisions of the United States Merit Systems Protection Board. Vol. 2. Washington, DC: U.S. Government Printing Office, 1980.

291. Vaughn, Robert G. "Whistleblowing and the Character of Public Employment." The Bureaucrat, 6 (Winter 1977), 29-34.

Emphasizes the fundamental importance of personal responsibility in the civil service, and the reluctance of courts to respond to the needs of whistleblowers. Vaughn suggests establishing an outside institution to review agency action against whistleblowers. Also see item 299.

292. Vogel, A. "Why Don't Employees Speak Up?" Personnel Administration, 30 (1967), 18-24.

293. Walters, Kenneth D. "Your Employees' Right to Blow the Whistle." Harvard Business Review, 53 (July-August 1975), 26-34, 161-162. See item 45.

*294. Weinstein, Deena. Bureaucratic Opposition: Challenging Abuses at the Work Place. New York: Pergamon Press, 1979.

Analyzes organizations as political systems instead of rational, neutral entities. Weinstein maintains the most do not have institutionalized procedures for dissent and have not recognized its legitimacy. Bureaucratic opposition is, therefore, interpreted as pathological rather than morally legitimate behavior.

295. Weinstein, Deena. "Opposition to Abuse Within Organizations: Heroism and Legalism." ALSA Forum, 4 (Fall 1979), 5-21.

296. Weinstein, Deena. "Bureaucratic Opposition: The Challenge to Authoritarian Abuses at the Workplace." Canadian Journal of Political and Social Theory, 1 (Spring/Summer 1977), 31-46.

*297. Weisband, Edward and Thomas M. Frank. Resignation in Protest: Political and Ethical Choices Between Loyalty to Team and Loyalty to Conscience in American Public Life. New York: Grossman, 1975.

Uses ad hoc examples, case studies and quantitative data to emphasize the debilitating organizational ethic of unquestioned loyalty. The percentage of officials who resign has declined substantially in this century. Most resign, not in protest, but "like gentlemen." Unlike England, there is no tradition of public protest resignation in America. Discusses the costs of a system based above all on the value of "team play."

298. "Whistleblower Reinstated at HEW." Science, 3 August 1979, p. 1.

*299. "Whistle-blowing Forum." The Bureaucrat, 6 (Winter 1977), 3-94.

Proceedings of the 1977 Conference on Whistle-blowing of the Government Accountability Project. Explores the rationale behind whistle-blowing and the kinds of protections needed. The opening session included several speeches by well-known experts. Alan Campbell, chairman of the Civil Service Commission, defended the administration's position on employee rights. Replies by whistle-blowers describing their experiences followed. Six workshops covered topics such as: the media, union programs, legislative branch, administrative procedures, litigation, the courts, and public interest groups. Concluding sessions examined the kinds of reform measures that would be needed to safeguard the whistle-blowers' domain.

300. Whitten, Les. "The Whistle Blowers." Harpers' Bazaar, September 1972, pp. 168-169.

Discusses Nader's Clearing House for Professional Responsibility, including an interview with its director.

301. Wright, Connie. "When Will We Whip Whistle Blowers?" Nation's Cities Weekly, 9 (June 1980), p. 3.

Reports the American Society for Public Administration's whistle-blowing statement (See item 219).

302. "You're Blowing the Whistle on Wrongdoing?" Washington, DC: The Ethical Society, n.d.

A folder offering the services of the Society to potential government whistle-blowers.

Section III

Government

B. Ethics and Corruption

303. Abrahamson, Bengt. Bureaucracy or Participation. Beverly Hills, CA: Sage, 1977.

304. Adair, John J. "How Vulnerable Are Federal Agencies to Fraud, Waste and Abuse?" Paper presented at the National Conference on Fraud, Waste, and Abuse, 5-7, October 1980, at the Pittsburgh Hilton, Pittsburgh, PA.

Discusses the mission of the General Accounting Office Task Force for the Prevention of Fraud to determine the scope of the problem, operate a nationwide telephone "hotline," and conduct "vulnerability assessments" to estimate the susceptibility of agencies and their programs to fraud and abuse.

305. Adams, Randolph K. An Analysis of Existing Ethical Guidelines and the Development of a Proposed Code of Ethics for Managers. Springfield, VA: National Technical Information Service, 1976. See item 55.

306. Allen, Robert F. "The IK in the Office." Organizational Dynamics, 8 (Winter 1980), 26-41. See item 57.

307. Armstrong, DeWitt C. and George A. Graham. "Ethical Preparation for the Public Service." The Bureaucrat, 4 (April 1975), 5-23.

Lists assumptions concerning ethical standards, noting, for example, that ethical foundations are laid in early years. Author assumes that although these foundations are established early in life the process of building a liveable superstructure continues throughout a life time. Consequently, professional schools can and should increase student perceptiveness of moral issues. Concludes by enumerating routes toward improved understanding.

308. Banfield, Edward C. "Corruption as a Feature of Governmental Organization." Journal of Law and Economics, 18 (December 1975), 587-606.

Offers a brief conceptual scheme for analyzing corruption which is then applied to business and governmental organizations.

309. Benson, George C. S. "Causes and Cures of Political Corruption." Studies in the Social Sciences, 14 (June 1975), 1-18.

310. Berg, Larry L., Harlan Hahn, and John Schmidhauser. Corruption in the American Political System. Morristown, NJ: General Learning Press, 1976.

"[P]olitical corruption in the United States is part of the political system rather than the result of the rise of an occasional 'evil man'" (from the Preface). Chapters discuss Watergate, voting behavior, systemic corruption, lobbying, and the electoral process.

311. Bernstein, Marver H. "Ethics in Government: The Problems in Perspective." National Civic Review, 61 (July 1972), 341-347.

Due to the compelling need for clearer guidance in identifying major sources of unethical conduct, state and local governments should undertake steps to alert their employees to ethical dilemmas. Ethical standards should aim to preserve the integrity of government by providing a sensible system of standards, sanctions, and effective administrative machinery.

312. Bequai, August. White Collar Crime: A 20th Century Crisis. Lexington, MA: Lexington Books, 1978. See item 67.

313. Boling, T. Edwin and John Dempsey. "Ethical Dilemmas in Government: Designing an Organization Response." Public Personnel Management, 10 (1981), 11-19.

Identifies types of ethical problems faced by public administrators. Suggests reforms in the tenor of organizational life through conceptual classification, whistle-blower protection, and a program of normative enrichment.

314. Boling, T. Edwin. "Organizational Ethics: Rules, Creativity and Idealism." Management Handbook for Public Administration. Ed. John W. Sutherland. New York: Van Nostrand Reinhold Co., 1978, chapter 3, pp. 221-253. See item 69.

315. Bollens, John C. and Henry J. Schmandt. Political
     Corruption: Power, Money and Sex. Pacific Pali-
     sades, CA: Palisades Publishers, 1979.

     "Through the use of case material, the book exam-
     ines different forms that the abuse of public office
     takes, the kind of people that get involved, the cir-
     cumstances in which such behavior arises, its impact
     on the political system, and the efforts to confine or
     eliminate it" (p. 8). Emphasizes corruption since
     1960.

316. Bowie, Norman E., ed. Ethical Issues in Government.
     Washington, DC: Urban Institute Press, 1981.

     Nationally known philosophers consider ethical is-
     sues that American politicians will face in the fu-
     ture.

317. Bowman, James S. "The Management of Ethics: Codes of
     Conduct in Organizations." Public Personnel Man-
     agement, 10 (1981), 59-66. See item 71.

318. Bowman, James S., ed. "Special Issue on Ethics in Gov-
     ernment." Public Personnel Management, 10
     (1981), entire.

     Consists of eight articles, 12 shorter essays,
     three case studies, a book review essay, current re-
     search notes, and an overview essay with an annotated
     bibliography. (See item 1321.) Also see T. Edwin
     Boling and John Dempsey, "Ethical Dilemmas in Govern-
     ment: Designing an Organizational Response" (item
     313).

319. Bowman, James S. "Ethics in the Federal Service: A
     Post-Watergate View." Midwest Review of Public Ad-
     ministration, 11 (March 1977), 3-20.

     Surveys attitudes of federal administrators. Con-
     cludes that while respondents demonstrate a high level
     or concern over both macro (government-wide) and micro
     (daily agency management) level ethics, some kind of
     institutional basis for professional conduct is neces-
     sary.

320. Bowman, James S. "Managerial Ethics in Business and Government." Business Horizons, 19 (October 1976), 48-54. See item 72.

321. Caiden, Gerald. "Public Maladministration and Bureaucratic Corruption: A Comparative Perspective." Paper presented at the National Conference on Fraud, Waste, and Abuse, 5-7 October 1980, Pittsburgh Hilton, Pittsburgh, PA.

   Emphasizes the persistence of corruption with a thorough explanation of the reasons it persists.

322. Caiden, Gerald E. and Naomi J. Caiden. "Coping with Administrative Corruption: An Academic Perspective." Dynamics of Development: An International Perspective. S. K. Shama, New Delhi: Concept Publishing, 1979, chapter 29, 478-494.

   Discusses methodological problems of studying corruption, causes of corruption, and effective ways to deal with it.

323. Caiden, Gerald. "Administrative Reform: A Prospectus." International Review of Administrative Sciences, 44 (1978), 106-120.

   A review and critique of types of administrative change from 1960-1978, with an emphasis on cross-cultural and trans-national developments. Highlights the incapacity of present administrative systems to deliver services or improve the quality of life. Stresses that many reform efforts are short-sighted, and that piecemeal measures change internal structures without delivering new outcomes. Caiden identifies "priorities for a continuing agenda" to address these problems.

324. Caiden, Gerald E. and Naomi J. Caiden. "Administrative Corruption." Public Administration Review, 37 (May/June 1977), 301-309.

   Analyzes the traditional, revisionist, and non-revisionist approaches to the study of corruption, concluding that these fail to recognize the existence of systematic corruption where wrong doing has become the norm. A number of illustrative hypotheses are included.

325. Caiden, Naomi. "Shortchanging the Public." Public Administration Review, 39 (May/June 1979), 294-298.

A book review essay that explores the origins of and potential solutions to corruption in American government.

326. Casey, James and Clifford G. Christians, eds. Free Expression in Democratic Societies. Urbana: University of Illinois Press, 1982.

327. Chandler, Ralph C. "Ethics and Public Policy." Commonwealth, May 1978, pp. 302-309.

"How can public administrators properly plant, bring to flower, and keep weeded a personal code of ethical performance . . .?" (p. 303). This question is discussed with reference to major historical scandals and key issues in public administration. "The problem of administrative ethics continues to be one of discretion . . . and pursuit of the public and good" (p. 308). Michigan's Public Act 196(1977) is analyzed as an example of legislation that effectively deals with ethical dilemmas.

328. Charlesworth, James C. "Ethics in America--Norms and Deviations." Annals of the American Academy of Political and Social Science, 363, (January 1966), 1-236.

Volume devoted to articles on the norms and deviations of ethics in American government, business, and the professions. It opens with a discussion on the flexibility of ethical codes of ethics in an attempt to determine whether the codes of ethics in public life should be absolute or relative. Unethical behavior in government is discussed, focusing on ethical problems of Congress.

329. Civiletti, Benjamin R. "Watergate Legislation in Retrospect." Talk given at the annual dinner of the University of Chicago Law School and Alumni Association, 25 April 1980, Chicago, IL.

Discusses four laws created in the wake of Watergate: the Freedom of Information Act, the Tax Reform Act, the Ethics in Government Act, and the Right to

Financial Privacy Act. Argues that these acts, while necessary and good in their intent, are overzealous and can hamper the service of justice and impede government efficiency.

330. Cleveland, Harlan. "Systems, Purposes, and Watergate." Public Administration Review, 34 (May/June 1974), 265-268.

Argues that "system thinking" has been deficient in enabling professionals to cope with ethical issues. Noting that a written code of ethics is never comprehensive enough to be a satisfactory guide to personal behavior, author proposes the self-question "If this action is held up to public scrutiny, will I still feel that it is what I should have done and how I should have done it?"

331. Cohen, David. "Responsible Managers and Accountable Institutions." The Bureaucrat, 7 (Winter 1978), 17-21.

President of Common Cause discusses the need to restore public confidence in government and steps being taken to achieve that end.

332. Comptroller General. Continuing and Widespread Weaknesses in Internal Control Result in Losses Through Fraud, Waste, and Abuse. Washington, DC: General Accounting Office, 1980.

Summarizes a series of earlier General Accounting Office (GAO) reports on internal control weaknesses in federal agencies. Repeatedly, GAO has found weaknesses in virtually all aspects of accounting operations. Recommends legislation that would place greater responsibility on agency needs for sound financial control systems.

333. Comptroller General. Federal Agency Standards of Employee Conduct Need Improvement. Washington, DC: General Accounting Office, 1979.

Finds the basic philosophy underlying the application of standards places the burden of responsibility on the employee to know standards, while agencies assume a passive role and react only to employee initiatives. Recommendations focus on financial issues.

334. Comptroller General, Fraud in Government Programs: How Extensive Is It? Can It Be Controlled? Vol. 1. Washington, DC: General Accounting Office, 1981.

Fraud is widespread and undermines the integrity of public institutions. Controls over federal programs are often inadequate or non-existent. Most fraud goes undetected. Some progress is being made, but more needs to be done.

335. Conklin, Patrick J., ed. Ethics, Leadership, and Interdependence. Charlottesville, VA: Federal Executive Institute, 1978.

Collection of three addresses delivered at the Executive Development Days Conference. The topics, individually and collectively, are concerned with ethics, the imperative of leadership, and the recognition of the reality of interdependence as the touchstone of both leadership and management.

336. Cooper, Melvin G. "Administering Ethics Laws: The Alabama Experience." National Civic Review, 68 (February 1979), 77-82.

Evaluates the Ethics Act passed in the 1973 session of the Alabama legislature, considered an extremely tough piece of legislation. Due to added amendments, the law is now too lenient and difficult to administer. Efforts began in 1979 to reach an effective balance by seeking further amendments.

337. Cooper, Terry L. The Responsible Administrator: An Approach to Ethics for the Administrative Role. Port Washington, NY: Kennikat Press, 1982.

"The first and most basic task is to illuminate the ethical situation of the public administrator; to understand . . . the problem of defining and maintaining the responsibility of his or her role" (p. 7). This book is a unique contribution to the literature that links individual decision making in the first three chapters with a democratic ethos for public administration in the last three chapters.

338. Cooper, Terry. "Citizenship in an Age of Scarcity: A Formative Essay on Ethics in Public Administration

Education." Paper presented at the Annual Meeting of the National Association of Schools of Public Affairs and Administration, 19-22 October 1980, Hilton Palacio del Rio Hotel, San Antonio, TX.

Asks "What is the ethical identity of the public administrator in today's era?" Proposes that the obligation of the civil servant be that of responsible citizenship.

339. Daley, Dennis M. "Ethics and Public Administration: Attitudes Toward Professionalism." Paper presented at the Annual Meeting of the American Society for Public Administration, 13-16 April 1980 at the San Francisco Hilton, San Francisco, CA.

Preliminary findings of a survey of state officials on professionalism are presented.

339a. Dempsey, John R. "Ethical Dilemmas in Government: Designing an Organizational Response." Paper prepared for presentation at the 1980 Annual Meeting at the American Society for Public Administration, San Francisco, April 13-16, 1980.

340. Dobel, J. Patrick. "The Corruption of a State." American Political Science Review, 72 (September 1978), 958-973.

Presents a theory that the corruption of a state involves changes in the social and political relations of the citizenry. Corruption, the moral incapacity of people to make commitments to the general good, is seen as part of the human condition. Structures to discourage these tendencies must be designed, including an increase in the amount of public participation in all aspects of political life.

341. Douglas, Jack D. and John M. Johnson, eds. Official Deviance: Readings in Misfeasance, and Other Forms of Corruption. Philadelphia: J. B. Lippincott Co., 1977.

Thirty-six selections address such issues as the meaning of official deviance, its changing forms, federal usurpations of power, official violence, police corruption, and solutions to deviance.

342. Dwoskin, Robert P. Rights of the Public Employee. Chicago: American Library Association, 1978. See item 1236.

343. Ealy, Steven D. "On the Ethical Basis of Bureaucratic Action: Democracy, Rationalization, and Communicative Competence." Paper presented at the Regional Conference of the American Society for Public Administration, 8 October 1979 at Albuquerque, NM.

   Considers three models (see title) that claim to provide a ground for bureaucratic activity.

344. Eddy, William B. "Credibility of the Public Managers: A Personal/Professional Issue." The Bureaucrat, 9 (Fall 1980), 11-16.

   In order to stimulate consideration of credibility, a series of propositions are examined [e.g., "Focusing directly on the credibility of the government . . . is of doubtful payoff. Working on the credibility of individual managers . . .may be useful: (p. 12)].

345. Edelhertz, Herbert and Charles Rogovin, eds. A National Strategy for Containing White Collar Crime. Lexington, MA: Lexington Books, 1980. See item 98.

346. Enhancing Government Accountability: A Program for Evaluating Accounting Controls and Improving Public Reporting. New York: Price, Waterhouse, 1979.

   Guide prepared for public officials to assess the effectiveness of their internal accounting control and reporting systems.

347. Ermann, M. David and Richard J. Lundman, eds. Corporate and Governmental Deviance: Problems of Organizational Behavior in Contemporary Society. 2nd Edition. New York: Oxford University Press, 1978. See item 104.

348. Erskine, Hazel. "The Polls: Corruption in Government." Public Opinion Quarterly, 37 (Winter 1973-74), 628-644.

   Survey results since 1935 are presented.

349. "The Ethics Squeeze on Ex-Government Lawyers." Business Week, 23 (February 1976), 82.

350. "Ethics (Symposium)." Public Interest, 63 (Spring 1981), entire issue. See item 106.

351. "Ethics in Government (Symposium)." American Economic Review, 67 (February 1977), 316-325.

352. Etzioni, Amitai. "Alternative Conceptions of Accountability: The Example of Health Administration." Public Administration Review, 35 (May/June 1975), 279-286.

    Four alternative conceptions of accountability are discussed and illustrated through examples in health administration: symbolic, political process, checks and balances, and guidance.

353. Evans, John H. III, Barry L. Lewis, and James M. Patton. "Mandated Public Sector Internal Control Systems as a Possible Deterrent to Fraud, Waste, and Abuse." Paper presented at the National Conference on Fraud, Waste, and Abuse, 5-7 October 1980, Pittsburgh Hilton, Pittsburgh, PA.

    Points out the need to control fraud in the public sector by comparing government and business in the context of the Foreign Corrupt Practices Act of 1977.

354. Feldman, Daniel L. Reforming Government: Willing Strategies Against Waste, Corruption, and Mismanagement. New York: Morrow, 1981

    Demonstrates methods for reforming government at all levels, and shows that unwieldy systems and apathy are as much a threat to stable government as corruption. Step-by-step analysis of the ways to investigate leads, evaluate evidence, and enlist support reveal how America's balance-of-powers system is working --and not working-- after two hundred years.

355. Feldman, Daniel L. "Combatting Waste in Government." Policy Analysis, 6 (Fall 1980), 467-477.

    Presents a framework for investigating and changing corruption and mismanagement in government. Describes successful applications of the format, and shows how the political interests of a legislator can be harnessed in such efforts.

356. Fleishman, Joel, Lance Liebman, and Mark Moore, eds. Public Duties: The Moral Obligations of Public Officials. Cambridge, MA: Harvard University Press, 1981.

Contributors include Sissela Bok, Donald P. Warwick, Dennis F. Thompson, and others as well as the editors.

357. Fleishman, Joel L. and Bruce L. Payne. Ethical Dilemmas and the Education of Policymakers. Hastings-on-Hudson, NY: The Hastings Center, 1980.

Part of the Hastings Center Monograph Series (see item 670) which provides a full treatment of ethical problems confronting policy analysts, presents results of a survey on teaching in the area, and makes recommendations for the future.

358. Fletcher, Thomas, Paula Gordon, and Shirley Hentzell. An Anticorruption Strategy for Local Governments. Washington, DC: National Institute of Law Enforcement and Criminal Justice, 1979.

Handbook describes the importance of the issue and the ethical basis of public service. A specific management control system is then presented in seven chapters. Concluding section examines obstacles to change and how to overcome them.

359. "Forum on Professional Standards.: The Bureaucrat, 6 (Summer 1977), 3-68.

360. Foster, Gregory D. "Law, Morality, and the Public Servant." Public Administration Review, 41 (January/February, 1981), 29-34.

"The law . . . fosters a particular way of looking at and responding to situations that is essentially amoral in nature . . ." (p. 29).

361. Freidman, Burton D. The Quest for Accountability. Chicago: Public Administration Service, 1973.

Discusses what it means for a public agency to be accountable, stages in the process of holding bureaucracy accountable, and means and problems in achieving fuller accountability in government.

362. Friedrich, Carl J. The Pathology of Politics: Violence, Betrayal, Corruption, Secrecy and Propaganda. New York: Harper and Row, 1972.

Examines four interdependent and mutually reinforcing aspects of politics, listed in the subtitle, that serve to maintain or develop the pathology.

363. Golembiewski, Robert T. "The MARTA Code of Ethics: Conflict Between . . . Private Interests . . . and Public Responsibilities." Unpublished monograph, Urban Mass Transportation Administration, Washington, DC, n.d.

364. Graham, George A. Ethical Guidelines for Public Administrators: Observations on Rules of the Games." Public Administration Review, 31 (January/February 1974), 90-92.

Conflicts of loyalty, involvement, and commitments lead to serious ethical problems for the administrator. Suggests guidelines by considering three questions: (1) how should administrators select input to decisions; (2) what are the limits of compromise; and (3) how should they implement decisions?

365. Greer, Scott, Ronald D. Hedlund, and James L. Gibson, eds. Accountability in Urban Society: Public Agencies Under Fire. Beverly Hills, CA: Sage, 1978.

A collection of fourteen original essays dealing with accountability and (a) professionalism; (b) political institutions; (c) controls; and (d) research design.

366. Gunn, Elizabeth M. "Administrative Responsibility: Operationalizing Theoretical Concepts." Paper presented at the 1981 Annual convention of the American Society of Public Administrators, The Renaissance Center, Detroit, MI, 12-15 April 1981.

Fully-documented review of the literature.

367. Halperin, Morton H., Jeffery J. Berman, Robert L. Boro-
     sage, and Christine M. Marwick. The Lawless
     State. New York: Penguin Books, 1976.

     Report on the crimes and abuses of the U.S. intel-
     ligence agencies. Reviews each agency's history of po-
     litical spying and presents two case studies, the CIA
     campaign against President Allende of Chile and the
     FBI vendetta against Martin Luther King.

368. Hartwig, Richard. "Ethics and Organizational
     Structure." The Bureaucrat, 9 (Winter 1980-81),
     48-56.

     Suggests that ethical dilemmas are inherent in the
     public service. A distinction should be made between
     personal and organizational ethics. Irreducible cri-
     teria must be used to determine moral behavior, and or-
     ganizational structure can be a crucial factor in de-
     termining the ethical meaning of employment for indi-
     viduals.

369. Haughey, John C. Personal Values in Public Policy:
     Conversations on Government Decision-Making. Ram-
     sey, NJ: Paulist Press, 1980.

     An introduction, nine essays, and a conclusion that
     explore ethics, theology, and decisionmaking in govern-
     ment. "This volume seeks to build bridges between the
     world of academe and the day to day execution of gov-
     ernmental responsibilities" (p.6). Each article is
     followed by a dialogue between scholars and practition-
     ers.

370. Heidenheimer, Arnold J., ed. Political Corruption:
     Readings in Comparative Analysis. New York:
     Holt, Rinehart, and Winston, 1970.

     A landmark collection of readings intended to "put
     the subject . . back onto the social sciences map" (p.
     v). Materials are organized in both structural analyt-
     ical and political geographic categories. Over 50 se-
     lections are grouped into four parts: the context of
     analysis, analysis of administrative corruption, analy-
     sis of electoral and legislative corruption, and cor-
     ruption and modernization.

371. Henry, Nicholas. "Toward a Bureaucratic Ethic." Public Administration and Public Affairs. 2nd ed. Englewood Cliffs, NJ: Prentice-Hall, 1980. chapter 6, pp. 131-145.

Traces the role of ethics in the evolution of the study of public administration, and recent theoretical attempts at defining a workable framework of moral choice for the public administrator.

371a. French, Peter A. Ethics in Government. Englewood Cliffs, NJ: Prentice-Hall, 1983.

Short monograph for those considering government service. The nine chapters cover the following topics: prudence and morality; dirty hands; the use of moral theories; the dictates of conscience; elected legislators; political executives and career bureaucrats.

372. Hershey, Cary. Protest in the Public Service. Lexington, MA: D. C. Heath Co., 1973.

A 92 page study of the causes and nature of federal employee protest activities, agency responses, and outcomes during the Vietnam War, 1967-1970. While the analysis predates the "Era of Whistle-blowing," (see Section I, "Introduction") it describes the conditions that would ultimately lead to it.

373. Hibbeln, M. Kenneth and Douglas H. Shumavon. "Structuring Administrative Discretion." Paper presented at the Annual Meeting, Western Political Science Association, 25-28 March 1981, at the Denver Hilton, Denver, CO.

In order to assemble, classify, evaluate, or communicate methods for affecting discretion, both the relevant literature and public administrators were surveyed. The former attached more significance to the issue then did the latter. Concludes that internal methods of control are a relatively unchartered area of investigation.

374. Jasper, Herbert N. "The Merit System: She Ain't What She Used to Be." The Bureaucrat, 8 (Winter 1979-80), 25-33.

Argues that recent reforms may greatly "increase the opportunities for abuse--and reduce the capacity to hold anyone accountable" (p. 25, emphasis original). Wonders why "the normal concern for the worst cases failed to forestall such sweeping legislation" (p. 32).

375. Johnston, Michael. Political Corruption and Public Policy in America. Monterey, CA: Brooks/Cole Publishing, 1982.

Provides three analytical perspectives for understanding corruption: personal, institutional and systemic. Three of the seven chapters are devoted to case studies of machine politics, police corruption, and watergate. Johnston offers several reforms and policy proposals noting the necessity of developing a realistic perspective on corruption in a democratic society.

376. Johnston, Michael. "Systematic Origins of Fraud, Waste, and Abuse." Paper presented at the National Conference on Fraud, Waste, and Abuse, 5-7 October 1980, Pittsburgh Hilton, Pittsburgh, PA.

377. Jones, D. Congressional Ethics. 2nd ed. Washington, DC: Congressional Quarterly, 1980.

A comprehensive historical overview is given of general issues and specific cases relating to Congressional ethics. Congressional efforts to regulate the behavior of Federal legislators are discussed.

378. Kernaghan, Kenneth. "Codes of Ethics and Public Administration: Progress, Problems and Prospects." Public Administration (UK), 58 (Summer 1980), 207-223.

Examines "Canadian developments affecting the ethical conduct of public servants; the form, content, and administration of codes of ethics; the benefits and costs of these codes. . ; and the implications of codes. . .for administrative responsibility" (p. 209).

379. Kernaghan, Kenneth. Ethical Conduct: Guidelines for Government Employees. Toronto: Institute of Public Administration of Canada, 1975.

Considers the need for and value of codes of ethics as well as the problems of conflict of interest, political activity and public comment, and confidentiality. Concludes with guidelines for ethical conduct in each of the problem areas. Great Britain, the United States, and Canada are discussed in terms of their attempts to deal with these issues.

380. Kernaghan, Kenneth. "Codes of Ethics and Administrative Responsibility." Canadian Public Administration, 17 (Winter 1974), 527-540.

Reviews recent Canadian experience in the sphere of ethical conduct among public employees. Discusses codes of ethics, their form, content, and administration, and the relationship of ethical conduct to administrative responsibility. Examines three propositions: first, that the development of a written code of ethics is a useful means of encouraging high ethical standards; second, that a code is preferable to a brief list of guidelines; and third, that the adoption of a written code is likely to enhance administrative responsibility.

381. Kreutzen, S. Stanley. "Protecting the Public Service: A National Ethics Commission," National Civic Review, 61 (July 1972), 339-342.

Proposes the creation of a national commission on ethics in government to render opinions on conflicts of interest and to provide continued guidance on ethical standards.

382. LeVine, Victor T. Political Corruption and the Informal Polity. New York: Panther Press, 1971.

Initial section of the book presents preliminary observations about corruption and suggests in a model some elements of the behaviors and processes involved in political corruption: the formal polity, political positions and roles, political goods and resources, exchange and conversion processes, informal political networks, and informal policy.

383. Lilla, Mark T. "Ethos, 'Ethics,' and Public Service." Public Interest, 63 (Spring 1981), 3-17.

"[H]owever inadequate the old public administration was . . . it did embody an ethos which prepared

the student . . . to take his place within a democratic government . . . [T]he ethics movement can only
hope to produce a new generation of casuists , not a
revived tradition of moral public service. The task
for which students are now unprepared is the responsible exercise of discretion . . ., and this new realm
of action is profoundly moral in nature" (pp. 8, 12,
16).

384. Linder, Stephen H. "Administrative Accountability:
Administrative Discretion, Accountability, and External Controls." Accountability, in Urban Society: Public Agencies Under Fire (item 365). pp.
181-196.

385. Lyman, Theodore R., Thomas W. Fletcher, and John A.
Gardiner. Prevention, Detection, and Correction
of Corruption in Local Government: A Presentation
of Potential Models. Washington, DC: Law Enforcement Assistance Administration, 1978.

"These program models are designed to summarize and
analyze the experience of local governments . . . in
preventing and responding to problems of official corruption" (p. iii). Subjects include the problems of
corruption, how to diagnose it, and internal and external remedies.

386. McCloskey, Paul N., Jr. Truth and Untruth: Political Deceit in America. New York: Simon and Schuster, 1972. See item 365.

Congressman and Presidential candidate McCloskey
discusses the need for faith, skepticism, and truth in
the executive branch, Congress, the judiciary, and the
press.

387. Mertins, Herman, Jr., ed. Professional Standards and
Ethics: A Workbook for Public Administrators.
Washington, DC: American Society for Public Admin-
istration, 1979.

Takes personal judgment rather than prescription as
a guide for people making ethical and practical decisions. Topics in this diagnostic workbook include
responsibility and accountability, commitment, conflicts of interest, public disclosure and confidentiality, and professional ethics.

Second edition (1982) is entitled Applying Professional Standards and Ethics in the Eighties: A Workbook and Study Guide for Public Administrators, coedited with Patrick J. Hennigan.

388. Miewald, Robert D. "Ethics and Administrators: A Review." Midwest Review of Public Administration, 13 (September 1979), 189-196.

Evaluates four 1978-1979 books related to the subject.

389. Miller, William Lee. Of Thee, Nevertheless, I Sing: An Essay in American Political Values. New York: Harcourt Brace Jovanovich, 1975.

Examines the cultural undergirding of American public life. Deals selectively with some well-known people in recent history, with Dwight Eisenhower, Adlai Stevenson, and John Kennedy serving as examples. Argues that the United States has a defective political culture. Discusses the paradoxes in the culture: democracy requires one set of values and American society teaches another; modern life requires a moral clarity that its own machinery inhibits; and twentieth century democracy requires a civic responsibility that its own characteristics discourage.

390. Mosher, Frederick C. et al. "Watergate: Its Implications for Responsive Government." Administration and Society, 6 (August 1974), 155-170.

Report prepared by a Panel of the National Academy of Public Administration that attempts to identify underlying flaws in the American system of government and to suggest directions for change, including statutory initiatives and constitutional amendments. The effectiveness of various codes of ethics depends upon continuing scrutiny of actions of public officials, provided by their colleagues in and out of government, the media, and general public. Ultimately, the moral quality of government depends on the standards of those who gain public office, and on the system of values they have internalized.

391. Murphy, Thomas P. "Ethical Dilemmas for Urban Administrators." Urbanism Past and Present, 4 (Summer 1977), 33-40.

Since most questions of public policy have inherent ethical implications, the manager may have to assess the impact of politics on administration, public accountability and the waste of resources, provisions for equal citizen access, the effect of secrecy on decisionmaking, and the use of inside knowledge for private gain.

392. National Academy of Public Administration. Ethics in the Public Service: Materials Prepared for a Pilot Training Session. Washington, DC: The Academy, 1979.

Includes group presentations, articles, copies of legislation, university course material, and bibliographies.

393. National Training and Development Service. "Ethical and Value Problems in Urban Management Dilemmas." Washington, DC: The Service, 1977.

394. Nigro, Felix A. and Lloyd G. Nigro. "Values and Ethics." Modern Public Administration. 5th ed. New York: Harper and Row, 1980, chapter 4, pp. 67-91.

Insufficient attention has been paid to the goals and means of organizations. Provides overview of practical and theoretical issues in administrative ethics.

395. Payne, Robert. The Corrupt Society: From Ancient Greece to Present Day America. New York: Praeger Publishers, 1975.

396. Peters, John G. and Susan Welch. "Political Corruption in America: A Search for Definitions and a Theory." American Political Science Review, 72 (September 1978), 974-984.

Lack of a clear definition of corruption has limited its systematic study. Offers a conceptual framework that formulates propositions and tests them using data from state legislators. Suggests future research possibilities.

397. Peters, Charles and John Rothchild, eds. Inside the System. 2nd ed. New York: Praeger, 1972.

A collection of articles from the <u>Washington Monthly</u> exposing government bureaucracy not only to the public but to others in the bureaucracy. The contributions, all from journalists, are divided into five sections: the Presidency, Capitol Hill, the Culture of Bureaucracy, Pressures from Outside, and the Realities.

398. Pursley, Robert D. and Neil Snortland. "Administrative Ethics and Responsibility." <u>Managing Government Organizations: An Introduction to Public Administration</u>. North Scituate, MA: Duxbury Press, 1980, chapter 3, pp. 73-104.

Explores administrative discretion, bureaucratic responsibility, administrative aggrandizement, the moral context of public management, codes of conduct, accountability, and unanswered questions in the field.

399. Reich, David. "Ethics." <u>Civil Service Journal</u>, 18 (January/March 1978), 24-26.

Describes the prevailing standards of ethical conduct for government employees. Discusses Executive Order 11222 issued in 1965 by President Johnson, part 735 of the Code of Federal Regulations, House Concurrent Resolution 175, commonly labeled "The Ten Commandments," and President Carter's proposed legislation (H. R. 6954).

400. Roebuck, Julian and Stanley C. Weeber. <u>Political Crime in the United States: Analyzing Crime By and Against Government</u>. New York: Praeger Publishers, 1978.

Seven types of political crime are delineated, and each is analyzed along four dimensions: action patterns, the goals of the offender, the legal status of the offense, and nature of the offense. "Our focus is on the criminal acts of persons . . ., committed during the normal course of their 'activities as employees . . ., that are intended to achieve organizational goals" (p. iv).

401. Rohr, John A. "Ethics for the Senior Executive Service: Suggestions for Management Training." <u>Administration and Society</u>, 12 (August 1980), 203-216.

402. Rohr, John A. Ethics for Bureaucrats: An Essay on Law and Values. New York: Marcel Dekker, 1978.

Provides a discussion of the dilemmas facing bureaucrats, the perspectives of scholars, and suggestions for educating administrators. Contends that regime values, as revealed by the Constitution and the Supreme Court, are the most appropriate focal points for normative reflection and guidance.

403. Rohr, John A. "Ethics for Bureaucrats." America, 128 (May 1973), 488-491.

Argues that since bureaucrats govern in a democratic regime through their administrative discretion, they can be held accountable for their behavior. The bureaucrat's problem is how to use discretionary authority to respond to people's values--specifically equality, freedom and property.

404. Rose-Ackerman, Susan. Corruption: A Study in Political Economy. New York: Academic Press, 1978.

Focuses on the relationships between government agents and citizens in two areas: legislative and bureaucratic corruption. Legislative corruption is analyzed in terms of a perfect democratic state, imperfect information, and interest groups. Bureaucratic corruption is explained in terms of bribery, misuse of monopolistic or regulatory powers, disorganized structures, and market failures.

405. Rosenbloom, David H. "Accountability in the Administrative State." Accountability in Urban Society: Public Agencies Under Fire (item 365), pp. 87-114.

406. Sawhill, John C. "A Question of Ethics." Newsweek, 29 October 1979, p. 27. See item 184.

407. Schaefer, Roberta R. "Democracy and Leadership: Reflections on Political Education of Civil Servants." Southern Review of Public Administration, 2 (December 1978), 345-374.

408. Scott, James C. Comparative Political Corruption. Englewood Cliffs, NJ: Prentice-Hall, 1972.

Different patterns of corruption are examined in political development and nation-building by analyzing the significance of political machines in various countries.

409. Sheehan, Neil and E. W. Kenworthy. Pentagon Papers. New York: Quadrangle, 1971.

410. Sikula, Andrew F. "The Values and Value Systems of Government Executives." Public Personnel Management, 2 (January/February 1973), 16-22.

A small survey of managers that shows personalities in selected careers have unique value systems. The instrumental characteristics most highly valued were honesty, responsibility, capability, helpfulness, and self-control.

411. Simons, Robert H. and Eugene P. Dvorin. Public Administration: Values, Policy and Change. Port Washington, NY: Alfred Publishing, 1977.

A comprehensive textbook that argues public administration is not value free, but "value-full."

412. Smigel, Erwin O. and Lawrence H. Ross, eds. Crimes Against Bureaucracy. New York: Van Nostrand Reinhold, 1970.

Seven contributors deal with issues such as public attitudes toward stealing from bureaucracies, ways in which those who steal avoid self definition as criminals, and methods of prevention.

413. Snyder, David P. "The Uncivil Servant." The Bureaucrat, 2 (Fall 1973), 310-314.

Reviews the changing state of bureaucratic risk-taking: in the 1950's, government took few risks; in the late 1960's, the bureaucracy itself became the risk-taker; in the 1970's, the concern is not whether to take risks, but how to minimize them.

414. Sobel, Lester A., ed. Post-Watergate Mortality. New York: Facts on File, 1978.

Reports on world events during the years immediately following Watergate. Topics include Watergate,

"Koreagate," Congressional ethics, corporate funds and political favors, the Carter administration's emphasis on ethics, financial abuses, and the continuing attack on corruption.

415. "Special Issue on ICMA Code of Ethics." Public Management, 63 (March 1981), entire.

Consists of a series of short articles describing the development and implementation of the International City Manager's Association Code.

416. Special National Workshop: Prevention and Detection of Fraud, Waste, and Abuse of Public Funds. Proceedings. Washington, DC: Law Enforcement Assistance Administration, 1979.

Workshop participants recommended strengthened commitment to corruption, an initiation of a public education campaign, development of model programs, and improvements in training courses.

417. "Special Report." Civil Liberties Review, 5 (September/October 1978), 6-49. See item 13.

418. "Special Section: Honesty/Ethical Standards." Gallup Opinion Index, 150 (January 1980), 7-29. See item 195.

419. Stahl, O. Glenn. "Loyalty, Dissent, and Organizational Health." The Bureaucrat, 3 (July 1974), 162-171.

Bases the proper balance between loyalty and dissent on four principles: loyalty and reasonable conformity are essential conditions of any concerted effort; executives seeking loyalty by surrounding themselves with "yes men" overlook valuable employees; encouraging diversity of opinion ensures higher loyalty; and subordinates involved in decision-making implement policy with fewer problems.

420. Stanley, John D. "Dissent in Organizations." Academy of Management Review, 6 (January 1981), 13-19. See item 36.

421. Stupak, Ronald J. "Ethics, Values, and the Public Service: A Values Clarification Module." Washington, DC: National Institute of Public Affairs, 1979.

Through the use of a variety of learning techniques, explores the multi-faceted nature of the topic.

422. Terapack, Richard G. "Administering Ethics Laws: The Ohio Experience." National Civic Review, 68 (February 1979), 82-84.

Examines the impact of the 1973 ethics law in Ohio, noting that the general purpose of the legislation was to restore public confidence. Statistics indicate that candidates for public office have not been driven away by financial disclosure, and that no mass resignations by appointed public officials due to financial disclosures have occurred.

423. Thomas, Theodore H. Ethical and Value Dilemmas in Urban Management Performance. Washington, DC: National Training and Development Service, 1977.

A set of activities designed to (a) demonstrate that ethical dilemmas are an intensely personal, deeply complex, everyday managerial problem; and (b) enlarge or expand the range of personally believable, effective, ethical options for action.

424. Thompson, Dennis F. "Moral Responsibility of Public Officials: The Problems of Many Hands." American Political Science Review, 74 (December 1980), 905-916.

Moral responsibility is difficult to ascribe to any single official concerned with decision-making in the modern state. The idea of personal responsibility is recommended as a useful approach to the problem. Also see items 767 and 994.

425. U.S. Department of Health, Education, and Welfare. Secretary's National Conference on Fraud, Abuse, and Error: Protecting the Taxpayer's Dollar. Conference Proceedings. Washington, DC: U.S. Government Printing Office, 1979.

Opening remarks, workshops, and discussion groups represent an exchange of information on ways to improve efficiency and integrity in HEW programs while continuing and enhancing the programs' ends.

426. U.S. Merit Systems Protection Board. The Other Side of the Coin: Removals for Incompetence in the Federal Service. Washington, D.C.: The Board, 1982.

Addresses the question of whether poor performers who cannot or will not improve are removed from the federal service. Statistical data regarding removal of federal employees because of inadequate performance is examined as well as attitudinal data describing the extent to which employees feel that they, or their bosses, are likely to be removed should performance be inadequate.

427. U.S. Merit Systems Protection Board. Breaking Trust: Prohibited Personnel Practices in the Federal Service. Washington, D.C.: The Board, 1982.

This 27 page monograph, the first in a series, examines prohibited personnel practices, such as those used against whistle-blowers, and the effectiveness of preventive mechanisms.

428. Wakefield, Susan. "Ethics and the Public Service: A Case for Individual Responsibility." Public Administration Review, 36 (November/December 1976), 661-666.

Argues, contrary to some recent literature stressing professional codes and institutional checks on administrative behavior, that the first line of defense against unethical conduct is the development of internalized values among employees.

429. Waldo, Dwight. "Reflections on Public Morality." Administration and Society, 6 (November 1974), 267-282.

Revision of a series of lectures including topics such as conflict between private and public morality, the necessity of public immorality (in order to be moral in some other sphere), and the prediction (for heuristic purposes) of how the future will change state and organizational forms.

430. Waters, James A. "Catch 20.5: Corporate Morality as an Organizational Phenomenon." Organizational Dynamics, 6 (Spring 1978), 3-19. See item 46.

431. Williams, J. D. "The Ethics of Management." Public Administration: The People's Business. Boston: Little, Brown, 1980, chapter 18, pp. 499-550.

   Examines the ethical dilemmas that make public administration difficult, although worth doing: what types of means to achieve what kind of goals; private gain at public expense; and how to secure the public interest. Problems, implications, and remedies of each dilemma are explored.

432. Wise, David. The Politics of Lying: Government Deception, Secrecy, and Power. New York: Random House, 1973.

   A detailed account of government misinformation and secrecy in the Eisenhower, Kennedy, Johnson, and Nixon administrations, an analysis of how this happened, and why Americans have come to feel frustrated, powerless, and distrustful of their elected leaders.

433. Zemke, Ron. "Ethics Training: Can We Really Teach People Right from Wrong?" Training, 14 (May 1977), 37-41. See item 217.

Section III

Government

C. Historical Literature

434. Amick, George. The American Way of Graft: A Study of Corruption in State and Local Government, How it Happens, and What Can Be Done About It. Princeton, NJ: Center for Analysis of Public Issues, 1976.

435. Benson, George C. S. Corruption in America. Lexington, MA: Lexington Books, 1978.

A descriptive account of the nature, origins and politics of municipal, state and federal corruption in the 19th and 20th centuries. Benson outlines the cost, theories, and control of corruption.

436. Boyd, James and Jack Anderson. Confessions of a Muckracker: The Inside Story of Life in Washington during the Truman, Eisenhower, Kennedy, and Johnson Years. New York: Random House, 1979.

437. Brooks, Robert C. Corruption in American Politics and Life. New York: Arno Press, 1974.

Reprint of an early classic.

438. Diamond, Martin. "Ethics and Politics: The American Way." The Moral Foundations of the American Republic. Edited by Robert H. Horowitz. Charlottesville, VA: University Press of Virginia, 1977, chapter 5, pp. 39-72.

Re-examines the Federalist understanding of civic virtue.

439. Eisenstadt, Abraham S., Ari Hoogenboom, and Hans L. Trefousse, eds. Before Watergate: Problems of Corruption in American Society. Brooklyn, NY: Brooklyn College Press, 1978.

A collection of 13 essays by historians covering the American Revolution, Federalist and Jacksonian Eras, the Reconstruction Period, the Gilded Age and World War I.

440. Joseph, Joan, ed. Political Corruption. New York: Washington Square Press, 1974.

Opening essay introduces the major cases of corruption in the federal government from Alexander Hamilton through Watergate. The readings which follow provide a picture of corruption as seen from many viewpoints: participants in the events themselves, critics and defenders of what has taken place, and those who suggest reforms.

441. Larson, James S. "Bureaucratic Corruption: An Historical Analysis." Paper presented at the Annual Meeting of the American Political Science Association, September 1981, New York Hilton, New York City, NY.

Analyzes upper level bureaucratic corruption in presidential administrations from 1869-1970. The results indicate that time variables are not associated with corruption: corruption has an equal chance of occurring during wartime, peacetime, or immediately before or after wars.

442. Lockard, Duane. "The 'Great Tradition' of American Corruption." New Society, 31 May 1973, pp. 486-488.

Offers explanations for the causes of corruption by pointing out that although local government corruption is not new, it was not until Watergate that some of its techniques reached the presidential level.

443. Miller, Nathan. The Founding Finaglers: An Account of the Corruption in the U.S. New York: McKay Co., 1976.

". . . [L]ong before Watergate, Americans have been alternately angered and entertained by the unbridled venality of their elected leaders without doing much about it" (p. vii). Emphasizes the period before 1900.

444. Payne, Robert. The Corrupt Society: From Ancient Greece to Present Day America. New York: Praeger, 1975.

445. Woodin, George B. The Shady Side of America: A Roundup of the Scoundrels, Deceivers, and Corrupters over 400-Odd Years Before Watergate. New York: Bold Face Books, 1974.

Incidents, facts, and attitudes of the leaders in American history have been kept from the public from the time of Columbus through Eisenhower.

Section IV

Science and Engineering

Albert Flores

A. Whistleblowing and Dissent

446. Alpern, Ken. "Engineers as Moral Heroes." Paper presented at the Second National Conference on Ethics in Engineering, 5-6 March 1982, at Bismark Hotel, Chicago, IL. Forthcoming in item 722b.

446a. Anderson, Robert M., et al. <u>Divided Loyalties: Whistle-Blowing at BART</u>. West Lafayette, IN: Purdue Research Foundation, 1980.

Examines the events which culminated in the firing of three engineers from the San Francisco Bay Area Rapid Transit (BART). Raises questions about the structure and functioning of large, technologically-oriented organizations and the behavior of professional employees in those organizations. Chronicles the surrounding events from different points of view and draws prescriptive conclusions concerning standards of behavior for individuals and organizations.

447. Baum, Robert J. "Whistleblowing." <u>Ethics and Engineering Curricula</u>. Hastings-on-Hudson, NY: The Hastings Center, 1980, pp. 61-66. See item 670.

Identifies aspects of whistle-blowing in need of future research: collective responsibility; conflicting truth claims; techniques for effectively blowing the whistle and managing dissent; attaching criminal liability to supervisors who override expert recommendation; and revision of codes of ethics to address whistle-blowing.

448. Bogen, Kenneth T. "Managing Technical Dissent in Private Industry: Societal and Corporate Strategies for Dealing with the Whistle-blowing Professional." <u>Industrial and Labor Relations Forum</u>, 13 (1979), 3-32.

An article based on the author's thesis (see item 449).

*449. Bogen, Kenneth T. "Whistleblowing by Technical Experts: Existing and Proposed Means of Protecting and Assisting the Technical Dissenter in Government and Industry." Unpublished thesis, Princeton University, 1978.

Surveys the organizational context for whistle-blowing and the unique characteristics of scientists and engineers as employees, followed by a review of 13 cases of dissent in regulatory agencies and industry. An analysis of existing forms of organizational assistance to whistle-blowing employees is presented, including the Civil Service Commission and other grievance procedures, management strategies, technical review board, ombudsmen, and related avenues. The role of the courts is examined, including a review of applicable federal statutes, common law, and proposals for reform. Finally, the function of professional societies in protecting technical whistleblowing through the enforcement of professional codes of ethics is discussed. Bogen predicts federal legislation will be enacted to prohibit retaliatory dismissal of legitimate whistle-blowers in the private sector. See also his "Managing Technical Dissent in Private Industry," item 448.

450.   Carter, Luther J. "Job Protection for 'Whistle Blowers' Being Tested." Science, 7 March 1980, p. 1057.

The state of Missouri challenged the right of a health physicist to seek federal protection from loss of his job at a state hospital where he "blew the whistle." He was ordered reinstated with back pay by the Department of Labor, but Missouri challenged the order which was based on the Eleventh Amendment.

*451.   Chalk, Rosemary, ed. Scientists as Whistle Blowers: A Report of the AAAS Committee on Scientific Freedom and Responsibility. Washington, DC: American Association for the Advancement of Science, forthcoming.

Consists of 20 edited and original contributions divided into four sections: "Scientists as Whistle Blowers," "Due Process Trends in the Workplace," "Professional Society Roles," and "Conclusions of the AAAS Committee on Scientific Freedom and Responsibility."

452.   Chalk Rosemary, and Frank von Hippel. "Due Process for Whistle-Blowers: Part 1 - The Professional's Dilemma." Mechanical Engineering, 102 (April 1980), 82.

Discusses the conflicting loyalties of engineers who might blow the whistle. Argues that organizations should develop due process procedures for dealing with dissenters in a fair and responsive manner. These could also protect the employer from those who would raise issues without reasonable grounds.

453. Chalk, Rosemary and Frank von Hippel. "Due Process for Whistle-Blowers: Part 2 - Who Should Protect Dissenters?" Mechanical Engineering, 102 (May 1980), 76.

Reviews attempts to protect whistle-blowers by professional societies, the courts, and Congress. Argues that making dissent public will raise, rather than lower, the quality of the policy-making process for technology.

454. Chalk, Rosemary and Frank von Hippel. "Due Process for Dissenting Whistle-Blowers." Technology Review, 81 (June/July 1979), 49-55. See item 232.

455. Chalk, Rosemary. "Scientific Society Involvement in Whistleblowing." Newsletter on Science, Technology and Human Values, (January 1978), 47-51.

456. "Engineers Who Blew the Whistle on BART Are Vindicated." American Machinist, September 1975, p. 73.

457. Fluegge, Ronald M. "Whistle-Blowing and Scientific Responsibility: The Management of Technical Dissent." Presentation at the 144th National Meeting of the American Association for the Advancement of Science, 12-17 February 1978, Washington, DC.

458. Fox, Cecil H. "Sakharov and Whistle-Blowing." Science, 30 May 1980, p. 976.

Discusses Andrei Sakharov of the Soviet Union, a scientist whistle-blower. Argues for the establishment of an international organization, analogous to Amnesty International, to publicize the plight of scientists who have fallen afoul of officialdom because of their beliefs.

459. Friedlander, Gordon D. "The Case of the Three Engineers vs. BART." IEEE Spectrum, 22 (October, 1974), 69-76.

An account of the events of the Bay Area Rapid Transit incident, based on interviews.

460. von Hippel, Frank. "Protecting the Whistle Blowers." *Physics Today*, October 1977, pp. 9-13.

Reviews James Olson's 1972 survey of the National Society of Professional Engineers whose findings include: 10 percent were required to do things which violated their sense of right and wrong; 40 percent felt restrained from criticizing employer's activities or products; 60 percent had expressed disapproval to employer; and most were in favor of professional society protection of whistle-blowers. Appraises protection mechanisms and points to their necessity since the potential dangers of technology are so high.

461. Holden, Constance. "Police Seize Primates at NIH Funded Lab." *Science*, 2 October 1981, p. 32.

Discusses the Montgomery County police raid on the Institute for Behavioral Research, which resulted in the seizure of seventeen allegedly abused monkeys. The raid resulted from inside information supplied by University of Maryland volunteer Alex Pacheco, a founder of an animal-rights group called People for Ethical Treatment of Animals.

462. Holden, Constance. "Scientist with Unpopular Data Loses Job." *Science*, 14 November 1980, p. 749.

A review of the case of a marine biologist dismissed after pressuring his company to include data potentially unfavorable to its clients in testimony before the Environmental Protection Agency.

463. Kennedy, Carol S. "Whistleblowing: Contribution or Catastrophe?" Paper presented at the American Association for the Advancement of Science, 15 February 1978, Washington, DC, See item 255.

464. "Laws Protect Whistle Blowers." *Bioscience*, 29 (June 1979), 388.

464b. Malin, Martin. "Current Status of Legal Protection for Whistleblowers." Paper presented at the Second National Conference on Ethics in Engineering, 5-6 March 1982, at Bismark Hotel, Chicago, IL. Forthcoming in item 722b.

465. Mitchel, Greg. Truth . . . And Consequences: Seven Who Would Not Be Silenced. New York: Dembner Books, 1982. See item 1381.

466. Nader, Ralph. "No Protection for Outspoken Scientists." Physics Today, July 1973, pp. 77-78.

    Discusses the defenseless position of scientists who want to speak or act on matters of conscience, pointing out that professional societies offer almost no protection. Nader argues the first step to advancing employees' rights is to develop the role of the public interest scientist. He calls for lobbying in Washington on behalf of public interest science, along with the establishment of a clearinghouse for jobs in the field, and some method of role-broadening. A scientist can perform many functions which include testifying to courts, agencies and Congress, and getting the right information to the public at the right time.

467. Niederhauser, Warren D. "Ethical Issues in Private Industry." AAAS Professional Ethics Project. Edited by Rosemary Chalk, Mark S. Frankel, and Sallie B. Chafer. Washington, DC: American Association for the Advancement of Science, 1980, p. 163.

    Short paper that discusses ethical issues in the American Chemical Society: 1) whistle-blowing; 2) theft of trade secrets; 3) hiring of competitors' employees to obtain trade secrets; 4) inventors' names on patent applications; and 5) proper recognition and credit for ideas.

468. Perrucci, Robert, Robert M. Anderson, Dan E. Schendel, and Leon E. Trachtman. "Whistle-Blowing: Professionals' Resistance to Organizational Authority." Social Problems, 28 (December 1980), 149164.

    Attempts to develop a series of hypotheses relevant to whistleblowing incidents by examining some of the structural features of organizations, and characteristics of professional work roles that increase the likelihood of resistance to organizational authority. Discusses the process by which professionals move toward an action of publicly opposing their organization at the risk of their own careers.

112

469. Perry, Tekla S. "Knowing How to Blow the Whistle."
IEEE Spectrum, 18 (September 1981), 56-61.

Advises that, despite the risks involved, engineers "should no longer always accept management's decisions passively." Recommends steps to follow in
reporting an employer's unethical and objectionable
practices to management, to professional societies, to
the government, and to the public. Discusses the
cases of eight well-known whistle-blowers.

*470. Raven-Hansen, Peter. "Dos and Don'ts for Whistle-
blowers: Planning for Trouble." Technology
Review, 82 (May 1980), 34-44.

Proposes guidelines for effective professional whistle-blowing: focus on the disclosure, not the personalities involved; use internal channels first; antici-
pate and document retaliation; and know when to give
up.

471. "The San Jose Three." Time, 16 February 1976, p.
78.

Describes three nuclear engineers who resigned from
General Electric because they believed that nuclear
safety was not technologically feasible.

472. Shapley, Deborah. "Don't Swallow the Whistle, Blow
It." Science, 27 April 1979, p. 389.

Examines little-known clauses in eight recent
pieces of federal legislation that could be used to
protect whistle-blowers. Employees can file under
these clauses, whether they work for a private or public organization, as long as the organization's activities are affected by one of these laws.

473. Steinacker, I. "Whistle-Blowing and Human Rights."
Communications of the ACM, 23 (1980), 659.

474. Union of Concerned Scientists. Testimony of Briden-
baugh, Hubbard and Minor Before the JCAE, February
18, 1976. Cambridge, MA: Union of Concerned Scientists, 1976.

An assessment of nuclear safety problems by three
experienced General Electric engineers who resigned in
protest over the industry's refusal to acknowledge ma-

jor safety deficiencies in nuclear power plants. Their testimony before the Joint Committee on Atomic Energy covered topics such as the Quality Assurance Program, design defects, personnel radiation exposure and the impact of human error on plant operations.

475. Unger, Stephen H. "The BART Case: Ethics and the Employed Engineer." Institute of Electrical and Electronic Engineers Committee on the Social Implications of Technology Newsletter, No. 6 (September 6, 1973), 6-8.

476. Wade, Nicholas. "Protection Sought for Satirists and Whistle Blowers." Science, 7 December 1973, pp. 1002-1003.

477. Weil, Vivian. "The Brown Ferry Case." Conflicting Loyalties in the Workplace. Edited by F. A. Elliston. Notre Dame, IN: Notre Dame University Press, forthcoming in item 717.

A chronology of events leading to the resignation of three General Electric engineers and one Nuclear Regulatory Commission (NRC) engineer. Briefly discusses: (1) the economic setting of the nuclear power industry; (2) the problems posed by increases in knowledge, especially of hazards and safety requirements; (3) the existence of a network of scientists and engineers heavily involved in the nuclear power industry; (4) the problem of adequate quality control; (5) the status and function of NRC and its ancestor, the Atomic Energy Commission; and (6) the problem of access by the public to information about nuclear power and its industrial development.

477a. Weisband, Edward. "Dissent, Ethical Autonomy and Team Play." Paper prepared for presentation at the Annual Meeting of the American Political Science Association, New York, August 31-September 3, 1978.

478. "Whistleblower Reinstated at HEW." Science, 3 August 1979, p. 1.

479. "Whistleblowers' Forum." New Engineer, 7 (May 1978), 37-41.

480. Zimmerman, Mark D. "Whistle-Blowing: The Perils of Professional Dissent." Machine Design, 12 March 1981, pp. 83-86.

Engineering problems possess several characteristics that can hamper potential whistle-blowing situations: (1) engineers tend to regard disputes as technical or personal in nature; (2) many issues require an assessment of risk which involves political and scientific considerations; and (3) an engineer may confuse proof in the technical sense with proof in the legal sense. Identifies seven tips for a would-be whistle-blower and concludes with a description of the ways management is meeting the challenge.

Section IV

Science and Engineering

B. Professional Responsibility

481. Alpern, Ken. "Engineers as Moral Heroes." Paper read at Second National Conference on Ethics in Engineering, 5-6 March 1982, at Bismark Hotel, Chicago, IL. Forthcoming in item 722b.

482. American Association for the Advancement of Science Professional Ethics Project. Agenda Book for the Workshop on Professional Ethics. Washington, DC: The Association, 1979.

   Designed as a preliminary project document that includes an agenda, list of participants, a brief discussion paper which reviews workshop topics, the guidelines for discussion groups, a short bibliography, and several excerpts from selected readings.

483. American Association for the Advancement of Science. Committee on Scientific Freedom and Responsibility: 1978 Annual Report. Washington, DC: The Association, 1978.

   Reviews yearly activities of the Committee, focusing on subcommittee reports, case review procedures, and issues such as professional rights and responsibilities.

484. American Association for the Advancement of Science, Committee on Scientific Freedom and Responsibility. 1975 Annual Report. Washington, DC: The Association, 1975.

   Recommends mechanisms to enable the AAAS to review specific instances in which scientific freedom is alleged to have been violated. The importance of due process in dealing with disputes arising from whistle-blowing is discussed. The report calls for an arbitration procedure that would involve hearings before a board with independent members and the right of appeal. It identifies difficulties associated with this procedure and possible solutions using the case of the three engineers who warned of dangerous deficiencies in the Bay Area Rapid Transit (BART) automatic control system. The concluding chapter stresses the need for scientists to have both the freedom to speak out and the responsibility to influence public policy.

485. Anderson, Robert M. Jr. "On the Design of Products." Paper presented at Workshop on Engineering Ethics:

Designing for Safety, 24-26 May 1982, Center for the Study of the Human Dimensions of Science and Technology, Rensselaer Polytechnic Institute, Troy, NY. See item 521.

Presents an overview of the product design process with an emphasis on describing how product safety considerations are incorporated during the design. Intended for non-technical readers, it can also be useful as a refresher for engineers currently involved in product design. Divided into six sections describing some of the practical techniques for dealing with the complexities and difficulties of designing safe products.

486. Barber, Bernard. "Some 'New Men of Power': The Case of Biochemical Research Scientists." Annals of the New York Academy of Sciences, 169 (1970), 519-523.

Responds to the charge that biomedical researchers, who now possess a great deal of power for doing both good and evil, are guilty of having mediocre ethics. Barber believes that although biomedical researchers have not acted irresponsibility , there is room for improving their ethical standards. Six ways are given for achieving this improvement including ethical training, codes of ethics, peer learning and control, review committees and limited legislation.

487. Baum, Robert J. and Albert Flores, eds. Ethical Problems in Engineering. Vol. 1, 2nd ed. Troy, NY: The Center for the Study of the Human Dimensions of Science and Technology, 1980.

Includes over 60 short articles on ethical issues encountered by practicing engineers. Five chapters cover the problem of professionalism, competitive practice, employed professionals and technology. Each chapter begins with an introduction explaining the issues and discusses the reading. Many articles have implications for whistle-blowing. Contains item 559.

488. Baum, Robert J. and Albert Flores, eds. Ethical Problems in Engineering. Vol. 2, 2nd ed. Troy, NY: The Center for the Study of the Human Dimensions of Science and Technology, 1980.

Contains some forty items, including cases illuminating ethical issues encountered by engineers in different contexts. Eight of the contributions discuss whistle-blowing.

489. Bayles, Michael D. "Acceptable Risk and the Public: Nonprofessional Involvement in Safety Design." Paper presented at Workshop on Engineering Ethics: Designing for Safety, 24-26 May 1982, Center for the Study of the Human Dimension of Science and Technology, Rensselaer Polytechnic Institute, Troy, NY. See item 521.

Examines two perspectives for determinating acceptable risk: the professional assessment (substantive) and the nonprofessional assessment (procedural). Bayles argues for the use of a design review board, similar to institutional review boards for experiments on human subjects. It would determine acceptable risk and indicate the type of instruction and safety warnings that should be given potential users.

490. Beetle, George R. "Engineering and Society: A Contemporary Challenge." Civil Engineering, 41 (February 1971), 51-53.

Argues that technologically complex social and environmental problems cannot be solved by citizens who lack technological knowledge, and yet engineers often remain detached from these problems. Individual engineers and professional societies should take the initiative in working through government and private enterprise to improve American life.

490a. Bell, Carlos G. Jr.. "One Ethical Problem Faced by the AEC and Its Contractors." Paper presented at the Second National Conference on Ethics in Engineering, 5-6 March 1982, at Bismark Hotel, Chicago, IL. Forthcoming in item 722b.

491. Boffey, Philip M. "Scientists and Bureaucrats: A Clash of Cultures on FDA Advisory Panel." Science, 26 March 1976, pp. 1244-1246.

Scientists serving in advisory capacities to federal agencies can face a variety of problems. Some were revealed at a meeting of the Toxicology Advisory

Committee of the Food and Drug Administration on the controversial color additive, Red Dye No. 2.

491a. Bok, Sissela. "Secrecy and Openness in Science: Ethical Considerations." Science, Technology, & Human Values, 7 (1982): 32-41.

492. Bok, Sissela. "Whistleblowing and Professional Responsibilities." Professional Engineer, 49 (June 19-79), 26-27.

Excerpt from a longer discussion of the questions surrounding whistle-blowing and how these may be addressed in teaching ethics and ethical codes.

492a. Boland, Richard J. Jr. "Organizational Control Systems and the Engineer." Paper presented at the Second National Conference on Ethics in Engineering, 5-6 March 1982, at Bismark Hotel, Chicago, IL. Forthcoming in item 722b.

492b. Boland, Richard J. Jr. "The Need for Organizational Power." Paper presented at the Second National Conference on Ethics in Engineering, 5-6 March 1982, at Bismark Hotel, Chicago, IL. Forthcoming in item 722b.

493. Brooks, Harvey. "Technology and Values: New Ethical Issues Raised by Technological Progress." Zygon, 8 (1973), 17-35.

Presents a concise overview of the many ethical and social issues that arise from the application of scientific knowledge in a technologically-based culture. These problems confront many scientists in diverse fields, and the whole of society as well.

494. Broome, Taft H. "New Developments in Engineering: The AAES Plan." Paper presented at the Second National Conference on Ethics in Engineering, 5-6 March 1982, at Bismark Hotel, Chicago, IL. Forthcoming in item 722b.

495. Buzzati-Traverso, Adriano. The Scientific Enterprise, Today and Tomorrow. Paris: United Nations Educational, Scientific, and Cultural Organization, 1977.

Discusses the triumphs of science, the responsibilities of the scientist, and the limits of science in the first five chapters. In the following six chapters, the sociological and bureaucratic structure of science, national policies and international politics, and current trends in organizations are considered. Finally, in three concluding chapters, the author traces the changes in the human implications of scientific advancement as our ideas of progress changed and new types of forecasts were made. He reviews current approaches to scientific ethics and values.

496. Carovillano, Robert L. and James W. Skehan, eds. Science and the Future of Man. Cambridge, MA: The MIT Press, 1970.

The proceedings of a symposium jointly sponsored by Boston College and the American Association for the Advancement of Science, 28-29 December 1969. Includes papers on the government and science, problems and responsibilities, and the university scientist.

497. Chalk, Rosemary. "Ethical Dilemmas in Modern Engineering." Technology and Society, 9 (March 1981), 1, 8-12.

Outlines the ethical concerns of professional societies, central issues in engineering ethics, and value conflicts in science and technology. Her conclusion suggests some specific activities through which professional groups can contribute to current work in engineering ethics.

498. Chalk, Rosemary, Mark S. Frankel, and Sallie B. Chafer. AAAS Professional Ethics Project: Professional Ethics Activities in the Scientific and Engineering Societies. Washington, DC American Association for the Advancement of Science, 1980.

The objectives of the project include: to identify moral activities in professional associations, describe their ethical principles, suggest areas of concern not addressed by them, and recommend a role for the societies in the area of professional ethics. The analysis is based on survey data from selected associations. Contains item 586.

499. Citizen's Commission on Science, Law and Food Supply. "A Report on Current Ethical Considerations in the

Determination of Acceptable Risk with Regard to Food and Food-Additives." McGraw-Hill Yearbook of Science and Technology. New York: McGraw-Hill, 1974.

500. Clark, Ian K. "Expert Advice in The Controversy About Supersonic Transport in The United States." Minerva, 12 (October 1974), 416-432.

Uses the case of the Supersonic Transport to show how the scientists' advice is used or misused, the ambiguous relationship between expert and politician, and the blurred distinction between technical policy questions.

501. Coughlin, Ellen K. "Educators, Scientists Fear New Federal Ethics Code." The Chronicle of Higher Education, 20 February 1979, pp. 1, 15.

Reviews the provisions of the Ethics in Government Act of 1978, which became effective on 1 July 1979, and indicates why there is a growing concern that the law's restrictions will discourage scientists and other scholars from working for federal agencies. Designed to cure conflict of interest in high-ranking government jobs, the Act places stringent restrictions on the contact a former executive-branch officer may have with the federal government.

502. Cournand, Andre and Michael Meyer. "The Scientist's Code." Minerva, 14 (Spring 1976), 79-96.

Reviews norms of scientific activity, assesses the stress to which the scientific code is currently being subjected, and suggests ways in which the code might be advantageously revised.

503. Decision Making for Regulating Chemicals in the Environment. Washington DC: The National Academy of Sciences, 1975.

504. "Defeat for Scientific Integrity: Scientists Testify in DDT Hearing." Business Week, 8 (July 1972), p. 60.

Discusses the conflict between environmentalists, scientists and the government over the pesticide DDT. It succinctly presents a case involving the ethical and social dilemmas which confront the scientist as a result of the application of his findings in the face of increasing political pressure.

505. Dierkes, Meinolf, Sam Edwards, and Bob Coppock, eds. Technological Risk: Its Perception and Handling in the European Community. Cambridge, MA: Oelgeschlager, Gunn, and Hain, 1982.

Thirteen essays on issues and programs discussed at a European conference on risk assessment. Contains a useful descriptions of Europe's reactions to particular health and safety problems.

506. Doderlein, Jan M. "Nuclear Power, Public Interest and the Professional." Nature, 264 (November 1976), 202-203.

Comments sharply on the roles of professionals and nuclear critics in light of the fact that in the case of complex technological decisions the public is unable to make a full evaluation and needs to trust some established professional and political mechanisms.

507. Donaldson, Thomas. "The Right to Behave Responsibly." Paper read at Second National Conference on Ethics in Engineering, 5-6 March 1982, Bismark Hotel, Chicago, IL. Forthcoming in item 722b.

508. Duncan Davies, Tom Banfield, and Ray Sheahan. The Humane Technologist. New York: Oxford University Press, 1976.

Intended to help technologists approach their increasing range of problems, extending beyond subjects in which they were trained into economics, politics, philosophy, and aspects of human behavior. This book describes problems, identifies modeling methods, and applies the planner's procedure to means for dealing with constraints such as finance, resource limitations, human willingness, and law and the environment.

509. Edel, Abraham. A Philosopher's View of the Social Responsibility of Scientists and Engineers." Journal of the Franklin Institute, 30 (August 1975), 113-114. See item 747.

510. Edsall, John T. "Scientific Freedom and Responsibility." Science, 16 May 1975, pp. 687-693.

An abbreviated version of the report of the American Association for the Advancement of Science (AAAS) Committee on Scientific Freedom and Responsibility. Discusses the role of professional societies as protectors of the public interest, the need for codes of ethics relating to the responsibility of employers and to the professional and personal conduct of employees, and mechanisms which will enable the AAAS to review specific instances in which scientific freedom is alleged to have been abridged.

511. Edsall, John T. "Two Aspects of Scientific Responsibility." Science, 3 April 1981, pp. 11-14.

Identifies two types of scientific responsibility: (1) for behavior associated with basic research and the communication of the results, and (2) for behavior dealing with problems that arise concerning social impact. A simple answer is difficult to give to a complex case, and a case is easily overstated to the general public. Referring to the Bay Area Rapid Transit System and two other cases, Edsall discusses the personal risk that whistle-blowers took and asserts that seeking the truth should be the principal concern of scientific workers.

512. Epstein, Samuel S., William J. Monsour, and Claire Nader, eds. Science, Technology and the Public Interest: Information, Communications and Organizational Patterns. Jeanette, PA: Monsour Medical Foundation, 1977.

Reports on an October 1973 conference which focused on professional responsibility, public interest groups and technical specialists. The 122-page document includes papers by Ralph Nader, Bjorn O. Gillberg, and George Wald.

513. Faulkner, Peter, ed. The Silent Bomb: A Guide to the Nuclear Energy Controversy. New York: Random House, 1977.

A joint effort, blending the skills and knowledge of engineers, scientists, and ecologists. Its covers the human, environmental, economic, and engineering aspects of the present nuclear power controversy and the contributing roles of government and industry.

Contains twenty-three chapters in five sections: the incident, the issue, the industry, the stances, and the prognosis.

514. Federation of American Scientists. "Scientific Responsibility." F.A.S. Public Interest Report, 29 (December 1976), 1-7.

Consists of short articles asking to whom public interest scientists are responsible (the scientific community or the citizenry) and how this responsibility can be expressed in standards dealing with practical problems, such as when to speak out, how to phrase conclusions, and how to get the public's attention. The simple view that scientists provide "facts" and policymakers then make choices is no longer adequate.

515. Federation of American Scientists. "New Ethical Problems Raised by Data Suppression." Federation of American Scientists Professional Bulletin, 2 (November 1974), 1-6.

516. Flores, Albert. "National Project on Engineering Ethics to Bring Together Engineers, Philosophers." Professional Engineer, 47 (August 1977), 26-29.

The National Project on Philosophy and Engineering Ethics will be funded by the National Endowment for the Humanities.

517. Flores, Albert. "Engineering Ethics." Business and Professional Ethics Newsletter, 1 (September 1977), 1-7.

Since the engineering profession has a short history and lacks homogeneity, ethical issues are obscured and lowered in significance. Flores argues that the engineering profession encounters ethical problems of the same kind and significance as those in the more traditional professions. A brief survey of the literature on engineering ethics and a selected bibliography are included.

518. Flores, Albert. "Philosophy and Engineering Ethics." Mechanical Engineering, 100 (1978), 4.

519. Flores, Albert. "Engineers' Professional Rights." Engineering Issues, 106 (October 1980), 389-396.

Notes that most codes of ethics of engineering societies fail to mention the "rights" of engineers.
Mentions three reasons to reverse this trend: (1)
most engineers practice their profession as employees
of industry or government and, consequently, their
rights are easier to ignore; (2) the failure to acknowledge the importance of rights may undermine authority
and lead to a loss of respect for professional judgment; and (3) without the autonomy and authority to
act on professional judgments, it is doubtful engineers can be held accountable for their activities
when these may be harmful to the public. Attempts to
sketch out a general theory of professional rights and
its justification. The last section deals with the
significance of rights of engineers.

520. Flores, Albert. "The Professional Rights of Engineers." Technology and Society, December 1980,
pp. 3-18.

521. Flores, Albert, ed. Designing for Safety. Proceedings of the First National Conference on
Engineering Ethics. Troy, NY: Center for the
Study of the Human Dimensions of Science and
Technology, Rensselaer Polytechnic Institute,
24-26 May 1982. Contains items 485, 489, 521b,
562, 578, 588, 596, 725, 776 and 827.

521a. Flores, Albert. "Designing for Safety: Organizational Influence on Professional Ethics." Paper presented at Workshop on Engineering Ethics: Designing for Safety, 24-26 May 1982, Center for the
Study of the Human Dimensions of Science and Technology, Rensselaer Polytechnic Institute, Troy, NY.
See item 521.

Describes some of the ways in which the design activities of engineers are structured by their employers to insure the end-product meets acceptable standards of safety.

522. Flores, Albert. "Organizational Influences on Engineers' Safety Attitudes." Applied Philosophy,
1:2 (Fall, 1982), 71-89.

Discusses Monsanto's oganizational mechanisms for
insuring that its engineering staff designs appropriate safety features into all its manufacturing oper-

ations and chemical processes. Aims at determining how these mechanisms encourage engineers to regard safety as an integral part of their design responsibilities, and to describe how engineers perceive these mechanisms as influencing their design practices. Argues that Monsanto supports its engineers in fulfilling professional and moral responsibilities for safety.

523. Flores, Albert, ed. "Organizational Influences on Engineers: Designing for Safety." Paper read at Second National Conference on Ethics in Engineering, 5-6 March 1982, at Bismark Hotel, Chicago, IL. Forthcoming in item 722b.

524. Florman, Samuel J. Blaming Technology: The Industrial Search for Scapegoats. New York: St. Martin's Press, 1981.

525. Florman, Samuel C. "Moral Blueprints." Harpers' Magazine, October 1978, pp. 30-33.

   Takes whistle-blowing as one issue in engineering ethics. Author is highly critical of its individualistic emphasis, stating that it is too simplistic, presumptive, and ineffective. Instead, he argues for more adequate solutions at the social and political level, largely through government rules and regulations.

526. Florman, Samuel C. The Existential Pleasures of Engineering. New York: St. Martin's Press, 1976.

   Tries to find answers to several questions about the nature of the engineering experience, and to answer criticisms of engineers as having brought civilization to the brink of ruin. Chapter Three entitled "Conscience, Error and Responsibility" argues that engineers have extensive social responsibilities.

527. Ford, Daniel F., Henry W. Kendall, and Lawrence S. Tye. Browns Ferry: A Regulatory Failure. Cambridge, MA: Union of Concerned Scientists, 1976.

   Findings of an independent investigation by the Union of Concerned Scientists of the Browns Ferry nuclear plant fire of March 22, 1975. Reviews the circumstances that led to the accident and allowed it to develop to such major proportions. Deficiencies in regulatory standards and practices are identified as the key contributors to the safety problems that arose.

528. "Guidelines to Professional Employment for Scientists and Engineers." Professional Engineer, 43 (February 1973), 37-44.

528a. Hacker, Sally. "Engineering the Shape of Work." Paper presented at the Second National Conference on Ethics in Engineering, 5-6 March 1982, at Bismark Hotel, Chicago, IL. Forthcoming in item 722b.

529. von Hippel, Frank. "Changing the Path of Least Resistance." Paper presented at the Symposium on

Whistle-Blowing and Scientific Responsibility. The Management of Technical Dissent in the Food and Drug Administration, Annual Meeting of the American Association for the Advancement of Science, 15 February 1978, at Washington, DC.

Argues that it is necessary to develop procedures which protect dissenting professionals and at the same time do not tie their organizations up in procedural knots. Discusses Ewing's proposed Bill of Rights for Employees and Carter's proposed Civil Service Commission reorganization. Favors (1) the requirement of written justifications from management for involuntary transfers, and (2) delegation of some authority to ombudsmen, hearing boards, or arbitration boards to deal with appeals concerning these transfers.

530. von Hippel, Frank. "Professional Freedom and Responsibility." Science, Technology and Human Values, January 1978, pp. 37-42.

Distinguishes ethics of competition among engineers from social responsibility of engineers in relations with employers. Considers electing more socially responsible executives to engineering societies, developing mechanisms such as mediation arbitration procedures, ombudsmen, grievance mechanisms, and more effective legislation.

531. Hollander, Rachelle. "Ecologists, Ethical Codes and the Struggles of a New Profession." The Hastings Center Report, 6 (February 1976), 45-46.

Uses the case of the "environmental professions," as a new profession in the process of drafting a code of ethics, to point out the inherent difficulties faced by any professional society, not only in the drafting and enforcing of an ethical code.

532. Holton, Gerald. "Scientific Optimism and Societal Concerns: A Note on the Psychology of Scientists." Ethical and Scientific Issues Posed by Human Uses of Molecular Genetics. New York: New York Academy of Sciences, 1976, pp. 82-101.

Analyzes existing studies on the psychology of scientists, and contends that a "better understanding of the psycho-dynamics of young scientists and of the societal pressures on them is needed in order to show us how to bring out more" of their social awareness.

533. Kardestuncer, Hayrettin, ed. Social Consequences of Engineering. San Francisco, CA: Boyd and Frazier, 1979.

Intended as a reader for courses in engineering or professional ethics. Examines a wide range of topics on the interaction of engineering and society.

534. Karjewski, Kathleen M. "Scientists and Social Responsibility: University of Delaware, July 1975." Technology and Culture, 18 (January 1977), 56-61.

Contains brief summaries of papers presented at a Conference On The Philosophy of Technology.

535. Kemper, John D. "Teaching Professionalism and Ethics," Civil Engineering, 48 (April 1978), 52-54.

Examines controversies surrounding the meaning of the term professionalism and the influences of these controversies on what should be taught in courses on professionalism. Warns against the pitfalls of propagandizing students.

536. Kennedy, Donald. "Law and the Assessment of Technological Risk." Talk given at symposium at the 144th

National Meeting of the American Association for the Advancement of Science, Washington, DC, 12-17 February 1978. Mimeographed.

537. Kipnis, Kenneth. "Engineers and the Paramountcy of Public Safety." Business and Professional Ethics 1 (Fall 1981): 77-92.

538. Kipnis, Kenneth. "Engineers Who Kill: Professional Ethics and the Paramountcy of Public Safety." Paper presented at Conference on Business and Professional Ethics, 15 May 1981, University of Illinois at Chicago Circle. Mimeographed.

    Articulates some of the principles of professional conduct that are implicit in the provision that engineers hold paramount the safety of the public. Also addresses the most pressing cases of professional misconduct in engineering. Attempts to sketch why and how engineering associations should take an expanded role in setting the conditions of professional practice.

539. Knight, Kenneth T. "Engineering Ethics." Mechanical Engineering, November 1979, pp. 38-41.

    Reports on recent developments in the engineering profession with respect to a code of ethics for engineers. This article includes the complete ASME Criteria for Enforcement of the Canons.

540. Kranzberg, Melvin, ed. Ethics in an Age of Pervasive Technology. Boulder, CO: Westview Press, 1980. See item 821.

541. Ladd, John. "The Quest for a Code of Professional Ethics." AAAS Professional Ethics Project: Professional Ethics Activities in Scientific and Engineering Societies. Rosemary Chalk, Mark Frankel and Sallie B. Chafer. Washington, DC: American Association for the Advancement of Science, 1980, pp. 154-159.

542. Ladd, John. "The Basis of Collective and Individual Moral Responsibility in Engineering." Paper read at Second National Conference on Ethics in Engineering, 5-6 March 1982, Bismark Hotel, Chicago, IL. Forthcoming in item 722b.

543. LaKoff, Sanford A., ed. <u>Science and Ethical Responsibility</u>. Reading, MA: Addison-Wesley, 1980.

   A collection of addresses and papers by scientists, scholars, and students dealing with ethical responsibility in areas such as arms control, bio-medical research, development assistance, and the role of scientists in political controversies.

544. Lambright, W. Henry. <u>Governing Science and Technology</u>. New York: Oxford University Press, 1976.

544a. Laurendeau, Norman M., "The Case for Corporate Ombudsmen." Paper presented at the Second National Conference on Ethics in Engineering, 5-6 March 1982, at Bismark Hotel, Chicago, IL. Forthcoming in item 722b.

545. Layton, Edward. <u>The Revolt of the Engineers</u>. Cleveland, OH: The Press of Case Western Reserve University, 1971.

   Examines engineering progressives who attempted to unify their profession and to use it as an instrument of social reform. Engineers developed two versions of professionalism, one which directed the engineer to independent action, and a second which linked the engineer to the business system. Traces the development of engineering from 1900 to 1940, arguing that it resulted primarily from the clash between these two versions.

545a. Leugenbiehl, Heinz C., "Moral Education and the Codes of Ethics." Paper presented at the Second National Conference on Ethics in Engineering, 5-6 March 1982, at Bismark Hotel, Chicago, IL. See item 722b.

545b. Levy, Edwin and David Copp, "Risk and Responsibility: Ethical issues in Decision Making." " Paper presented at the Second National Conference on Ethics in Engineering, 5-6 March 1982, at Bismark Hotel, Chicago, IL. Forthcoming in item 722b.

546. Lichter, Barry D. and Michael P. Hodges. "Perceptions of Engineers' 'Professionalism' in the Chemical Industry." Paper read at Second National Conference on Ethics in Engineering, 5-6 March 1982, Bismark Hotel, Chicago, IL. Forthcoming in item 722b.

547. List, Peter. "Engineers' Responsibilities Within Institutions: Some Reminders." Business and Professional Ethics, 2 (Fall 1978), 4-5.

Over 80 percent of practicing engineers work for large corporations or government agencies, and often lack the necessary autonomy to significantly affect institutional directives. Hence, attributions of moral responsibility to engineers must be made only when the possibility of individual initiative is taken into account.

548. Lowrance, William W. Of Acceptable Risk: Science and the Determination of Safety. Los Altos, CA: William Kaufman, 1976.

549. Marlowe, Donald E. "Engineering on Trial." Engineering Education, 67 (April 1977), pp. 662.

549a. Martin, Brian. "The Scientific Straightjacket: The Power Structure of Science and the Suppression of Environmental Scholarship." The Ecologist 11 (1981): 33-43.

550. May, Larry. "Professional Action and Professional Liability." Paper read at Second National Conference on Ethics in Engineering, 5-6 March 1982, Bismark Hotel, Chicago, IL. Forthcoming in item 722b.

551. Medvedev, Zhores A. Nuclear Disaster in the Urals. New York: Random House, 1979.

A documented account of the 1957 explosion of nuclear waste that devastated an area of the Urals the size of Rhode Island. Discusses the attempts made by the American and British atomic energy agencies to keep it from the public. Includes a new afterword on a U.S. study that finally supports the author's findings.

551a. Montgomery, D.J., "Categorization of Human Goals in an Engineer's Idiom." Paper presented at the Second National Conference on Ethics in Engineering, 5-6 March 1982, at Bismark Hotel, Chicago, IL. Forthcoming in item 722b.

552. Mozur, Allan. The Dynamics of Technical Controversy. Communications Press, 1981.

Aims to explain controversies about the products of science and technology and to suggest how these controversies may be used as an effective means for technological assessment. Suggests regularities in behavior that often occur across the class of technical controversies.

553. Nelkin, Dorothy. "Ethical Issues Facing Scientists in the Public Sector." AAAS Professional Ethics Project Professional Ethics Activities in Scientific and Engineering Societies. (Item 498, pp. 160-166).

554. Nelkin, Dorothy. Controversy: Politics of Technical Decisions. Beverly Hills, CA: Sage, 1979.

Identifies the many complex factors involved in the public debate over issues of importance to society. Both the scientist and nonscientists will gain an understanding of the scientific and political issues involved in the debate.

555. Nelkin, Dorothy. "Scientists and Professional Responsibility: The Experience of American Ecologists." Social Studies of Science, 7 (February 1977), 75-96.

Examines the effect of political involvement on the organization of a scientific discipline. Two major changes are (1) a shift from a scientific concern with maintaining standards to a professional concern with controlling practitioners working publicly, and (2) a concern with maintaining autonomy. As scientists move closer to the market, they will inevitably give up many privileges of the gown.

556. Nelkin, Dorothy. "Changing Images of Science: New Pressures on Old Stereotypes." Harvard Newsletter, January 1976, 21-31.

Points out the serious implications for science that result from its potential for social utility. These implications are in the form of threats to the autonomy of science that arise from a complex interaction of outside pressures, the scientists' perception of these pressures and professional concern with maintaining the integrity of science.

557. Norman, Colin. "Science vs. the Public." Nature, 262 (July 1976), 163-165.

Analyzes the conflict between groups of scientists, city officials and Cambridge, Mass. residents over plans to conduct recombinant DNA research at Harvard and MIT.

558. Olson, James. "Engineers' Attitudes Towards Professionalism, Employment, Social Responsibility." Professional Engineer, 42 (August 1972), 30-32.

Results of 775 responses to questionnaires mailed to 110 NSPE members: 117 were required to violate conscience, 447 felt restricted from criticizing employer, only 667 rank public's interest over employers. Though 817 claim they would refuse to work on a project injurious to the public, 687 say they would resign and 557 would protest. When placed in that situation, 6 percent sought transfer, 87 resigned, 167 refused work, and 247 refused client's commission.

559. Otten, Jim. "Organizational Disobedience." Ethical Problems in Engineering. (Item 487), pp. 182-186.

Examines and defines 'organizational disobedience' (of which whistleblowing is one example), its rationale, moral justification, and limits.

560. Perrucci, Robert. "In the Service of Man: Radical Movements in the Professions." Sociological Review Monograph 20. Paul Halmos. Keele, England: University of Keele, 1973, pp. 179-194.

Deals with the "radical caucuses" or separatist movements within the major professions. Describes the conditions under which they emerge, the composition of their membership, and the specific nature of their goals and strategies. Finally, Perrucci analyzes four dilemmas confronting radical movements and specifies conditions necessary for their continuity and effectiveness.

561. Perrucci, Robert. "Engineering: Professional Servant of Power." American Behavioral Scientist, 13 (March/April 1971), 119-133.

Suggests that one of the major problems facing American society is that its technological elite, i.e., its engineers, do not constitute an independent power base. The two main factors operating against the development of engineering as an autonomous profession are the background and motivational characteristics of persons attracted to the occupation and the diversity of the professional community itself. Engineering activities call for a profession that not only has the technical skills to deal with societal problems, but also has both a strong commitment to serve human welfare and the independent power to determine the way in which its talents are used. Suggests that such a profession does not now exist.

562. Perrucci, Robert. "Organizationalism and the Limits of Technique." Paper presented at Workshop on Engineering Ethics: Designing for Safety, 24-26 May 1982, Center for the Study of the Human Dimensions of Science and Technology, Rensselaer Polytechnic Institute, Troy, NY. See item 521.

Maintains that the engineering profession, as it currently stands, continues to serve the economic and political interests of only a segment of our society. Examines the forces that influence the actions of organizations to set limits on the autonomy of its professional employees, and evaluates the concept of professionalism as it is currently used in order to identify its function as ideology.

563. Perrucci, Robert and Joel E. Gerstl. The Engineers and the Social System. New York: John Wiley and Sons, 1969.

Eleven original essays concerned with the analysis of the engineering profession in the context of the social systems within which it functions. Four themes are developed: the historical and occupational setting of the profession, the processes of recruitment and socialization, the nature of the work roles and organizations, and the links between careers and society.

564. Perrucci, Robert and Joel E. Gerstl. Profession Without Community: Engineers in American Society. New York: Random House, 1969.

565. Perry, Tekla. "Five Ethical Dilemmas." IEEE Spectrum, 18 (June 1981), 53-60.

A collection of five hypothetical events: suppression of an energy-saving invention; industrial risks to society; secrets that could hurt the client; lying to get a contract; and company practices. The situations are analyzed and discussed by a philosopher, a volunteer for the IEEE Member Conduct Committee, an attorney, a manager, and five engineers.

566. Pletta, Dan and George Gray. "Engineering Accountability vs. Corporate Responsibility." Paper read at Second National Conference on Ethics in Engineering, 5-6 March 1982, at Bismark Hotel, Chicago, IL. Forthcoming in item 722b.

567. Pletta, Dan. "Coupling Economics with Ethics for Employed Engineers." Professional Engineer, 47 (July 1977), 21-24.

568. Pollard, Robert D., ed. The Nugget File. Cambridge, MA: Union of Concerned Scientists, 1979.

Excerpts from the government's special file on nuclear power plant accidents and safety defects obtained by the Union of Concerned Scientists under the Freedom of Information Act.

*569. Primack, Joel and Frank von Hippel. Advice and Consent. New York: Basic Books, 1974.

Examines how scientists have been carrying out their political responsibilities. The way in which technical experts make their services available to society can significantly affect the distribution of political power. Authors note that scientists may inadvertently contribute to a technological dictatorship. The challenge to the scientific community, therefore, is to strengthen the government's science advisory system by making it more open and less vulnerable to subversion and to promote "public-interest science." Several case studies are included to provide examples of the controversies over technology. Two main themes are developed: the limitations on the effectiveness of the government advisor, and the importance of the public interest scientist in keeping the policy-making process honest.

570. Ravetz, Jerome R. Scientific Knowledge and Its Social Problems. New York: Oxford University Press
1973.

571. Reagan, Charles E. Ethics for Scientific Researchers.
Springfield, IL: Charles C. Thomas, 1971.

572. "Reprint Series on Scientific Freedom and Responsibility." Washington, DC: American Association for
the Advancement of Science , 1981.

Twenty articles and editorials explain the ethical
and moral role of the scientist today. Each can be ordered separately or as a complete set.

573. Rescher, Nicholas. Unpopular Essays on Technological
Progress. Pittsburgh, PA: University of Pittsburgh Press, 1980.

The eight essays, most of which are revised versions of previously published articles, include philosophical discussions of modern technology in relation
to human happiness, the environment, endangered species, health care, justice, and economics.

574. Rose, Steven and Hilary Rose. "Social Responsibility
(III): The Myth of the Neutrality of Science."
Impact of Science on Society, 21 (1971), 137-149.

Argues for four suggestions: that scientists must
become aware of the social, political and economic
pressures effecting the development of science; that
scientists must learn to communicate with the community and fellow scientists; that problems of science education are not addressed; and that scientists ask themselves how they can best use their skills to serve the
people.

575. Schinzinger, Roland. "The Ethical Problems of Regulating Engineering Practice." Paper read at Second
National Conference on Ethics in Engineering, 5-6
March 1982, at Bismark Hotel, Chicago, IL. Forthcoming in item 722b.

575a. Schinzinger, Roland and Mike W. Martin. "Engineering
as Social Experimentation: A Sharing of Responsibilities Among Engineers, Managers, and the Public."
1980 ASEE Annual Conference Proceedings.

575b. Schinzinger, Roland and Mike W. Martin. "Responsib-
ility and Engineering as Social Experimentation."
Paper prepared for a meeting of the Society for the
Study of Professional Ethics. American Philosophi-
cal Association, Pacific Division. San Francisco:
March, 1980.

576. Schott, Richard L. "The Professions and Government:
Engineering as a Case in Point." Public Administration Review, 38 (March/April 1978), 126132.

Provides an introduction to the engineering profession, examines its influence on government, and raises
issues which surround the role of engineers in the public service.

577. Sergerstedt, Torgny, ed. Ethics for Science Policy.
Oxford: Pergamon Press, 1979.

Contains the proceedings of a Nobel Symposium held
in Sweden in 1978. The group asked what rules or restrictions should be applied to scientific research
and who should decide on priorities and limitations.

578. Sinclair, George. "Unethical Conduct or Professional
Incompetence?" Paper presented at Workshop on Engineering Ethics: Designing for Safety, 24-26 May 19-
82, Center for the Study of the Human Dimensions of
Science and Technology, Rensselaer Polytechnic Institute, Troy, NY. See item 521.

Asserts that engineering graduates today have to be
regarded as "paraprofessionals," who have been trained
but have little idea of how to function as professionals. The real problem facing the engineering profession is widespread incompetence rather than unethical
behavior. Sinclair notes that conspicuous examples of
this are easily found whereas case histories relating
to unethical conduct are difficult to locate.

579. Slowter, Edward S. "Engineering Ethics and Professional Societies." Business and Professional Ethics,
3 (Spring 1980), 4-5.

Notes that efforts to implement an engineering-
wide code of ethics have been hampered by the fragmen-
tation of the profession and various state-by-state approaches to the problem. Recent developments show

promise. Once a unified statement of ethical principles is developed, the engineering profession can
concentrate on the larger task of making the code enforceable.

580. Smith, W. Eugene and Aileen M. Smith. Minamata.
New York: Holt, Rinehart, and Winston, 1975.

Chronicles the story and cover-up of mercury poi-
soning in Minamata, Japan. Using illustrative photo-
graphs, authors present a subjective account of the
complexities involved in the situation.

581. Southgate, A. J. "Professional Ethics and Secrecy in
Science." Search, 8 (September 1977), 305-307.

Reports on a recent public scientific forum in New
Zealand which concluded that there is a need for freedom of information laws and codes of ethics for scientists. The forum also recommended development of "a
special tribunal which could swiftly and impartially
investigate cases in which scientists claimed that information vital to the public welfare was being kept
secret." Emphasized the barriers to communication of
scientific issues directly to the public and urged the
New Zealand scientific societies to adopt codes of ethics emphasizing the responsibility of scientists to in-
form the public.

582. St. Clair, J. B. "Ethics and Engineering: A Two-Way
Bridge." Chemical Engineering Progress, 75
(August 1979), 27-30.

Discusses perceptions of engineers and connections
between the educational process and engineering practice. Concludes that engineers should understand
their own ethical standards and consider the perceptions and values of the society in which they operate.
Then they would present themselves as responsible professionals.

582a. Taylor, James. "Borrowing from Philosophers for the
Engineering Classroom." Paper presented at the
Second National Conference on Ethics in Engineer-
ing, 5-6 March 1982, at Bismark Hotel, Chicago, IL.
Forthcoming in item 722b.

583. Thompson, Paul B. "Ethics and Probabilistic Risk Assessment." Paper read at Second National Conference on Ethics in Engineering, 5-6 March 1982 at Bismark Hotel, Chicago, IL. Forthcoming in item 722b.

584. Tribe, Laurence H., Corinne S. Schelling, and John Voss, eds. When Values Conflict. Cambridge, MA: Ballinger, 1976.

Contains nine essays on the philosophy of environmental protection. Authors are member of a group sponsored by the American Academy of Arts and Sciences to study the problems of environmental decisionmaking. One of the main problems is how to incorporate what the study calls "fragile" values into the "hard" values which can reasonably be quantified.

585. Unger, Stephen H. Controlling Technology: Ethics and the Responsible Engineer. New York: Holt, Rinehart, and Winston, 1982.

586. Unger, Stephen H. "How Engineering Societies Can Bolster Professional Ethics." AAAS Professional Ethics Project. (Item 498), pp. 165-166.

587. Unger, Stephen H. "How to Be Ethical and Survive." IEEE Spectrum, 16 (December 1979), 56-67.

Discusses conflicts that engineers may have with managerial decisions. Lists steps that engineers may take in such situations and the role of engineering societies in such conflicts.

588. Unger, Stephen. "Role of Engineering Schools in Promoting Design Safety." Paper presented at Workshop on Engineering Ethics: Designing for Safety, 24-26 May 1982, Center for the Study of the Human Dimensions of Science and Technology, Rensselaer Polytechnic Institute, Troy, NY. See item 521.

Suggests guidelines and observations in regard to the question "How Safe Is Safe Enough?" Discusses the relations among safety, reliability, and maintainability. Argues that engineering schools should teach design safety through engineering ethics courses, colloquial, special seminars, films, and field trips.

589. Values and the Public Works Professional. Rolla,
     MO: University of Missouri-Rolla, 1980.

   Proceedings of a workshop supported by the National Endowment for the Humanities and the National Science Foundation, and held in Boston. It aimed to help
   public works professionals achieve a greater awareness
   of their role. Presentations include "The Social Responsibility of Engineers and Scientists: A Philosophical Approach" (Robert Ladenson); "The Limits of Professional Responsibility" (Robert Baum); and "Values
   and Professional Practice" (Marvin Manheim).

589a. Walters, H.J. and R.L. Vandenberg. Proposed Policy
     and Procedures for Differing Professional Opin-
     ions. Published for the Nuclear Regulatory Commis-
     sion. Office of Management and Program Analysis,
     Washington, DC: GPO, October 1979.

590. Weart, Spencer. Scientists in Power. Cambridge,
     MA: Harvard University Press, 1979.

   Gives an account of the events that paved the way
   first to the atom bomb and later to nuclear power.
   Weart recounts not only the history of a science and
   its technological outgrowth, but the cultural and social atmosphere that nurtured these events.

591. Weil, Vivian. "Bottom-Line Moral Obligations for Engi-
     neers." Paper presented at Conference on Business
     and Professional Ethics, 15 May 1981, University of
     Illinois at Chicago Circle. Mimeographed.

   A rebuttal to Kipnis (see item 538). Weil addresses his two principles and concludes that although
   they clarify the issue of paramountcy of public safety
   they do not quite succeed. Suggests an alternative
   principle and argues for a moral obligation to scruti-
   nize the practices of employees.

592. Weil, Vivian. Report of the Workshops on Ethical
     Issues in Engineering. Chicago, IL: Center for
     the Study of Ethics in the Professions, Illinois
     Institute of Technology, 1979.

   Summaries of presentations made during workshops at
   the Illinois Institute of Technology in July 1979. Appendices contain the works of the participants, possi-

ble curriculum plans for courses on engineering ethics, and a discussion of the Goodrich Airbrakes case.

593. Weil, Vivian. "Moral Issues in Engineering: An Engineering School Instructional Approach." Professional Engineer, October 1977, pp. 35-37.

594. Weinberg, Alvin M. "The Many Dimensions of Scientific Responsibility." Bulletin of the Atomic Scientists, 32 (November 1976), 21-24.

Discusses various dimensions of the scientist's social responsibility: publicizing the faults; speaking to the public; and delineating the line between scientific knowledge and scientific ignorance.

595. Welch, B. L. "Deception on Nuclear Power Risks: A Call for Action." Bulletin of the Atomic Scientists, 36 (September 1980), 50-54.

Reviews the discrepancies between what the public has been told regarding the risks associated with nuclear energy and what the scientific evidence actually suggests. Contends that it is the scientific community's ethical responsibility to publicly acknowledge the abuse of scientific information, to see that such offenses are punished, and to erect defenses against such misuse.

596. Wilson, Donald E. "Social Mechanisms for Controlling Engineer's Performance." Paper presented at Workshop of Engineering Ethics: Designing for Safety, 24-26 May 1982, Center for the Study of the Human Dimensions of Science and Technology, Rensselaer Polytechnic Institute, Troy, NY. See item 521.

Examines primary social mechanisms for controlling engineer's professional performance: civil law, criminal law, administrative law and peer review. Concludes that these mechanisms are not effective particularly in small and medium-size organizations, and that existing mechanisms should be established.

597. Wright, Gayle N. "Employer Recognition Program Responsive to Member's Views." Professional Engineer, 46 (October 1976), 45-46.

598. Ziman, John. "Social Responsibility (I): The Impact
of Social Responsibility on Science." Impact of
Science on Society, 21 (1971), 113-122.

Argues that scientists are responsible for the consequences of their discoveries. Ziman criticizes society for turning out narrow specialists and calls for
scientists to form a loyal opposition against the irresponsible use of science.

Section V

Selected Professions

A. Law

599. "The ABA's Retreat from Whistle-blowing." Business Week, 31 August 1981, p. 56.

Discusses the ABA's new draft of the revised code of ethics that upholds the rules requiring lawyers to keep client information secret. This draft appears to reverse a previous provision on whistle-blowing.

600. Abramson, Gil A. and Stephen M. Silvester. "Restrictions in the Right of an Employer to Discharge at Will: The Action of Wrongful Discharge." Federal Bar Newsletter Journal, 20 (September, 1981), 177182.

Conflicting court decisions and vague legal standards mandate new legislation on discharging employees.

601. Association of Trial Lawyers of America. "Tinkering with the First." Trial, 9 (May/June 1973), 34-38.

Evaluates policy questions in proposals to create a journalist's privilege against disclosure of sources of information. Contends that the privilege should attach only to information received under a promise of confidentiality and should extend only to professional journalists.

602. "Attorney-Client Privilege - Fixed Rules, Balancing, and Constitutional Entitlement." Harvard Law Review, 91 (December 1977), 464-487.

Inconsistencies in judicial applications of attorney-client privilege are examined, and a model that reflects social costs and benefits is proposed. Three non-utilitarian justifications for the privilege are considered. It is argued that criminal defendants have such a right, but that the claims of other clients to this privilege must be subject to rigorous balancing.

603. Brill, Steven. "When A Lawyer Lies, Is It His Young Associate's Duty to Blow the Whistle or Keep His Mouth Shut?" Esquire, 19 December 1978, p. 23.

604. Burke, Maureen H. "The Duty of Confidentiality and Disclosing Corporate Misconduct." Business Lawyer, 36 (January 1981), 239-295.

Proposed standards governing a corporate lawyer's obligation to disclose client wrongdoing.

605. Callan, J. Michael and H. David. "Professional Responsibility and the Duty of Confidentiality: Disclosure of Client Misconduct in an Adversary System." Rutgers Law Review, 29 (1976), 332-396.

Defines legal and ethical principles relevant to an attorney's voluntary disclose of past, continuing, or intended misconduct of a client. Sets up a framework to evaluate and determine obligations to disclose. Notes the uncertainty prevailing in this area and indicates a need for clearly defined standards.

*606. Christiansen, Jon P. "A Remedy for the Discharge of Professional Employees Who Refuse to Perform Unethical or Illegal Acts: A Proposal in Aid of Professional Ethics." Vanderbilt Law Review, 28 (May 1975), 805-840.

Examines the duties demanded of professionals (particularly attorneys and accountants) in the proper exercise of their ethical responsibilities, and analyzes the methods for enforcing professional ethics. The limitations of traditional master-servant theory are discussed as they relate to "abusive discharge," and an attempt is made to create a legal remedy for the dissenting employee.

607. "Developments in the Law: Conflicts of Interest in the Legal Profession," Harvard Law Review, 94 (April 1981), 1244-1503.

Discusses the contemporary problems in conflicts of interest besetting the legal profession today. Conflicts in various kinds of practice are examined, including private practice, criminal, poverty, government and public interest law. Concludes with an analysis of sanctions and civil remedies available to deal with violations of the Code of Professional Ethics and the rights of clients.

608. Donagan, Alan. "Justifying Legal Practice in the Adversary System." Center for Philosophy and Public Policy Working Group on Legal Ethics, 1981. Mimeographed.

*609. Estreicher, Samuel. "At-Will Employment and the Prob-
      lem of Unjust Dismissal: The Appropriate Judicial
      Response." New York State Bar Journal, 54 (April
      1982), 146-149ff.

      Examines the evolution of the uniquely American
      employment-at-will doctrine, why it needs re-examin-
      ation, the scope of appropriate judicial action and
      recent cases, and objections to change.

610. "The Ethics Squeeze on Ex-Government Lawyers." Busi-
     ness Week, 23 February 1976, p. 82.

      Lawyers hold a high proportion of the top jobs in
      the federal government, and when they leave govern-
      ment service many gravitate to Washington law firms.
      The result is a chronic ethical dilemma. The new con-
      cern for professional ethics may transfer the problem
      to the law firms themselves, forcing a major change in
      their relationships with corporations and govern-
      ment.

611. Exum, James G. Jr. "The Perjurious Criminal Defend-
     ant: A Solution to His Lawyer's Dilemma." Social
     Responsibility: Journalism, Law, Medicine. Vol.
     6. Lexington, VA: Washington and Lee University,
     1980.

612. Ferren, John M. "The Corporate Lawyer's Obligation to
     the Public Interest." Business Lawyer, 33 (March
     1978), 1253-1289.

      Presents a hypothetical ethical dilemma involving a
      lawyer and a client. Addresses the question whether,
      if ever, the lawyer-client relationship need not be
      honored in view of a higher public interest.

613. Frankel, Charles. "Review of ABA Code of Professional
     Responsibility." University of Chicago Law Re-
     view 43 (1976), 874-886.

      Reviews the Code of Professional Responsibility.
      and compares it with earlier ones. Criticizes the
      fact that it is not embedded in an explicit examina-
      tion of the issues raised by differences between pro-
      fessional and general ethical codes. It also fails to
      encourage non-adversary methods of social dispute res-
      olution and does not adequately address the changing
      circumstances of modern legal practice.

614. Freedman, Monroe. <u>Lawyers' Ethics in an Adversary</u> <u>System</u>. Indianapolis, IN: Bobbs-Merrill Co., 1975.

Topics include the nature of limitations on lawyer-client confidentiality and advocacy; the problems of the perjured client; impeaching a truthful witness; and ethical aspects of the prosecutorial function. Discusses proposals for certification of trial lawyers and compares the British system of a bifurcated bar with the American bar.

615. Fried, Charles. "The Lawyer as Friend: The Moral Foundations of the Lawyer-Client Relation." <u>Yale</u> <u>Law Journal</u>, 85 (1976), 1060-1089.

Evaluates two criticisms of the traditional conception of the lawyer as completely devoted to his client's interest to the point of doing things for his client which he would not do for himself. First, professional loyalty to one's client is said to demand an allocation of the lawyer's time which does not always maximize the greatest good for the greatest number of people. The author rebuts this criticism saying that it is morally right that the lawyer advocate his client's interest ahead of the collective interest providing he offers good counsel. Second, advocacy is said to provide unfair advantages for the client while harming his adversary. The author responds by stating that the lawyer is morally entitled to represent his client's interest so long as he stays within the law and maintains his personal integrity.

616. Geraghty, James A. "Structural Crime and Institutional Rehabilitation--A New Approach to Corporate Sentencing." <u>Yale Law Journal</u>, 89 (December 1979), 353-375.

Analyses "structural crimes' in which no member of a corporation can be found criminally culpable because no one has acted in a criminally liable manner or because no one can be convicted of intentional misconduct. Suggests a redefinition of punishment: sentences should impose significant penalties on managers whose departments generate crimes; internal operational procedures should be modified to reduce the likelihood of recurrence; corporate probation should be instituted to monitor compliance.

617. Gross, Kent. "Attorneys and Their Corporate Clients: SEC Rule 2(E) and the Georgetown 'Whistle Blowing' Proposal." Corporation Law Review, 3 (Summer 1980), 197-227.

The Institute for Public Interest Representation petitioned the Securities and Exchange Commission (SEC) to define the responsibilities of an attorney who discovered that a client had perpetrated a fraud on the SEC. The Institute sought a requirement that the attorney disclose securities law violations to the corporate Board of Directors. Gross suggests that the bar itself promulgate guidelines for reporting to the Board.

618. Harrison, Michelle H. "Confidentiality of Attorney-Client Consultations in the Prison Setting." New England Journal on Prison Law, 3 (Spring 1977), 539-548.

Factors limiting prisoners' rights to private consultation with their attorneys are examined. Three major factors which have limited the right to private consultation are identified.

619. Hazard, Geoffrey C., Jr. Ethics in the Practice of Law. New Haven: Yale University Press, 1980.

Believes the legal profession is going through a crisis of public and self confidence. Identifies three problems in legal ethics: (1) there remain serious questions as to what ethical rules are all about; (2) a lawyer's professional function consists of providing counsel for clients about how to escape or mitigate the law's obligation; and (3) the tension between the client's position (resulting from the professional connection) and the position of equality (general principles of morality and legality accorded to all). Consists of eleven chapters which discuss such topics as conflict of interest, unpopular clients, the adversary system, and advice and consent.

620. Hazard, Geoffrey C., Jr. "An Historical Perspective On The Attorney-Client Privilege." California Law Review, 66 (September 1978), 1061-1091.

Outlines the scope of the modern attorney-client privilege and traces its historical development from Elizabethan times to the present.

621. Hershman, M. "The Murky Divide--Professionalism and Professional Responsibility--Business Judgment and Legal Advice--What is a Business Lawyer?" Business Lawyer, 31, 1 (1975), 457-463.

Summarizes a panel discussion on the professional responsibility of business lawyers and the murky divide between sound business judgment and astute legal advice. Hershman focuses mainly on the attorney's role in representing a multinational U.S. corporation which has made secret payments to a foreign intermediary in return for favorable consideration. Should he resign or "blow the whistle" on moral grounds? Two opposing views emerged. The first requires resignation while the second permits individual discretion depending on the circumstances.

622. Hipler, H. M. "Turning Point Between Lawyer and Accomplice." Trial, 12 (May 1976), 48-50.

Discusses some of the ethical problems faced by a lawyer when a client arrives for legal consultation with a weapon used in a crime. Hipler concludes that the lawyer-client privilege does encompass words, signs, and acts communicated by the client. However, a distinction is made between communications in reference to a past crime (which are privileged) and communications in reference to commission of a future crime or fraud (which are not). A lawyer should not advise a client to dispose of a murder or assault weapon during legal consultation because the lawyer risks becoming an accessory.

623. Hoffman, Junius. "On Learning of a Corporate Client's Crime or Fraud: The Lawyer's Dilemma." Business Lawyer, 33 (March 1978), 1389-1431.

The lawyers' duty to disclose--or not disclose--their corporate client's crime or fraud will require weighing a number of competing considerations. The conflicts in the canons of the American Bar Association Code of Professional Responsibility primarily concern protection of the client's interest and the lawyer's responsibility to other segments of society.

624. Issalys, Pierre. "Professions Tribunal and the Control of Ethical Conduct Among Professionals." McGill Law Journal, 24 (Winter 1978), 588-626.

Describes the administrative structure created by the National Assembly Act of 1973, with its Professional Code, that regulates Canadian professions. The author considers peculiar features of legal rules governing discipline among members of the professions and the relationship of these rules to other branches of the legal system.

625. Jacobs, Myra R. "Ethical Quandary--The Extension of Attorney/Client Privilege to Communication of Past Crimes." Case and Comment, 81 (July/August 1976), 24-28, 30, 32-33, 36-39.

Conflicting attorney and client rights are discussed including the client's right against self-incrimination and the right to counsel. Jacobs concludes that protections afforded defendants in these instances extend to their attorneys as well.

626. Jowell, Jeffery L. Law and Bureaucracy: Administrative Discretion and the Limits of Legal Action. New York: Dunellen Publishing, 1975.

627. Keenan, Patrick A., Stuart C. Goldberg and G. Griffin Dick, eds. Proceedings From the National Conference on Teaching Professional Responsibility. Detroit: University of Detroit School of Law, 1979.

Presents various perspectives on the ethical conduct of lawyers and sets forth the conference recommendations on improved teaching of professional ethics. A well-designed course in professional responsibility must be required by every law school, and continuing education programs should include materials on professional ethics. Topics include innovations in the teaching of professional responsibility, student perceptions of attorney ethics, scrutinizing legal education, and moral conflicts in the profession.

628. Kelso, C. Kevin and Charles D. Kelso. "Conflict, Emotion and Legal Ethics." Pacific Law Journal, 10 (January 1979), 69-93.

The Code of Professional Responsibility can help resolve psychological and emotional conflicts at different stages in the lawyer-client relationship. A classification scheme is presented that relates psychological and ethical dilemmas interrelate to assist lawyers by encouraging responsible professional conduct. Other conflicts discussed relate to the lawyer's needs for recognition and self-aggrandizement, feelings of psychological responsibility for the client's moral status, and concerns about fees, competence, client rejection of advice, and case outcome.

629. Kipnis, Kenneth. Legal Ethics. Englewood Cliffs, NJ: Prentice-Hall, forthcoming.

630. Landesman, Bruce. "Confidentiality and the Lawyer-Client Relationship." Utah Law Review, (1980), 765-786.

Focuses on the differences between the proposed Model Rules of Professional Conduct and the presently enforced Code of Professional Responsibility. Section One discusses the differences in regard to confidentiality in the lawyer-client relationship. The following two sections address the moral basis, complexity, and limits of confidentiality. Part four analyzes the various arguments given for the view that very little, if anything, should be disclosed by the lawyer. A concluding section proposes that the motive for greater disclosure stems from obligations to third parties and the lawyer's own moral autonomy.

631. Law Reform Commission of Canada. Evidence, 12 Professional Privileges Before the Courts. Philadelphia: Lea and Febiger, 1974.

This report considers the problem of professional privileges before the Court which can extend to lawyers, clergy, physicians, and others. It attempts to clarify the principles that underlie the recognition of the right to professional secrecy.

632. Lefstein, N. "Criminal Defendant Who Proposes Perjury--Rethinking the Defense Lawyer's Dilemma." Criminal Law Review, (1979), 481-508.

Three ways that have been proposed for a defense lawyer's handling of a client's revelation of an intent to commit perjury are critiqued, and a preferred approach to the issue is presented.

633. "Legal Ethics and the Destruction of Evidence." Yale Law Journal, 88 (July 1979), 1665-1688.

The argument presented is that the Code of Professional Responsibility should be amended to cover evidence destruction. Attorneys should not be free to change the nature of the facts available to future adversaries since this threatens basic assumptions of the adversary system. The attorney-client privilege should not protect the attorney who advised or assisted in the destruction of evidence. Some enforcement mechanism is needed to ensure compliance with this rule.

634. Luban, David. <u>The Adversary System Excuse</u>. College Park, MD: Center for Philosophy and Public Policy, University of Maryland, 1981.

Discusses the adversary system, and the means of justifying or not justifying it. Luban maintains that the system leads to morally objectionable results, especially regarding attorneys who employ morally reprehensible means, though sanctioned by the system, to help their clients.

635. Luban, David. "Corporate Counsel and Confidentiality." <u>Ethics and the Legal Profession</u>, ed. Frederick Elliston. Buffalo, NY: Prometheus Books, forthcoming.

Argues that corporate counsel, acting objectively and to prevent future harm, has an obligation to blow the whistle on executives and other employees who deliberately commit serious crimes or other wrongs. Arthor contends that appeals to justice or human dignity fail to establish a duty or privilege of confidentiality especially for corporations.

636. Luban, David. "Professional Ethics, A New Code for Lawyers." <u>Hastings Center Report</u>, 10, 3 (June 1980), 11-15.

Criticizes the American Bar Association's Proposed Rules of Professional Conduct, arguing that the provisions requiring disclosure of information obtained from a client which affects the interest of third parties are ineffective. Luban argues that the rules provide only illusory protection for effected third parties because they give the attorney too much discretion.

637. Morgan, Thomas and Ronald Rotunda. Professional Responsibility Problems and Materials. Mineola, NY: The Foundation Press, 1976.

638. Myers, Alan C. "The Attorney-Client Relationship and the Code of Professional Responsibility: Suggested Attorney Liability for Breach of Duty to Disclose Fraud to the Securities and Exchange Commission." Fordham Law Review, 44 (May 1976), 1114-1144.

      The imposition of increased obligations and liabilities on securities lawyers threatens not only attorneys but the quality of their representations as well. Myers examines the possible consequences of the current expansion of liability, and suggests what the securities lawyers' obligations and liabilities should be under an appropriate sections of the Code of Professional Responsibility.

639. "Note: Client Fraud and the Lawyer: An Ethical Analysis." Minnesota Law Review, 62 (1977), 84-118.

640. Polster, Dan A. "Dilemma of the Perjurious Defendant--Resolution, Not Avoidance." Case Western Reserve Law Review, 28 (Fall 1977), 3-40.

      Proposed solutions to the ethical dilemma confronting the criminal defense lawyer whose clients perjure themselves are assessed. An alternative solution is proposed in which the attorney is required to inform the client at the outset of the attorney-client relation that the attorney will disclose any perjury on the client's part. This solution would provide honesty in the attorney-client relationship while preserving the integrity of the judicial process.

641. Postema, Gerald J. "Moral Responsibility in Professional Ethics." New York University Law Review, 55, 1 (April 1980), 63-89.

      Argues for new conception of professional ethics in which lawyers must acknowledge personal responsibility for their conduct. Suggests that a new code of responsibility is required because the current one allows lawyers to ignore the social and moral costs of their actions, and to do as professionals what they would not do as individuals.

642. Pye, A. Kenneth. "Role of Counsel in the Suppression of Truth." Duke Law Journal, 4 (October 1978), 921-959.

To illuminate the role of defense counsel in the suppression of truth in criminal cases, this article explores the nature of the legal profession and uses a hypothetical armed robbery case to illustrate conduct by the defense counsel that ultimately does not serve the public interest.

643. "Recent Development In the Law of Confidentiality." Microfiche. Atlanta, GA: American Business Law Association, 1976.

Case law initiating significant changes in two areas of the law of confidentiality is reviewed: decisions limiting confidentiality is reviewed: client/attorney relationship and cases concerning consensual sexual acts.

644. Reichstein, Kenneth. "Criminal Law Practitioner's Dilemma--What Should The Lawyer Do When His Client Intends to Testify Falsely?" Journal of Criminal Law, Criminology and Police Science, 61 (March 1970), 1-10.

Discussion of American Bar Association's canons of professional ethics and a study which sampled lawyers' views regarding clients intending to commit perjury.

645. Simon, William H. "The Ideology of Advocacy: Procedural Justice and Professional Ethics." Wisconsin Law Review, 78 (1978), 29-144.

Discusses the ideology of advocacy as the profession's defense to criticism of its morally neutral stance and evaluates three justifications: (1) the Hobbesian view that individuals are entitled to use whatever means are necessary to achieve their own ends; (2) the Purposivist view that law is regarded as a technical apparatus for the advancement of social norms; and (3) the Ritualist view that adversary proceedings are a public ceremony designed to show that something is being accomplished. Examines procedural limitations of all three.

646. Sommer, A. A., Jr. "Disclosure of Management Fraud." Business Lawyer, 31 (March 1976), 1283-1293.

Sommer, a Commissioner with the Securities and Exchange Commission (SEC), examines the problems associated with corporate failure to comply with the SEC disclosure rules. The issue of materiality which is at the core of the problem probably has caused the greatest amount of uncertainty. The number of dollars involved in a matter is not the sole determinant of materiality, but is disclosable if payments and bribes relate to significant amount of business.

647. Tankersley, Michael W. "The Corporate Attorney-Client Privilege: Culpable Employees, Attorney Ethics, and the Joint Defense Doctrine." Texas Law Review, 58 (April 1980), 809-843.

While corporations' needs for expert legal advice are increasing, the attorney-client privilege has been eroded by a failure to agree on how and when the privilege should apply to corporations. It is suggested that the privilege should be extended to all corporate employees who are personally responsible for acts that have affected the organization's legal position.

648. "A Tempest at the SEC." Business Week, 4 May 1981, p. 58.

The Securities and Exchange Commission, in efforts to establish standards of conduct for corporate lawyers, declares lawyers will be expected to notify the Directors whenever it appears that companies persist in violating securities laws. Lawyers contend that this decision makes clearer what they must do within their companies to press the issue further and prove they have not aided and abetted.

649. A Tug-Of-War over Confidentiality." Business Week, 23 June 1980, pp. 34-37.

Association of Trial Lawyers of America has proposed a code to tighten attorneys' obligations of confidentiality, in opposition to the American Bar Association's proposals which would make it easier for attorneys to make disclosures. Both proposals are sketched.

650. Volcansek, Mary L. "Codes of Judicial Ethics: Do They Affect Judges' Views of Proper Off-the-Bench Behavior?" American Business Law Journal, 17 (1980), 493-505.

Analysis of responses to questionnaire sent to Texas judges. Discusses respondent's perceptions of the propriety of judicial action in business and political milieux in light of recent revisions to judicial code.

651. Wasserstrom, Richard. "Lawyers as Professionals: Some Moral Issues." Human Rights, 5 (Fall 1975), 1-24.

Examines two moral criticisms of lawyers: (1) the lawyer-client relationship renders the lawyer amoral or immoral and (2) the lawyer-client relationship is objectionable because the lawyer treats the client in both an impersonal and paternalistic fashion.

652. "When Must a Lawyer Blow the Whistle?" Business Week, 21 May 1979, p. 117.

Reports the submission to the Securities and Exchange Commission (SEC) of a petition by the Institute for Public Representation. It urged the Commission to promulgate rules relating to corporate counsels' duties toward management, directors, shareholders, and the general public. The regulations would require attorneys to report instances of fraud and unlawful acts to management and the board of directors, or the SEC, if management failed to act. The author presents views of the Institute, the Commission, and corporate attorneys.

653. Wice, R. "Private Practice of Criminal Law - Life In The Real World." Criminal Law Bulletin, 14 (September/October 1978), 381-409.

Examines the workday, acquisition and retention of clients, fees, incomes, lawyer-client relationships, and basic questions of ethics of criminal lawyers. The major areas of ethical concern were shown to be confidentiality, emotional neutrality, and maintenance of professional relationships.

654. Wolfram, Charles W. "Client Perjury." Southern California Law Review, 50 (1977), 809-870.

Discusses various aspects of perjury: risks to both the perjurer and his attorney; professional rules; theoretical background; and attorneys' duties.

Points out the vagaries in the American Bar Association Code and the California Rules of Professional Conduct. Recommends new, specific rules. In civil cases Wolfram would require that attorneys withdraw if their client insists on presenting perjured testimony. In the case of surprise perjury attorneys should immediately move for a recess and remonstrate with their client to correct the perjury. Perjury known in advance should be disclosed to the fact finder. With respect to criminal cases, the only difference would be to allow the witness (accused) the right to take the stand despite the attorney's opposition.

Section V.

B. Other Fields

655. American Bar Association. Future of 'Newsman's Privilege' --The Whither and Whether of Disclosure for Newspersons. Washington, DC: ABA, 1975.

A panel discussion transcript dealing with the current status of federal legislation to shield newspersons from being forced to reveal sources of information.

656. Bagot, C. N. H. Two Problems of Confidentiality in Probation. Ontario: Butterworth and Scarborough, 1977.

The discretion of the probation officer in bringing parole violations to the attention of the supervising court and his/her claim to privilege as a witness before authorities other than the supervisory court are examined.

657. "Benefit-Risk Ratio--New Test in Malpractice Cases-- Introduced by Retired Surgeon Who Blows Whistle On His Profession." Current Medicine for Attorneys, 23 (1976), 21-27.

658. Benjamin, James J., Keith G. Stanga, and Robert H. Strawser. "Disclosure of Information Regarding Corporate Social Responsibility." Managerial Planning, 27 (Winter 1978), 23-27.

Results of 52 questionnaires sent to management accountants on the means and content of corporate disclosure.

659. Bossy, Mike. "Blow the Whistle on Dirty Hockey." Sport, 70 (June 1980), 8.

660. Boyle, C. "Confidentiality in Correctional Institutions." Canadian Journal of Criminology and Corrections, 18 (January 1976), 26-41.

The administrative and rehabilitative considerations of maintaining the confidentiality of personal, medical, and psychiatric information on inmates are debated, and general safeguards for information control are suggested. Recommends that information exchange only occur on a horizontal level between professionals who have a legitimate need for the information.

661. Brown, James and Michael J. Collins, eds. Military Ethics and Professionalism. Washington, DC: National Defense University Press, 1981.

Contains five essays covering such topics as the moral and ethical foundations of professionalism in the military, and competence and ethics in the military profession.

662. Callahan, David and Sissela Bok, eds. Ethics Teaching in Higher Education. New York: Plenum Press, 1980.

Presents a number of papers and special studies prepared for The Hastings Center Project on the Teaching of Ethics in Higher Education. These papers were heavily drawn upon for preparation of the Center's Report and develop in a more comprehensive way issues treated in other publications of the Project (see item 670).

663. Carmichael, D. R. "Behavioral Hypotheses of Internal Control." The Accounting Review, 45 (April 1970), 235-245.

Argues that internal control systems are supposed to influence human behavior. Therefore, the nature of control will be influenced by the assumptions about human behavior held by accountants who design control systems. Compares these assumptions to recent empirical studies of organizational behavior and concludes that many assumptions in control system design have been invalidated.

664. Corsini, L. S. "The Auditor's Role and Corporate Misdeeds." National Public Accountant, 21 (November 2, 1976), 18-20.

665. Elliot, Robert K. and John J. Willingham. Management Fraud: Detection and Deterrence. Princeton, NJ: Petrocelli Books, 1980. See item 99.

666. Florida State University and Center for Professional Development and Public Service. Proceedings From the 23rd Annual Conference on Corrections. Edited by V. Fox. Tallahassee, FL: Florida State University, 1978.

Twenty-seven presentations on ethical dimensions in corrections, ethics in the formulation and implementation of correctional policies, ethical traditions and correctional training, prison counseling and the dilemma of confidentiality, and a responsibility model of correctional ethics. Also discussed were the emergence of correctional employee rights and their impact on the evolution of correctional law, equal employment opportunity and affirmative action for criminal justice administrators, persuasive communication in hiring ex-offenders, victim compensation and offender restitution, community supervision and the use of volunteers.

667. Gorovitz, Samuel, Andrew L. Jameton, Ruth MacKlin, John M. O'Conner, Eugene V. Perrin, Beverly Page St. Clair, and Susan Sherwin, eds. Moral Problems in Medicine. Englewood Cliffs, N.J.: Prentice-Hall, 1976.

Examines the moral dimensions of decision making in medicine and the biological sciences. Major sections deal with philosophy, problems in the physician-patient relationship, concerning life and death issues, and moral problems on a social scale. Over eighty readings address these issues from a philosophical point of view.

668. Gunn, Albert E. "Cost Effectiveness? It's Time to Blow the Whistle." Critical Care Medicine, 6 (September/October 1978), 352-353.

Discusses the trend toward preventive health care at the expense of acute care, which may lose a major part of its funding. Doctors and hospitals will then be forced to manage sick people with shorter hospital stays and less equipment. For the medical profession to retain credibility, it should speak up.

669. The Hastings Center. "In The Service of the State: The Psychiatrist As Double Agent." The Hastings Center Report Special Supplement, April 1978.

Twenty-four page transcript of a conference co-sponsored by the American Psychiatric Association and The Hastings Center on the psychiatrist's conflicting loyalties in the service of the state: prisons, military and mental hospitals.

*670. The Hastings Center. The Teaching of Ethics in Higher Education: Nine Monographs. Hastings-on-Hudson, N.Y.: The Center, 1980.

Subjects include teaching ethics in higher education (see item 662), law, journalism, bioethics, business (item 171), the social sciences, engineering, (item 447) and policy analysis (item 357).

671. Herbsler, J. D. and J. J. Berman. "When Psychologists Aid in the Voir Dire--Legal and Ethical Consideration." Social Psychology and Discretionary Law. Lawrence Edwin and Irving R. Stuart. New York: Van Nostrand, 1979, pp. 21ff.

Legal and ethical considerations raised by the use of social science techniques to aid in voir dire are discussed.

672. Hirsch, Harold L., MD. "When to Blow the Whistle on Patient Threats." Practical Psychology for Physicians, 2 (December 1975), 66-67.

Deals with the tradition of the physician-patient privilege versus society's right to protection. Reviews the legal problems of blowing the whistle. Recommends revealing only that information which physicians professionally believe is a "clear and present danger" to the public.

673. Isabell, David B. "An Overview of Accountants' Duties and Liabilities Under the Federal Securities Laws and a Closer Look at Whistle-Blowing." Ohio State Law Journal, 35 (1974), 179-261.

Addresses the question of accountants' responsibilities within a framework of the kinds of factual situations in which accountants' duties and liabilities may arise; the kinds of liability that may be incurred for failure to discharge his/her duties; the particular sources of the duties enforceable under the securities laws; and the varying degrees of exigence that characterize such duties.

674. Kennedy, Carol S., M.D. "One Doctor's Fight for Reform." Medical Dimensions, 7 (May 1978), 25-27.

Chronicles the investigation into the Federal Drug Administration (F.D.A.) begun in 1974. Dr. Kennedy, a a psychiatrist in the Neuropharmacological Division, charges laxity in protecting the public and harassment of critics. Concludes with recommendations for greater accountability through less secrecy, careful evaluation of industry raw data, limited but open contacts between F.D.A. officials and industry, and more extensive premarketing studies.

675. Knerr, C. R. and J. D. Carroll. "Confidentiality and Criminological Research--The Evolving Body of Law." Journal of Criminal Law and Criminology, 69 (Fall 1978), 311-321.

The evolving body of law concerning the confidentiality of communications between a criminologist and his subject is reviewed, with attention to problems experienced by researchers, and statutory and constitutional protection.

676. Knerr, C. R. and J. D. Carroll. "Social Scientists and the Courts--The Development of a Testimonial Privilege." Social Science Journal, 15 (January 1978), 103-113.

Essay examines legal issues related to confidentiality in social science research, with emphasis on the question of whether researchers must disclose confidential information when ordered to do so in criminal proceedings. Social and behavioral scientists commonly conduct their research under an expectation of confidentiality.

677. Levine, R. S. "Child Advocacy and the Psychotherapist." Voices, 13 (Fall 1977), 77-80.

Certain states have enacted legislation requiring therapists to report suspected cases of child abuse to authorities. This conflicts with the notion of privileged information and presents certain ethical problems for the psychotherapist. The role of the psychotherapist in the growing movement of concern for the rights of children is examined.

678. Levy, Charles. "The Code of Ethics of the National Association of Social Workers: A Case Study in Code Development." Paper presented at the meeting on Professional Ethics, Institute of Society, Ethics

and the Life Sciences, The Hastings Center, 18-19 September 1980, Harvard Faculty Club, Boston, Mass.

679. Levy, Charles S. <u>Social Work Ethics</u>. New York: Human Sciences Press, 1976.

In discussing the background, premises, and substance of social work ethics, it becomes evident that ethical social work practice depends more upon the awakening in the social worker of concern about his /her ethics than upon external regulatory devices. A rationale and procedures are suggested for social work education, and principles are offered, affecting the relationship of the social worker to clients, third parties, employers, and colleagues.

680. Marcuse, Peter. "Professional Ethics and Beyond: Values in Planning." <u>AIP Journal</u>, 42 (July 1976), 264-274.

Looks at professional ethics in planning from two perspectives. The first, internal, explores what professional ethics now imply for the practicing planner. The second, external, questions the social value of planning and looks at ethics in that broader sense. Examines five cases, suggesting the types of problems with which ethics in planning must deal. Describes obligations under current ethics and their application to selected issues, (e.g. autonomy, allegiance, guild loyalty, loyalty, and dissent). Concludes by looking beyond professional ethics to the area of planning theory and identifies six different approaches to ethics.

681. Molner, S. F. "Trapped Bedfellows--A Comment on Windle and Neigher." <u>Evaluation and Program Planning</u>, 1 (1978), 109-112.

This commentary on an article discussing the ethical problems evaluators face (see item 702) agrees with the points made by Windle and Neigher and adds five more evaluation models which can cause problems.

682. Moser, S. Thomas. "Meeting the Challenge of the Corporate Watergate Phenomenon." <u>International Auditor</u>, 35 (April 1978), 19-25.

Discusses recent cases and dubious practices that auditors may encounter. Outlines the "triangle of corporate accountability and governance." Suggests guidelines for auditors in the questionable practices area.

683. Nejelski, P. Social Research in Conflict with Law and Ethics. Cambridge, MA.: Ballinger Publishing, 1976.

Papers from a 1974 conference on the conflict of social research with law and ethics held at the University of Bielefeld, West Germany. Eleven essays deal with such topics as legislative proposals for regulating social research, the role of professional organizations, and methodological solutions to conflicts.

684. Nejelski, P. and K. Ffinsterbusch. "Prosecutor and the Researcher--Present and Prospective Variations on the Supreme Court's Branzburg Decision." Social Problems, 21 (Summer 1973), 3-21.

Suggests social scientists compare their situation to newspersons who refuse to disclose their sources of information. Authors feel that social scientists should begin to organize their efforts to obtain a judicially recognized privilege to protect confidential data.

685. Nejelski, P. and L. M. Lerman. "Researcher-Subject Testimonial Privilege--What To Do Before The Subpoena Arrives." Wisconsin Law Review, 1971, 1085-1148.

Concentrates on the problem of the consequences, if any, should a researcher be compelled to reveal confidential information about individuals in his/her testimonial privilege would be the best vehicle for protecting this relationship from outside demands.

686. Oakes, Andra N. "Protecting the Rights of Whistleblowers and the Accused in Federally Supported Biomedical Research." Washington, DC: President's Commission for the Study of Ethical Problems in Medicine and Biomedical and Behavioral Research, n.d. (mimeograph).

Explores, through three case studies and a brief survey of existing law, what safeguards exist at the institutional, associational, state and federal levels to protect the interests of both whistle-blowers and accused when allegations of research misconduct and reprisals for whistle-blowing occur. Closes with suggestions for reform.

687. Orzack, Louis H. and Annell L. Simcoe, eds. The Professions and Ethics: Views and Realities in New Jersey. New Brunswick, NJ: Bureau of Educational Research and Development, Rutgers University Graduate School of Business, 1982.

Contains fourteen papers and four workshop summaries of Rutgers University's Professional Forum held November 17, 1981. Papers cover ethical issues in the regulatory process, nursing, psychology, dentistry, education, pharmacy, social work, and public accounting. Contains items 706 and 743.

688. Paul, Robert E. "Tarasoff and the Duty to Warn: Toward a Standard of Conduct that Balances the Rights of Clients Against the Rights of Third Parties." Professional Psychology, 8 (1977), 125-128.

689. Popiel, D. J. "Confidentiality in the Context of Court Referrals to Mental Health Professionals." American Journal of Orthopsychiatry, 50 (October 1980), 678-685.

Problems of confidentiality and professional ethics faced by mental health professionals who accept client referrals from the judiciary or allied agencies are explored, and a possible solution is proposed.

690. Porterfield, Bob. "Why Investigative Reporting Is Dying." Editor and Publisher, 14 March 1981, p. 60.

Former Anchorage Daily News reporter and two-time Pulitzer Prize winner Bob Porterfield discuss why investigative reporting is dying. Argues that reporters are kept too busy with their beats, newspapers rely on leaks by whistle-blowers, and many journals avoid controversial subjects in order to build advertising.

691. Reamer, Frederick G. "Fundamental Ethical Issues in Social Work: An Essay Review." Social Service Review, (1979), 53.

692. "Report of the Task Force on the Role of Psychology in the Criminal Justice System." American Psychologist, 33 (December 1978), 1099-1113.

Key ethical issues for psychologists in the criminal justice system are identified, and seven recommendations regarding the ethical practice of psychology are presented.

693. Shannon, Thomas A. "Whistle Blowing and Countersuits: The President's Commission and Fraudulent Research." IRB, 3 (August/September 1981), 6-7.

694. Siler, Tom. "College Grid Coaches Vow to Blow Whistle on Cheaters." Sporting News, 2 February 1980, p. 22.

695. Simon, Gottlieb C. "Psychologist As Whistle Blower Case Study." Professional Psychology, 9 (May 1978), 322-340.

Psychologists who practice as salaried employees may find that their professional responsibilities to clients are in conflict with the demands of their organizations. This problem is illustrated in the firing of Veterans Administration (VA) psychologist who objected, first internally and then publicly, to VA policies that they believed jeopardized the health and well-being of their patients. The organizational responses to this incident reveal a series of threats to the integrity of professional practice in institutional settings.

696. Todaro, G. J. "Piercing the Newsman's Shield--The Supreme Court and the States Assess Privilege Legislation." Capital University Law Review, 3 (1974), 53-76.

Brief discussion of the 1972 case of Branzburg vs. Hayes, the difficulties with the nineteen state statutes which provide legislative protection to newspersons, and a review of the case law interpreting these statutes.

697. Tortorella, A. N. "Physician-Patient Privileged Communications." Trial, 9 (March/April 1973), 59-63.

Overview of privilege when a communication is or is not privileged and who can accept the privilege, with New York cases used as an example of one state's rulings.

698. "University Blows Whistle on Library Troublemakers." American Libraries, 10 (September 1979), 456.

699. Veatch, Robert. "Medical Ethics: Professional or Universal?" Harvard Theological Review, 65 (October 1972), 531-559.

700. Weissman, J. C. and B. R. Berns. "Patient Confidentiality and the Criminal Justice System--A Critical Examination of the New Federal Confidentiality Regulations." Contemporary Drug Problems, 5 (Winter 1976), 531-552.

A critical review is presented of the 1975 supplement to the Code of Federal Regulations regarding protection of the confidentiality of alcohol and drug abuse patient records.

701. "When Audit Rules Clash With Legal Ethics." Business Week, 14 April 1975, p. 72.

Tighter accounting rules are bringing auditors into direct conflict with corporate lawyers over the issue of how much information about a company's internal affairs must be revealed publicly. Accountants are alarmed since the court case of Ernst and Ernst which resulted in the danger that auditors can be held liable for not knowing what they should have know about their company. Lawyers are fearful that complying with requests for more information about company affairs violates their own code of ethics by divulging client confidences.

702. Windle, C. and W. Neigher. "Ethical Problems in Program Evaluation--Advice for Trapped Evaluators." Evaluation and Program Planning, 1 (1978), 97-107.

The ethical standards of psychologists, formulated by the American Psychological Association, are reviewed and their application to program evaluations is discussed. Program evaluation models are examined. Ethical problems inherent in each model, and the problems which arise when the models are combined, are presented.

Section VI

Philosophical Literature

A. Whistleblowing and Dissent

703. Bok, Sissela. "Whistleblowing and Professional Respon-
     sibility," <u>New York University Education Quar-
     terly</u>, 11 (Summer 1980), 2-10. See item 224.

704. Bok, Sissela. "Whistleblowing and Professional Respon-
     sibilities." <u>Ethics Teaching in Higher Education</u>.
     Daniel Callahan and Sissela Bok. New York:
     Plenum Press, 1980, chapter 11, pp. 277-295. Based
     on item 703.

705. Bowie, Norman. "Blowing the Whistle and Other 'Why Be
     Moral Questions.'" <u>Business Ethics</u>. Englewood
     Cliffs, NJ: Prentice-Hall, 1982, chapter 7, pp.
     138-149.

     Analyzes whistle-blowing as morally justified
     wherever one (a) acts for appropriate moral motives;
     (b) has exhausted internal channels (except in special
     circumstances); (c) verified that inappropriate ac-
     tions have or will occur; (d) analyzed danger as seri-
     ous, immediate, and specific; (e) behaves commensurate
     with one's responsibility for avoiding and/or exposing
     moral violations; and (f) has some chance of success.

706. Chalk, Rosemary. "Ethical Issues in the Work of the
     Professional." (Item 687), pp. 12-17.

     Suggests three categories of ethical issues: the
     duty to inform, to warn, and to ensure equitable ac-
     cess to professional services and information. Con-
     tains a brief discussion of conflicts among ethical
     principles, and possible responses. Concludes that
     personal, self-directed moral reflection is conspicu-
     ously absent in the professional literature.

707. DeGeorge, Richard T. "Workers' Rights, Obedience, and
     Whistleblowing." <u>Business Ethics</u>. New York:
     Macmillan, 1981, chapter 9, pp. 147-165.

708. DeGeorge, Richard T. "Ethical Responsibilities of En-
     gineers in Large Organizations: The Pinto Case."
     Paper presented at the National Conference on Engi-
     neering Ethics, 20-22 June 1980, at Rensselaer Poly-
     technic Institute, Troy, NY.

     Summarizes the Pinto Case and raises questions
     about the responsibility of the engineers involved.
     Argues that blowing the whistle is morally permitted

when three conditions are met and morally obligatory when two further conditions are met. Concludes that that automobile companies should not have the last or exclusive word on how much safety to provide, and that the purpose of engineering ethics should be to restructure organizations.

708b. DeGeorge, Richard. "Whistleblowing: Prohibited, Permitted Required." Conflicting Loyalities in the Workplace, edited F. A. Elliston. See item 717.

Argues that whistleblowing is permitted under the following conditions: serious and considerable harm is threatened; the employee has reported the threat to his or her immediate superior; if the superior does nothing, one exhausts all internal avenues. It is required if two further conditions are met: the employee has reasonable evidence; and going outside the organization is likely to succeed in bringing about the desired change.

709. Donaldson, Thomas. "Employee Rights." Corporations and Morality. Englewood Cliffs, NJ: Prentice-Hall, 1982, chapter 7, pp. 129-157.

Dissent is one employee right (along with privacy and political participation) that is examined from a legal, historical and moral perspective. Classifies moral rights as traditional, modern, ·and manifesto. Identifies strategies to establish employee rights.

710. Donaldson, Thomas. "International Whistleblowing." Conflicting Loyalities in the Workplace, edited F. A. Elliston. See item 717.

Discusses the employee in a multinational corporation who wishes to complain about a corporate practice not permitted in his home country but permitted in the country in which he works. After developing the notion of the right to dissent in international perspective, he asserts that whistleblowing is justified if the members of one's home country would not regard the practice as permissible if they lived under similar conditions of economic development. Alternatively, it is justified if it is possible to conduct business in the country in which one works without the practice in question, or if the practice clearly violates a basic human right.

711. Elliston, Frederick A. "Anonymous Whistleblowing." Business and Professional Ethics, 1 (Spring 1982), 39-58.

Briefly surveys the popular literature and scholar's efforts to define whistle-blowing. Appraises anonymous whistle-blowing according to three factors: the seriousness of the harmed threatened, the probability of unfair retaliation, and the social roles.

712. Elliston, Frederick A. "Anonymity and Whistle-Blowing." Journal of Business Ethics, 1 (Summer 1982), 167-177.

Defines whistle-blowing and anonymity, and defends anonymous whistle-blowing against charges that it breaches professional etiquette, obstructs the discovery of truth, is unfair, or will cause organizational disorder.

713. Elliston, Frederick A. "Civil Disobedience and Whistleblowing: A Comparative Appraisal of Two Forms of Dissent." Journal of Business Ethics, 1 (Spring 1982), 23-28.

Argues that whistle-blowers are the civil disobedients of the 1970's and 1980's, and that principles used to evaluate the latter can be extended to the former--freedom of speech, higher moral law, and appeals to the public good.

714. Elliston, Frederick A. "Whistleblowing: A Moral Appraisal." Paper presented at the Western Division Meeting of the American Philosophical Association, 24 April 1981, Milwaukee, WI.

Examines the conflicting rights of professionals and their employers by identifying the conditions under which whistle-blowing is permitted and when it is mandatory.

715. Elliston, Frederick, John Keenan, Paula Lockhart and Jane van Schaick. Professional Dissent: Methodological and Moral Issues. Chicago: Illinois Institute of Technology, 1983.

Report of a project sponsored by EVIST that identifies various theoretical questions that arose in the

course of research on blowing the whistle: the definition of whistleblowing; theories about individual characteristics, organizational structures and environment
that explain when it will occur; relations between researchers and reporters, interviewing techniques and
protecting the confidentiality of research subjects.

716. Elliston, Frederick, John Keenan, Paula Lockhart and
Jane van Schaick. Professional Dissent: Strate-
gies and Options. Chicago: Illinois Institute of
Technology, 1983.

Report of a project sponsored by EVIST that identifies various strategies for blowing the whistle
through media, professional associations, consultants,
the Congress, community groups and the Inspector General. Each is analyzed in terms of several factors:
professional role, individual characteristics, organizational structure, the issue and the historical context. Authors define successful dissent from three
different perspectives: personal, objective, and
legal.

*717. Elliston, Frederick A., ed. Conflicting Loyalties in
the Workplace. Notre Dame, IN: University of
Notre Dame Press, forthcoming.

Contains items 477, 710, 717, 721, 795, 1242.

Includes essays which address such topics as the
concept of whistleblowing, employee rights and freedom
of speech in the workplace, professionals as whistle-
blowers, the role of professional societies, a legal
analysis of professional dissent, and strategies for
professional dissent.

718. Hill, Thomas E. Jr. "Symbolic Protest and Calculated
Silence." Philosophy and Public Affairs, 9 (Fall
1979), 83-102.

A philosopher explores conflicting approaches to in-
justice--symbolic protest and calculated silence.

*719. James, Gene G. "Whistle Blowing: Its Nature and Jus-
tification." Philosophy in Context, 10 (1980),
99-117.

Discusses whistle-blowing, pointing out the reasons for its infrequency. Deterrents include organi-

zational loyalty, self-interest, the threat of prosecution, and laws which forbid the release of information. James reviews laws which encourage whistle-blowing, but notes that they are ineffective. He analyzes criticisms against whistle-blowing and defends its importance on the grounds that dissenters are the only people in their organizations willing to take a stand for an ideal.

720. Johnson, Deborah. "The Concept of Whistle-Blowing." Forthcoming in items 716 and 717.

Identifies the characteristic features of whistle-blowing and distinguishes these from aspects often found in a case of whistle-blowing, but not essential to it. A definition is proposed and defended.

720a. Johnson, Deborah. "Successful Whistleblowing." Unpublished paper. RPI: Troy, NY.

Conditions under which whistle-blowing can be categorized as successful include: the wrongdoing stops or is prevented; there is a policy change; the organization is prosecuted and convicted; or individuals are able to avoid becoming victims of wrongdoing.

721. Ladenson, Robert F. "Freedom of Expression in the Corporate Workplace." Ethics in Business and the Professions. Forthcoming in items 100 and 717.

Examines two kinds of arguments in support of freedom of expression in business corporations: (1) the volunteer public guardian approach, which stresses immediate benefits to society from making the climate in corporations more conductive to free speech; and (2) the fundamental liberty approach, which suggests that that freedom of expression is an inherent right grounded in basic principles of social morality. Using the second approach, Ladenson argues that corporate employees should be free to speak without fear of sanctions even when they make false allegations.

722. Oldenquist, Andrew. "Loyalties." Journal of Philosophy 79:4 (April 1982) pp. 173-193.

722a. Weil, Vivian, ed. Beyond Whistle-Blowing. Chicago: Illinois Institute of Technology, 1983.

The Proceedings of the Second National Conference on Ethics in Engineering. Papers are divided into 6 sections: (1) Moral Choice and Professional Duty; (2) Engineers and Regulation; (3) Risk Assessment and Decision Making; (4) Creating an Ethical Work Environment; (5) Responsibilities of the Professional Societies; and (6) a panel on Case Study and Teaching.

Section VI

Philosophical Literature

B. Ethics and Responsibility

723. Adams, Guy B. "Ethics in Organization Theory and Behavior." Unpublished paper, Evergreen State College, Olympia, WA. n.d.

Uses as its point of departure that "in the organizational world, choice and decision have long been seen as a matter of economics, not ethics ..." (p. 1).

724. Barry, Vincent. Moral Issues in Business. Second edition. Belmont, CA: Wadsworth Publishing Co., 1983.

A textbook/reader in which each chapter considers a set of business issues (e.g., personnel actions, ecology, consumer relations) and how ethical theories may be applied to them.

725. Baum, Robert J. "Institutional Obstacles to Design." Paper at Workshop on Engineering Ethics: Designing for Safety, 24-26 May 1982, Center for the Study of the Human Dimensions of Science and Technology, Rensselaer Polytechnic Institute, Troy, NY. See item 521.

Identifies philosophical issues underlying engineering design safety. Outlines a course of action that could increase the extent to which hazards are recognized and eliminated.

726. Bayles, Michael D. "Acceptable Risk and the Public." Paper presented at Workshop on Engineering Ethics: Designing for Safety, 24-26 May 1982, Rensselaer Polytechnic Institute, Troy, NY. See item 489.

727. Bayles, Michael D. Professional Ethics. Belmont, CA: Wadsworth Publishing Co., 1981.

Chapters one and two discuss the scope of professional ethics, what can be expected from its study, and the relations between professional norms and ordinary ethical norms. Chapters three through six analyze the substantive obligations of professions and professionals. The last chapter reviews methods to ensure that professionals conform to ethical norms.

728. Bayles, Michael D. "Problems of Clean Hands: Refusal to Provide Professional Services." Social Theory and Practice, 5 (Spring 1979), 165-181.

Argues against the standard views when a professional is asked to provide services to a client whose conduct is thought to be morally wrong.

729. Beauchamp, Tom L. and Norman E. Bowie, eds. Ethical Theory and Business. Englewood Cliffs, NJ: Prentice-Hall, 1979.

A set of sixty-five interrelated readings arranged to reflect a controversy among authors by demonstrating the strengths and weaknesses of alternative positions. The editors survey two major ethical theories (utilitarian and deontological) as related to business in the opening chapter, while the remaining eight sections contain fourteen case studies, legal opinions, and contributions from philosophers and business people. Suggested supplementary readings are included. Contains item 782.

730. Beauchamp. Tom L., ed. Ethics and Public Policy. Englewood Cliffs, NJ: Prentice-Hall, 1979.

A collection of twenty-nine readings by philosophers attempting to show the importance of critical analysis and ethical theory for the resolution of social controversies, arranged in an order which reflects widely divergent viewpoints. Issues include racial and sexual discrimination, criminal punishment and the death penalty, civil disobedience, war, moral enforcement, abortion, and biomedical technology.

731. Behrman, Jack N. Discourses on Ethics and Business. Cambridge, MA: Oelgeschlager, Gunn, and Hain, 1981. See item 64.

732. Benjamin, Martin. "Can Moral Responsibility Be Collective and Non-Distributive?" Social Theory and Practice, 4 (Fall 1976), 93-106.

Argues that attributions of moral responsibility for collective action must be analyzed in terms of individual moral responsibility. Benjamin proceeds by analyzing descriptions of moral responsibility and focusing on an example of a vigilante committee that is responsible for an injustice against a cowboy.

733. Bowie, Norman E., ed. Ethical Issues in Government. Washington, DC: Urban Institute Press, 1981. See item 316.

734. Callahan, Daniel. "Do Special Ethical Norms Apply to
     Professions?" (Item 687), pp. 4-11.

     Begins by identifying several different kinds of
     conflicts confronting professionals today: conflicts
     among values within a profession, conflicts between
     professional values and broader societal values, and
     conflicts between personal values and professional
     values. Callahan then draws further distinctions
     among the types of moral problems that arise for pro-
     fessionals: personal-moral dilemma, ethical problems
     of institutional structures and arrangements, and mor-
     al problems posed by certain methodologies or tech-
     niques. His concluding section addresses the question
     of whether ethical norms apply to professions. He pro-
     vides both affirmative and negative answers.

735. Callahan, Daniel and H. Tristram Engelhardt, Jr., eds.
     The Roots of Ethics. New York: Plenum Publish-
     ing, 1982.

     Examines the philosophical foundations of ethics,
     the importance and relevance of religion for ethical
     viewpoints, the ways science can illuminate our na-
     ture as knowers and valuers, and the extent to which
     moral philosophy can account for our roles as scien-
     tists.

736. Caplan, Arthur L. and Daniel Callahan, eds. Ethics
     in Hard Times. New York: Plenum Publishing,
     1982.

     Represents an effort to see what the current per-
     ception of hard times means for ethical inquiry. In-
     vestigated are the feasibility of legislating
     morality, the moral propriety of selfishness and
     egoism, the role of ethics in resolving on-going
     policy debates, and the nature of tolerance in a
     pluralistic society.

737. Carens, Joseph H. "Institutional Loyalty and Public
     Responsibility: The Ethics of Whistle-blowing."
     Paper presented at the Annual Meeting of the Mid-
     west Political Science Association, 15-18 April
     1981 at the Stouffer's Inn, Cincinnati, OH.

     A political theorist compares civil disobedience
     and whistle-blowing through the application of John
     Rawls' theory of justice.

738. Carey, Toni Vogel. "Institutional Versus Moral Obliga-
     tions." Journal of Philosophy, 74 (October
     1977), 587-589.

     Commenting on a symposium paper by Peter French,
     Carey argues against French's thesis that the paradig-
     matic function of moral ought judgments is to resolve
     institutional conflicts of duty. Conflict aside, we
     enter or quit an institution (e.g., marriage) on the
     basis of moral ought judgments, and we establish or
     abolish institutions (e.g., slavery) on that same
     basis.

739. Carpenter, Stanley R. "Philosophical Issues in Tech-
     nology Assessment." Philosophy of Science, 44
     (December 1977), 574-593.

740. Cooper, Terry L. "Ethics, Values and Systems." Jour-
     nal of Systems Management, 30 (September 1979), 6-
     12.

     An analysis of the ways in which cognitive pro-
     cesses are related to and affected by values and eth-
     ics. Cooper examines ethical problems implied by wide-
     spread use of systems analysis. Of particular impor-
     tance are (1) boundary definitions that create ethical
     externalities; (2) identification of goals and objec-
     tives in which only subordinate goals receive analysis
     and evaluation; (3) gratification which limits value
     and goal input from persons without qualitative skill
     or quantifiable objectives; and (4) componentiality,
     by which persons in organizations fail to take respon-
     sibility for the impact of the whole system.

741. DeGeorge, Richard T. and Joseph A. Pichler, eds.
     Ethics, Free Enterprise, and Public Policy. New
     York: Oxford University Press, 1978.

     A collection of essays by philosophers dealing with
     ethical considerations in the business world. The
     first two readings address the questions of ethics,
     business, and public policy. The next three present
     opposing, but representative, approaches to justice
     for the economic system. The remaining essays discuss
     specific issues of morality and business (e.g., ethi-
     cal considerations in civil remedies, public service
     strikes, advertising). Although the theme of morality

is evident in all the essays, the sub-theme of the possible role of government in remedying inequities and
injustices in dominant.

742. Donaldson, Thomas. "The Right to Behave Responsibly."
Paper read at Second National Conference on Ethics
in Engineering, 5-6 March 1982, at Bismark Hotel,
Chicago, IL. See item 722b.

743. Donaldson, Thomas and Patricia H. Werhane, eds. Ethical Issues in Business: A Philosophical Approach.
Englewood Cliffs, NJ: Prentice-Hall, 1979.

Contains fifty essays and fourteen case-studies
drawn from modern and traditional philosophical material on business problems, divided into four parts:
Philosophical Issues in Business Ethics; Economics,
Values, and Justice; Rights, Liability and the State;
and Business in Modern Society.

744. Donaldson, Thomas. "Ethics in the Business Schools:
A Proposal." National Forum, 58 (Summer 1978),
11-14. See item 77.

745. Downie, Robert S. Roles and Values. London:
Methuen, 1971.

Examines the demands of social and political institutions as they impinge on individual values and responsibility. Downie uses the concept of social role
to connect institutional duties and individual responsibility, divided into eight chapters: "The Nature of
Social Ethics;" The Principles of Social Morality;"
"Responsibility;" "Authority, Legitimacy, and Representation;" "The Morality of Government Action;" Persons
and Roles;" "Resenting, Forgiving, Punishing, and Par-
doning;" and Moral Change and Moral Improvement."

746. Durland, William R. and William H. Bruening, eds.
Ethical Issues: A Search for the Contemporary
Conscience. Palo Alto, CA: Mayfield Publishing,
1975.

The thirty-two selections argue that part of our
present difficulties stems from a general lack of understanding of the nature of morality and from the
failure to think of contemporary issues in terms of

188

morality. Readings are divided into seven sections: religion and morality, law and morality, pacifism and violence, medical and environmental ethics, government and business, sex and liberation, and rights, race, and human dignity.

747. Edel, Abraham. "A Philosopher's View of the Social Responsibility of Scientists and Engineers." Journal of the Franklin Institute, 300 (August 1975), 113-114.

Claims that the issue is not whether science and engineering always had a pattern of responsibility which they ignored. Rather what is the task of reconstruction in a world that is undergoing massive transformation?

748. Ellin, Joseph, Michael S. Pritchard, and Wade L. Robinson, eds. Ethics in Business and the Professions. New York: Humana Press, forthcoming.

749. Feinberg, Joel. "Collective Responsibility." Doing and Deserving: Essays in the Theory of Responsibility. Princeton, NJ: Princeton University Press, 1970, chapter 9, pp. 222-251

While in standard cases of responsibility there can be no liability without contributing fault, unusual cases can have solid rationales. Feinberg examines strict liability, vicarious liability and collective liability in this context.

750. Flores, Albert. "On the Rights of Professionals." Ethics in Business and the Professions. Joseph Ellin; Michael Pritchard; and Wade Robinson. New York: Humana Press, forthcoming.

751. Flores, Albert and Deborah G. Johnson. "Collective Responsibility and Professional Roles." Ethics, 93 (April 1983), 537-545.

752. Flores, Albert. "The Philosophical Basis of Engineering Codes of Ethics." Engineering and the Humanities. James H. Schaub. New York: Wiley, 1981.

753. Freedman, Benjamin. "A Meta-Ethics for Professional Morality." Ethics, 89 (October 1978), 1-19.

Argues that what is moral for a professional may conflict with the requirements of ordinary morality (exemplified through medical and psychotherapeutic confidentiality). This conflict is similar to, but stronger than, those conflicts which can be generated by acquired moralities in general, such as promise-keeping. Standard deontological and act-utilitarian explanations are clearly inadequate to explain this conflict. Freedman constructs a theory that differs in important respects from rule-utilitarianism.

754. French, Peter A. "The Corporation as a Moral Person." American Philosophical Quarterly, 16 (July 1979), 207-215.

Defends the position that Davidsonian agency is a necessary and sufficient condition for moral personhood. French argues that corporations qualify as Davidsonian agents by virtue of the fact that their internal decision-making structure provides the means for the prediction of corporate intentionality.

755. French, Peter A. "Types of Collectivities and Blame." The Personalist, 56 (Spring 1975), 160-169.

756. French, Peter A., ed. Individual and Collective Responsibility. Cambridge, MA: Schenckman Publishing Co., 1972.

Discussion of the moral and legal questions of individual and collective responsibility in the massacre at My Lai.

757. Gewirth, Alan. "Institutions and Obligations." Morals and Values. Marcus G. Singer. New York: Scribners, 1977, pp. 348-363.

Institutional obligations are defined by rules which constitute the institution. These obligations are tentative and dependent on whether or not the institution itself is justified.

758. Goldman, Alan H. "Business Ethics: Profits, Utilities, and Moral Rights." Philosophy and Public Affairs, 9 (Spring 1980), 260-286.

Asks if business managers make decisions using special professional norms instead of ordinary moral norms. Goldman assesses the arguments for and against the moral primacy of profit maximization as the principal norm of business ethics, and concludes that the case for strong role-differentiation in business, according to the maximization-of-profit principle, cannot prevail.

759. Goldman, Alan H. The Moral Foundations of Professional Ethics. Totowa, NJ: Rowman and Littlefield, 1980.

Professional roles require norms and principles to guide their well-intentioned conduct. This requirement, which justifies activity in otherwise prohibited ways, is appraised in four contexts: politics, law, medicine and business.

760. Grady, J. E. "Royce and Kant: Loyalty and Duty." Journal of the British Society for Phenomenology, 6 (October 1975), 186-193.

Sequel to a previous article, "Marcel and Hope: Loyalty and the Person." Loyalty is a "natural" principle, and a formal conception of duty is utilized to complement the concrete meaning of loyalty. Both articles are chapters from Grady's book Without Good and Evil: An Introduction to the Logic or Ontology of Value.

761. Hampshire, Stuart, ed. Public and Private Morality. New York: Cambridge University Press, 1978.

Examines a Machiavellian question: What are the limits to be set on grossly immoral and cruel practices which sometimes protect great public causes? Asks if a "moral threshold" is crossed when people assume a public role to represent the will and interests of others. Chapter titles include "Morality and Pessimism," and "Public and Private Morality;" "Politics and Moral Character;" "Ruthlessness in Public Life;" "Rights, Goals and Fairness;" and "Liberalism."

762. Hanson, Donald W. and Robert B. Fowler, eds. Obligation and Dissent: An Introduction to Politics. Boston: Little, Brown, 1971.

An anthology divided into four parts: political obligation; morality, law, and enforcement; forms and limits of dissent; and obligations and dissent in time of war. The aim of Hanson's introductory essay is "to consider political philosophy, and how it differs from other types of intellectual activity which strive to form or express value judgments in politics" (p. x).

763. Hill, Ivan. "Common Sense and Everyday Ethics." Washington, DC: Ethics Resource Center, 1980.

Raises these questions: "What are Ethics?" "Why Be Ethical?" "How Does One Decide What's Ethical?" "What About Lying?" "Can Ethics Be Taught?" "What Should Our Priorities Be?"

764. Hoffman, Michael and Jennifer Mills Moore, eds. Ethics and the Management of Computer Technology. Cambridge, MA: Oelgeschlager, Gunn and Hain, 1982.

Contains papers and discussions on the ethical management of computer technology from Bentley College's Fourth National Conference. Covers positions on a broad array of ethical issues in the management of computer technology. Some are optimistic about a future enhanced by the capabilities of computers; other are more circumspect.

765. Hoffman, W. Michael and Thomas J. Wyly. The Work Ethics in Business: Proceedings of the Third National Conference on Business Ethics. Cambridge, MA: Oelgeschlager, Gunn, and Hain, 1980. See item 142.

766. Hoffmann, W. Michael, ed. Proceedings of the Second National Conference on Business Ethics: Power and Responsibility in the American Business System. Washington, DC: University Press of America, 1979.

A collection of papers sponsored by the Center for Business Ethics at Bentley College, whose primary purpose is to provide a nonpartisan atmosphere for the exchange of ideas on business ethics in an industrial society. Deals with a wide range of issues, including accounting ethics, corporate boards, employee freedoms, the philosophical foundations and nature of the corporation, and environmental protection.

767. Howard, Kenneth W. "Must Public Hands Be Dirty?" Journal of Value Inquiry, 11 (Spring 1977), 29-40.

Investigates the function of morality in politics by appraising the thesis "It is easy to get one's hands dirty in politics and it is often right to do so." Howard questions two consequences: that politics is radically different from individual activities; and that politicians are radically different men. He argues that if we consider politics as an extension of our own lives, its moral conduct becomes our responsibility. See item 794.

768. Johansen, Elaine. "Institutional Guidelines for Managing Ethical Conflicts: An Overview of Moral Dilemmas and Organization Culture in Political Institutions." Paper presented at the Annual Meeting of the American Society of Public Administration, 12-15 April, 1981, Detroit, MI.

Examines the selection of the correct unit of analysis when studying ethics. Past studies have focused on individual moral dilemmas, and much must be done to construct appropriate analytical models.

769. Johnson, Deborah G. "Moral Accountability in Corporations." Southwestern Journal of Philosophy, (forthcoming).

770. Johnson, Elmer W. "Corporate Leadership and The Judeo-Christian Vision." Paper presented at Conference on the Judeo-Christian Vision and the Modern Business Corporation, 15 April 1980, University of Notre Dame, Notre Dame, IN. Mimeographed.

Begins by discussing two inter-related phenomena that have prevented us from identifying principles of corporate accountability: the adversarial approach and the self-interest approach to executive motivation. Johnson then examines the legal doctrine of fiduciary responsibility from several perspectives focusing on the "business judgement" rule. This rule states "in effect that absent a showing of bad faith or gross abuse of discretion, the business judgment of directors and officers will not be interfered with by the courts" (p. 15).

771. Jones, Donald G., ed. Business, Religion and Ethics. Cambridge, MA: Olegeschlager, Gunn, and Hain, 1982.

Contains twenty essays written by senior business executives, ordained clergy, and professors of ethics. They focus on two questions: What is the proper role of business in society? What is the proper role of religion in economic affairs?

772. Kipnis, Kenneth. "Engineers and the Parmountcy of Public Safety." Business and Professional Ethics, 1 (Fall 1981), 77-92.

773. Kipnis, Kenneth. "Professional Ethics," Business and Professional Ethics, 2 (Fall 1978), 2-3.

Argues against the notion that general ethical principles are sufficient to appraise the moral responsibilities of professionals. Kipnis maintains that universal principles may be necessary, but they cannot fully explain the specialized responsibilities of the professions. Indeed, the exclusive attention to principles having universal application may blind professionals to their special responsibilities.

774. Kipnis, Kenneth. "Professional Responsibility and the Responsibility of the Professions." Ethics in Business and the Professions. See item 748.

An analysis of the concept of responsibility, showing how the professions come to be recognized as professions with distinctive responsibilities. Kipnis argues that it is through the institutionalization of a code of ethics that professions put into effect recognition of their responsibilities.

775. La Boetie, Etienne. The Politics of Obedience: The Discourse of Voluntary Servitude. New York: Free Life Edition, 1970.

La Boetie's call for civil disobedience, mass non-violent resistance to tyranny, stems from two premises: the fact that all rule rests on the consent of the masses, and the great value of natural liberty. In three parts, he addresses the question why people obey a government, the concepts of liberty versus servitude, and the extent to which the foundation of tyranny lies in the networks of corrupted people who have an interest in maintaining the tyranny.

776. Ladd, John. "Philosophical Remarks on Professional Responsibility in Organizations." Paper presented at

194

Workshop on Engineering Ethics: Designing for Safety, 24-26 May 1982, Center for the Study of the Human Dimensions of Science and Technology, Rensselaer Polytechnic Institute, Troy, NY. See item 521.

Attempts to disentangle the meaning of "responsibility," and comments on some of the abuses of the term. Ladd sets forth four kinds of responsibility: role, causal, liability, and capacity. In the concluding section he discusses a fifth type, one particularly apposite to the engineering profession: organizational responsibility.

777. Ladd, John. "The Quest for a Code of Professional Ethics." AAAS Professional Ethics Project: Professional Ethics Activities in Scientific and Engineering Societies. Edited by Rosemary Chalk, Mark Frankel and Sallie B. Chafer. Washington, DC: American Association for the Advancement of Science, 1980, pp. 154-159.

778. Ladd, John. "Morality and the Ideal of Rationality in Formal Organizations." Monist, 54 (October 1970), 488-517.

Deals with the moral problems that arise out of the interrelationships between individuals and formal organizations. Ladd argues that certain facets of the organizational ideal are incompatible with ordinary principles of morality. The dilemma thereby created is one source of alienation in our society.

779. Levy, Edwin and David Copp. "Risk and Uncertainty: Ethical Issues in Decision-Making." Paper read at Second National Conference on Ethics in Engineering, 5-6 March 1982, at Bismark Hotel, Chicago, IL. Mimeographed. See item 722b.

780. McDonald, Lee C. "Three Forms of Political Ethics." Western Political Quarterly, 31 (March 1978), 7-18.

Historical, theoretical, and philosophical analysis of the subject.

781. Martin, Mike W. and Benjamin Freedman. "An Exchange on Professional Morality." Ethics, 91 (July 1981), 619-633.

Whereas some use the case of medical confidentiality as a model, Martin suggests that ordinary moral rights, such as the right to privacy, can explain the special obligations of a professional. He lists distinctions between professional and ordinary morality and specifies the complex requirements of being a professional.

782. Michalos, Alex C. "The Loyal Agent's Argument." Ethical Theory and Business, (item 729), pp. 338-347.

Constructs a generalized argument which would appeal to persons who perform immoral or illegal actions on behalf of their employer. Michalos proceeds to analyze the "loyal agent's argument" with the conclusion that it does not stand the test.

783. Morris, Christopher W. "Moral Constraints, Prisoners' Dilemmas, and The Social Responsibilities of Corporations." Paper presented at Conference on Business and Professional Ethics, 15 May 1981, University of Illinois-Chicago Circle. Mimeographed.

Using the notion of a Prisoners' Dilemma, Morris develops an analysis of the misleading debate over the "social responsibilities of corporations." He clarifies the issues ultimately at stake in the debate and shows how these are related to issues in moral theory.

784. Penn, William. "Kohlberg and Professional Ethics." Paper presented at Conference on Business and Professional Ethics, 15 May 1981, University Illinois --Chicago Circle. Mimeographed.

Penn shares his perceptions and those of his Masters of Business Administration students on the practical value of a Business Ethics Course which made use of Lawrence Kohlberg's theory of moral development. When polled at the end of the semester, an overwhelming majority of the students (19 out of 20) thought that a business ethics course should be a part of the education of all business students.

785. Pettigrew, Andrew. The Politics of Organization Decision Making. London: Tavistock, 1973.

An expanded version of Pettigrew's earlier article on information control. He provides a detailed case study of one organization, and particularly the role

of power in innovative decision making about computer
Oardware. He concentrates on relationships among computer specialists, computer companies, and the board
of directors. He includes a complete literature review relevant to political behavior in technologically advanced organizations.

786. Platt, Thomas W. "The Concept of Responsible Dis-
     sent." Social Theory and Practice, 1 (Fall 19-
     72), 41-51.

787. Regan, Tom. Just Business: Essays in Business Eth-
     ics. New York: Random House, 1982.

788. Rescher, Nicholas. Unpopular Essays on Technological
     Progress. Pittsburgh, PA: University of Pitts-
     burgh Press, 1980. Cited as item 573.

789. Russell, Avery. "Applied Ethics: A Strategy for Fos-
     tering Professional Responsibility." Carnegie
     Quarterly, 28 (Spring/Summer 1980), 1-7.

790. Sayre, Kenneth and Kenneth E. Goodpaster. "An Ethical
     Analysis of Power Company Decision-Making." Val-
     ues in the Electric Power Industry. Notre Dame,
     IN: University of Notre Dame Press, 1977.

791. Simmons, Alan J. Moral Principles and Political Obli-
     gations. Princeton, NJ: Princeton University
     Press, 1979.

792. Sites, W. Kilmes and Barbara C. Blossom. Ethics in
     Perspective and Practice. Dobbs Ferry, NY: Oce-
     ana Publications, 1972.

Includes discussions of decision-making, types of
ethics, political philosophy, and sex.

793. Walsh, W. H. "Pride, Shame and Responsibility." The
     Philosophical Quarterly, 20 (January 19780), 1-13.

Beginning with the fact that people take pride in
and feel shame about the activities of groups of which
they are members, Walsh examines whether this is mis-
guided or makes sense, given the nature of responsibility.

794. Walzer, Michael. "Political Action: The Problem of Dirty Hands." <u>Philosophy and Public Affairs</u>, 2 (Spring 1973), 160-180.

   In political life, "we claim to act for others..., rule over others, and use violence against them. It is easy to get one's hands dirty ..., and it is often right to do so." Also see item 767.

795. Weil, Vivian. "The Brown's Ferry Case." Forthcoming. in item 716.

796. Winthrop, Henry. "The Strain of Loyalty and the Anguish of Commitment." <u>The Human Context</u>, 3 (July 1971), 404-410.

Section VII

Theoretical Literature

A. Professional Conduct

797. D'Andrade, Kendall, Jr. "Pre-Conditions for Whistle-Blowing." Unpublished paper, University of Illinois-Chicago Circle, n.d.

Discusses seven, admittedly restrictive, conditions that must be fulfilled before an employee is obligated to blow the whistle.

798. Davis, Gary. "Self Interest and the Professional Society." Business and Professional Ethics, 3 (Spring 1980), 3-4.

Notes that although professional societies officially serve to protect both the practitioner and professional standards, these societies are often perceived as showing more concern for the former than the latter. This is not necessary because a profession embodies a shared, principled tradition capable of seeing beyond the immediate interests of any given member.

799. Gross, Ronald and Paul Osterman, eds. The New Professionals. New York: Simon and Schuster, 1972.

A collection of thirteen essays which discuss a growing national movement among the new professionals. Three underlying assumptions are identified: (1) a concern for social change; (2) accountability or control by clients; and (3) an attack on the credential system.

800. Harries-Jenkins, G. "Professionals in Organizations." Professionals and Professionalization. Edited by John A. Jackson. Cambridge: Cambridge University Press, 1970, chapter 3, pp. 53-107.

801. Hirschman, Albert L. Exit, Voice, and Loyalty. Cambridge: Harvard University Press, 1970. See item 19.

802. Illich, Ivan, et al. Disabling Professions. London: Marion Boyers, 1977.

"[N]ew professions, dominant, authoritative, monopolistic, legalized--and, at the same time, debilitating, and effectively disabling the individual have become exclusive experts of the public good" (pp. 19-20).

803. Issalys, Pierre. "Professional Tribunal and the Control of Ethical Conduct Among Professionals." McGill Law Journal, 24 (Winter 1978), 588-626.

804. Knight, Jonathan. "The AAUP Experience." Paper presented at Second National Conference on Ethics in Engineering, 5-6 March 1982, Bismark Hotel, Chicago, IL. See item 722b.

805. Krishnan, Rama. "Business Philosophy and Executive Responsibility." Academy of Management Journal, 16 (December 1973), 658-659. See item 152.

806. Lerner, Max. "The Shame of the Professions." Saturday Review, 1 November 1975, pp. 10-12.

807. Lockhart, T. W. "Professional Societies and the Enforcement of Professional Codes." Business and Professional Ethics, 3 (Spring 1980), 1-3.

   Argues that it is justifiable for professional societies to enforce their codes of ethics and that the enforcers should be judged not as moral visionaries but as individuals trying to use their special abilities, perspectives, and positions to discharge their responsibilities.

808. McDonald, Lee C. "Three Forms of Political Ethics." Western Political Quarterly, 31 (March 1978), 7-18. See item 780.

Section VII

Theoretical Literature

B. Ethics and Responsibility

809. Alexander, Kenneth O. "On Work and Authority: Issues in Job Enlargement, Job Enrichment, Worker Participation and Shared Authority." The American Journal of Economics and Sociology, 34 (January 1975), 43-54.

Contends that although theory and practice point to decreased productivity and increased worker dissatisfaction in an authoritarian workplace, management and unions continue to protect their traditional roles, denying both worker and society the potential benefits of change. Alexander concludes by identifying factors that suggest corruption will continue and increase in the future.

810. Boland, Richard J. "Organizational Control Systems and the Engineer: The Need for Organizational Power." Paper presented at the Second National Conference on Ethics in Engineering, 5-6 March 1982, Bismark Hotel, Chicago, IL. See item 722b.

811. Boling, T. Edwin. "The Management Ethics Crisis: An Organizational Perspective." Academy of Management Review, 3 (April 1978), 360-365. See item 70.

812. Bradley, David and Roy Wilkie. The Concept of Organization: An Introduction to Organizations. London: Blackie, 1974, chapter 6, pp. 84-100.

"These issues are fundamental. First . . ., our own behavior is a function of values. Secondly, organizations . . . will endorse certain values . . . Thirdly, society is largely a conjunction of organizations . . ." (p. 90). Managers are seen as "the moral custodians of the goals of organizations" (p. 96).

813. Brown, David S. "The Effect of Size on Morality: The Villain Is in the Living Room." Paper presented at the Annual Meeting of the American Society for Public Administration, 13-16, April 1980, at the San Francisco Hilton, San Francisco, CA.

"[T]he purpose of this paper [is] to explore some of those factors which relate bigness to immorality; to indicate what is happening because of it; and to suggest what . . . to do about it" (p. 15).

814. Carmichael, D. R. "Behavioral Hypotheses of Internal Control." The Accounting Review, 45 (April 1970), 235-245. See item 663.

815. Chermiss, Cary. Staff Burnout: Job Stress in the Human Services. Beverly Hills, CA: Sage, 1980. See item 1349.

816. Dunshire, Andrew. Control in a Bureaucracy. New York: St. Martin's Press, 1978.

Elaborates a theory about control in a bureaucracy. The superior-subordinate relationship is analyzed and models of control processes are examined in terms of monitoring subordinates and achieving compliance.

817. Galbraith, Jay. Designing Complex Organizations. Reading, MA: Addison-Wesley, 1973.

A complement to organizational development theory. Galbraith examines the alternative structures organizations may develop, and argues that these alternatives will be reactions to increased uncertainty of organizational tasks. The need to process more information leads to the creation of slack resources, self-contained units, investment in vertical information systems, or the creation of lateral relations. Galbraith compares the costs and benefits of four adaptations, and concludes that the first is the natural tendency, but the last is the most effective if its problems are managed well.

818. Garson, G. David and Michael P. Smith, eds. Organizational Democracy: Participation and Self-Management. Beverly Hills, CA: Sage, 1976. See item 121.

819. Hanan, Mack. "Make Way for the New Organization Man." Harvard Business Review, 49 (July/August 1971), 128-138.

Proposes that organizations are faced with adapting to the needs of a new breed of "organization men" who are concerned with individual rights, advancement for accomplishment, and self-fulfillment rather than security in the company. Hanan suggests that firms which cannot make the required adjustments will face a serious personnel gap in the future. He calls for greater horizontal structure, participation, and emphasis on ideas rather than position.

820. Hunnius, Gerry, G. David Garson, and John Case, eds. Worker's Control: A Reader on Labor and Social Change. New York: Random House, 1973.

"Worker's control means democratizing the workplace . . ." (p. ix). Consists of 23 essays dealing with the issues of self-management.

821. Kranzberg, Melvin, ed. Ethics in an Age of Pervasive Technology. Boulder, CO: Westview Press, 1980.

Edited papers from a symposium held in Israel in 1974. The contributors examine the causal role of technology in contemporary ethical dilemmas; ask if traditional ethics can provide guidance to deal with the problems created by new technology; consider ways in which ethical principles can be translated into action; and discuss the social responsibilities of those involved in the world of technology so that morality and power can be joined.

822. Keeley, Michael. "Organizational Reality." Paper presented at Conference on Business and Professional Ethics, 15 May 1981, University of Illinois-Chicago Circle. Mimeograph.

Re-examines the controversy concerning the reality of social groups. Keeley, an organizational theorist, raises questions about the realist theories that have long dominated the social science literature on organizations.

823. Lawler, Edward E. III and John Grant Rode. Information and Control in Organizations. Santa Monica, CA: Goodyear, 1976.

Designed as a basic text for use in management and business, this book goes beyond a simple review of current knowledge and practice. Lawler and Rhode provide a comprehensive literature review on the conception, processes, structures, and problems with control in organizations. They systematically employ an original typology of control characteristics and elaborate: (1) characteristics of censor measures; (2) nature of standards; (3) source of discrimination; (4) pattern of communication; (5) speed of communication; (6) frequency of communication; (7) type of activity; and, (8) source of motivation. Contains a ten-page bibliography.

824. Levin, Virginia. "Ethical Standards Between Public and Private Executives: Is There a Difference?" Paper presented at the Annual Convention of the American Society for Public Administration, 13-16 April 1981, at the San Francisco Hilton, San Francisco, CA.

The basis for differences in ethical standards between public and private executives depends on whether they are part of a large organization. Structural factors such as size, hierarchy, degree of organizational loyalty, and the need for survival influence the moral standards which guide behavior.

825. Van Maanen, John. "People Processing: Strategies of Organizational Socialization." Organizational Dynamics, 7 (Summer 1978), 19-36.

Identifies seven dimensions of socialization, together with their often fateful consequences for individuals and organizations. He emphasizes that "much of the control over individual behavior in organizations is the direct result of the manner in which people are processed" (p. 35).

826. May, Larry. "Vicarious Agency." Paper presented at Conference on Business and Professional Ethics, 15 May 1981, University of Illinois-Chicago Circle. Mimeograph.

Attempts to set out the underpinnings of a theory of corporate agency and briefly discusses some of the conditions for corporate responsibility for harm. May contends that "corporations have a peculiar property of only being able to act vicariously" and therefore "the fiction that corporations are full-fledged moral or legal agents should not be sustained. Instead they should be given a distinct moral and legal status of their own, where they have to satisfy special conditions before they can be held liable or responsible" (p. 2).

827. Perrucci, Robert. "Organizational Imperatives, the Ideology of Professionalism and the limits of Technique." Paper presented at Workshop on Engineering Ethics: Designing for Safety, 24-26 May 1982, at Rensselaer Polytechnic Institute, Troy, NY. Mimeographed. See item 521.

828. Perrucci, Robert, Robert M. Anderson, Dan E Schendel, and Leon E. Trachtman. "Whistle-blowing: Professionals' Resistance to Organizational Authority." Social Problems, 28 (December 1980), 149-164. See item 468.

829. Pettigrew, Andrew. The Politics of Organization Decision Making. London: Tavistock, 1973. See item 785.

830. Pettigrew, Andrew. "Information Control as a Power Resource." Sociology, 6 (May 1972), 187-204.

Examination of the influence of (1) organizational position on an incumbent's ability to control information and (2) information control on decision outcomes in a major industrial equipment purchasing decision. Although limited to one case study, these observations are useful in pointing out the different forms of organizational power and the ability of centrally located subordinates to control decision input to their superiors.

831. Pfeffer, Jeffrey and Gerald Salancik. The External Control of Organizations. New York: Harper and Row, 1978.

Seven contributions deal with issues such as public attitudes toward stealing from bureaucracies, ways in which those who steal avoid self-definition as criminals, and methods of prevention.

832. Reisman, W. Michael. Folded Lies: Bribery, Crusades, and Reform. New York: Free Press, 1979.

Studies the myth system and operational code surrounding bribery.

833. Steward, Lea P. "When Organizational Socialization Fails: A Case Study of a Non-Conforming Enclave." Paper presented at the Central States Speech Association Annual Convention, April 1981 at Chicago, IL.

A theory-directed examination of the Bay Area Rapid Transit (BART) whistle-blowing incident based on Leed's concept of protest absorption: legitimizing non-conforming behavior which strengthens the organization.

*834. Stewart, Lea P. "'Whistle Blowing': Implications for Organizational Communicataion." <u>Journal of Communication</u>, 80 (Autumn 1980), 90-101.

Notes reasons for the neglect of systematic studies of whistle-blowing incidents, and provides a literature review. Stewart examines whistle-blowing by analyzing 51 cases to derive a model of the steps through which incidents progress. From this model it is possible to generalize about the nature of whistle-blowing and how it fits into communication patterns in organizations.

835. Stewart, Lea Pestel. "The Enthnography of a Whistle Blowing Incident: Implications for Organizational Communicataion." Ph.D. dissertation, Purdue University, 1979.

A study of the 1972 Bay Area Rapit Transit (BART) whistle-blowing incident as a communicative event. The theoretical framework used in the study is developed from the literature on bureaucratic and professional conflict. Stewart sees organizations as political systems, and provides descriptions of 51 specific whistleblowing events. She proposes a framework for identifying the conditions under which a whistle-blowing incident is likely to occur, the organizational response to the dissenter, and the steps through which the whistle-blowing is likely to progress.

836. Stout, Russell, Jr. <u>Management or Control? The Organizational Challenge</u>. Bloomington, IN: Indiana University Press, 1980.

"Management and control are critical activities in all organizations. What is important . . . is which orientation dominates. The manager's task is to discern which situations call for management and which call for control" (p. 17).

837. Strother, George. "The Moral Code of Executives: A Watergate-inspired Look at Barnard's Theory of Exec-

utive Responsibility." Academy of Management Review, 1 (April 1976), 13-22.

Presents an interpretive summary of Chester Barnard's theory, and its implications for the study of organizational and executive behavior. Executive codes of conduct are formed from three influences: organization as a technical and social system, personal history of the manager, and the executive's role perception.

838. Teft, Stanton, K., ed. Secrecy: A Cross-Cultural Perspective. New York: Human Sciences Press, 1980.

Social, cultural, historical, political, and organizational demensions of secrecy are explored in essays by professionals from a variety of social science desciplines. The topics include aspects of secrecy and privacy, the politics of secrecy, secrecy in business and bureaucratic society, and a comparative perspective.

839. Weinstein, Denna. Bureaucratic Opposition: Challenging Abuses at the Work Place. New York: Pergamon Press, 1979. See item 294.

840. Weinstein, Deena. "Opposition to Abuse Within Organizations: Heroism and Legalism." ALSA Forum, 4 (Fall 1979), 5-21. See item 294.

841. Whisler, Thomas L, Harold Meyer, Bernard H. Baum, and Peter F. Sorenson, Jr. "Centralization of Organizational Control: An Empirical Study of Its Meaning and Measurement." Journal of Business, 40 (Janauary 1967), 10-26.

Focuses on three measures of control: (1) individual compensation; (2) perceptions of interpersonal influence recorded on a questionnaire; and (3) the span of control in the formal organization.

842. Zald, Mayer N. and Michael A. Berger. "Social Movements in Organizations: Coup d'Etat, Insurgency, and Mass Movements." American Journal of Sociology, 83 (January 1978), 823-861.

Organizational change and conflict are conceptualized in terms of coup d'etat, bureaucratic insurgency, and mass movements which differ in their breadth, location in organizational social structure, goals, and tactics. Whistle-blowing is a form of insurgency that occurs when an insurgent deviates from loyalty norms to describe the disjunction between organizational functioning and public expectations. The reaction will depend upon the cost of compliance with the insurgents' demands and the priorities of the organization. A number of illustrative hypotheses are given.

Section VIII

Daily Newspaper and Popular Magazine Articles

843. "Aftermath of Begelman Scandal [sic]: New CPI Counsel, Rap and Praise 'Whistle-blowers,' Times Suit." Variety, 10 May 1978.

844. "Allied Offer Aims at Kepone Problem." Chemical and Engineering News, 7 February 1977, p. 7.

845. "Allied Has Hard Time Disposing of Kepone," Chemical and Engineering News, 29 November 1976, p. 6.

846. "Air Force Critics of Fitzgerald Upgraded Again," Federal Times, 4 May 1981.

847. "The ABA's Retreat from Whistle-blowing." Business Week, 31 August 1981, p. 56. See item 599.

848. Anderson, Jack. "Bureaucrats Grind Up Meat Expert." Washington Post, 13 September 1980.

849. Anderson, Jack. "Fitzgerald Vendetta: Another Chapter." Washington Post, 1 November 1980.

850. Anderson, Jack. "Making Waves Dampens Career of AID Officer," Washington Post, 10 October 1981.

851. Anderson, Jack. "Senate Postpones Touchy Justice Probe." Washington Post, 9 October 1980.

852. Anderson, Jack. "Two Who Talked Are Shifted." Washington Post, 17 July 1979.

853. Anderson, Jack. "Watchdog Unit Gets Kicked in the Teeth." Washington Post, 25 September 1980.

854. Anderson, Jack. "Whistle Blowers Have Rights Too." Washington Post, 15 April 1979.

855. Anderson, Jack. "Whistleblower's Fate." Washington Post, 19 April 1981.

856. Andronicos, Bill. "Foreign Service Act Draws Assault from Study Group." Federal Times, 19 November 1979.

857. Andronicos, Bill. "GAP Favors Independent Inspector General at State." Federal Times, 28 January 1980.

858. Angle, Martha and Robert Walters. "Whistle-blowers, Beware!" Newspaper Enterprise Association, 2 May 1979.

859. "Armor for Whistle-blowers." Business Week, 6 July 1981, p. 97. See item 000.

860. Arnold, Martin. "Proposed New Criminal Code Arouses Press's Fears on Secrecy." New York Times, 28 May 1975, p. 4.

861. "As I See It: To Tell or Not To Tell." Forbes, 1 February 1976, pp. 41-43. See item 002.

862. "Atom Agency to Study Ouster of Complaining Worker," New York Times, 30 March 1978, p. 17.

863. Ayres, James B. "Corporate Free Speech Is Upheld. Reaction: It's a Major Blow to Consumers." The Boston Globe, 27 April 1978.

864. Badhwar, Inderjit. "A Whistleblower's Taste of Ethics." Federal Times, 4 August 1980.

865. Badhwar, Inderjit. "Analyzing the Hoax of Hoaxes." Federal Times, 25 August 1980.

866. Badhwar, Inderjit. "CSC Reopens Case of 'Swine Flu' Critic." Federal Times, 18 September 1978.

867. Badhwar, Inderjit. "FDA Gave a Scandal and Nobody Came." Federal Times, 1 August 1977.

868. Badhwar, Inderjit. "GAP Right for the Times." Federal Times, 12 June 1978.

869. Badhwar, Inderjit. "MSPB Said to Weaken Key Whistleblower Shields." Federal Times, 26 November 1979.

870. Badhwar, Inderjit. "Merit System Policeman Accused of Copping-Out." Federal Times, 8 October 1979.

871. Badhwar, Inderjit. "MSPB Fails Free Speech Exam." Federal Times, 7 January 1980.

872. Badhwar, Inderjit. "No Man Is So High." Federal Times, 3 September 1979.

873. Badhwar, Inderjit. "OPM Faces Challenge on Cutting Legal Fees." Federal Times, 16 June 1980.

874. Badhwar, Inderjit. "Social 'Deviants' Have Rights Too." Federal Times, 21 July 1980.

875. Badhwar, Inderjit. "Whistleblowers Top FBI's List of Least-Wanted." Federal Times, 26 November 1979.

876. Basler, Barbara. "Olympic Fieldhouse Undergoes Repairs." New York Times, 25 January 1980, p. 15.

877. Basler, Barbara. "Quality of Olympics Work Questioned." New York Times, 1 January 1980, p. 21.

878. Bedell, Sally and Don Kowet. "Blowing the Whistle on TV's Sports Reporters." TV Guide, 12 December 1981, p. 47.

879. Ben-Horin, Daniel. "The Sterility Scandal: What Happened When Two Young Filmmakers Uncovered a Health Fiasco That Rocked the Chemical Industry." Mother Jones, May 1979, p. 51.

880. Bennetts, Leslie. "Employees: The Latest to Declare Independence." Chicago Tribune, 4 July 1979.

881. "Big Crusade of the '80's: More Rights for Workers." U.S. News and World Report, 26 March 1976, pp. 86-87.

882. "Blowing the Whistle." Detroit News, 15 April 1980.

883. Blumenthal, Ralph. "KLM Payments Face Investigation." New York Times, 19 April 1979, p. 16.

884. Boffey, Philip M. "Scientists and Bureaucrats: A Clash of Cultures on FDA Advisory Panel." Science, 26 March 1976, pp. 1244-1246. See item 491.

885. Boyd, James. "The Indispensable Informer." Nation, 5 May 1979, p. 495. See item 1369.

886. Bredemeier, Kenneth. "District Inspector is Transferred in Dispute over Leaking Radiation." Washington Post, 3 November 1979.

887. Brill, Steven. "When A Lawyer Lies, Is His Young Associate's Duty to Blow the Whistle or Keep His Mouth Shut?" Esquire, 19 December 1978, p. 23.

888. Britain: Dividends From Blowing the Whistle on Oil-gate." Business Week, 23 October 1978, p. 64. See item 008.

889. Brodt, Bohita. "AID Abuse Link Works Amid Gestapo Charges." Chicago Tribune, 17 July 1980.

890. Burnham, David. "Experts Reportedly Knew of Flaw in Reactors in '77." New York Times, 25 May 1979, p. 10.

891. Burnham, David. "How Corruption Is Built into the System--And a Few Ideas for What to Do About It." New York Magazine, 21 September 1970, pp. 30-39.

892. Burnham, David. "Legality of National Security Agency's Purchases Challenged in Suit." New York Times, 5 February 1980, p. 20.

893. Burnham, David. "Some Legislators See 2 Recent Trails as Caster Crackdown on Release of Information." New York Times, 12 July 1978, p. 12.

894. Burnham, David. "Trial of 2 for Espionage May Inhibit Leaks of Government Information." New York Times, 1 May 1978, p. 12.

895. Carlson, Peter. "Government Whistleblower: The Hero in a Tragedy." Boston Herald American, 19 November 1978.

896. Carter, Luther J. "Job Protection for 'Whistle Blowers' Being Tested." Science, 7 March 1980, p. 1057. See item 450.

897. Causey, Mike. "Agencies Liable for Legal Fees." Washington Post, 25 July 1980.

898. Causey, Mike. "Ask Not for Whom the Whistle Blows." Washington Post, 10 August 1979.

899. Causey, Mike. "Better Job Needed for Whistle-Blowers." Washington Post, 24 October 1979.

900. Causey, Mike. "Bureau Will Aid Whistle-Blowers." *Washington Post*, 4 November 1979.

901. Causey, Mike. "Fledgling Outfit Carries Big Stick." *Washington Post*, 13 February 1979.

902. Causey, Mike. "Free Legal Aid Seen for Whistle Blowers." *Washington Post*, 6 December 1979.

903. Causey, Mike. "Government Reform Hailed as Success." *Washington Post*, 25 January 1980.

904. Causey, Mike. "Hot-Line Tip Phone for G.S.A." *Washington Post*, 15 November 1978.

905. Causey, Mike. "Merit Board Rules for Hospital Employee." *Washington Post*, 28 February 1979.

906. Causey, Mike. "Postal Clerk Wields a Mighty Pen." *Washington Post*, 17 May 1979.

907. Causey, Mike. "VA Whistle Blowers Win Transfer Stays." *Washington Post*, 8 April 1980.

908. Causey, Mike. "Watchdog Hotline Gives 2,000 Leads." *Washington Post*, 12 March 1979.

909. Causey, Mike. "Whistle Blower Defender Resigns." *Washington Post*, 19 December 1979.

910. Causey, Mike. "Whistle Blowers to Get Rewards." *Washington Post*, 21 May 1979.

911. Causey, Mike. "WhistleBlowers." *Washington Post*, 15 October 1980.

912. Chandler, Ralph C. "Ethics and Public Policy." *Commonwealth*, May 1978, pp. 302-309. See item 327.

913. "Civil Service Reform Act Bringing a Rise in Dismissals." *New York Times*, 12 November 1980, p. 24.

914. Clark, Louis and Thomas Devine. "To Protect the Whistle-Blowers." *Washington Star*, 6 May 1980.

915. Clever, Dick. "Bureaucratic Fumbling Blamed For Hindering Air-safety Systems." *Seattle Daily Times*, 31 October 1981.

916. Clever, Dick. "Probe of F.A.A. Charges." Seattle Daily Times, 2 November 1980.

917. Clines, Francis X. and Bernard Weintraub. "Briefing." New York Times, 1 October 1981, p. 28.

918. "Commerce Told to Air Sex Charges at Census." Federal Times, 13 April 1981.

919. Cook, Daniel D. "Whistle-Blowers--Friend or Foe?" Industry Week, 5 October 1981, pp. 50-54, 56. See item 11.

920. Coote, Anna. "The Whistle-blower's Reward." New Statesman, 7 March 1980, p. 345.

921. "Coping with Employee Lawsuits." Business Week, 27 August 1979, pp. 66, 68.

922. "Corporate Free Speech Is Upheld. High Court Overturns Mass Spending Law, 5-4." The Boston Globe, 27 April 1978.

923. Coughlin, Ellen K. "Educators, Scientists Fear New Federal Ethics Code." The Chronical of Higher Education, 20 February 1979, pp. 1, 15. See item 501.

924. "Court Gives Fitzgerald Long-Awaited Victory." Federal Times, 9 March 1981.

925. Crewdson, John M. "Former F.B.I. Agent Tells Investigators of Widespread Abuse and Corruption." New York Times, 20 January 1979, p. 8.

926. Crewdson, John M. "Jury Picking Begins in Nuclear Contamination Case." New York Times, 7 March 1979, p. 2.

927. "Critics Predict Problems for Appraisal Systems." Federal Times, 2 June 1980.

928. D'Antonio, Michael. "Blowing the Whistle on Federal Waste." Family Weekly, 16 August 1981.

929. "Dealing with The Poisoners." Washington Post, 20 August 1979.

930. "Defeat for Scientific Integrity:" Scientists Testify in DDT Hearing." Business Week, 8 July 1972, p. 60. See item 504.

931. "The Defense of Liberty: The Constitutional Guarantees Are Not Self-Executing." Center Magazine, 12 (November/December 1979), 41.

932. "Dr. Szilaird Szabo Dismissal from Lawrence Livermore Laboratory." New York Times, 26 June 1979, p. 16.

933. Dudar, Helen. "The Price of Blowing the Whistle." New York Times Magazine, 30 October 1977, pp. 41-42.

934. "The Ethics Squeeze on Ex-Government Lawyers." Business Week, 23 February 1976, p. 82. See item 610.

935. "Ethics Rules: An Empty Exercise." Industry Week, 21 June 1976, pp. 7-8. See item 105.

936. Ewing, David W. "Business and the Bill of Rights: Free Speech From Nine to Five." Nation, 15 June 1974, pp. 755-766. See item 110.

937. Ewing, David W. "Canning Directions: How the Government Rids Itself of Trouble-makers." Harper's, August 1979, pp. 16, 18, 22. See item 238.

938. Ewing, David W. "Protecting 'Whistle-Blowers'." New York Times, 1 September 1977, p. 21.

939. "F.B.I. Agent Charging Cover-Up Sues 3 Superiors." New York Times, 18 February 1979, p. 23.

940. "Federal Nonsecrecy." New York Times, 12 November 1978, p. 49.

941. "Federal Waste Tied to Aides' Fear of Speaking Out." New York Times, 6 December 1977, p. 13.

942. "The Fear of Reprisal in Exposing Waste." Seattle Daily Times, 24 July, 1980.

943. Feaver, Douglas B. "Inspectors Generals Chase Waste: 'Junkyard Dogs' Told To Keep Up Work." Washington Post, 8 December 1981.

944. "Editors Say 'Whistle-Blowing' Should Be Encourage." New York Times, 1 May 1980, p. 2.

945. Edsall, John T. "Scientific Freedom and Responsibility." Science, 16 May 1975, pp. 687-693. See item 510.

946. Edsall, John T. "Two Aspects of Scientific Responsibility." Science, 3 April 1981;, pp. 11-14. See item 511.

947. "The Embattled Businessman." Newsweek, 16 February 1976, pp. 56-60. See item 101.

948. "Engineers Who Blew the Whistle on BART are Vindicated." American Machinist, September 1975, p. 73.

949. "Final Resting Place for Kepone." Chemical Week, 26 July 1978, p. 16.

950. Flores, Albert. "The Professional Rights of Engineers." Technology and Society, December 1980, pp. 3-4.

951. Florman, Samuel C. "Moral Blueprints." Harpers' Magazine, October 1978, pp. 30-33. See item 525.

952. "For the Protection of Whistle-Blowers." New York Times, 9 August 1978, p. 20.

953. Fox, Cecil H. "Sakharov and Whistle-Blowing." Science, 30 May 1980, p. 976. See item 458.

954. Frankel, Glen. "Foster Parents Sue Prince William County." Washington Post, 27 December 1980.

955. Franklin, Ben. "Federal Workers' Right to Dissent Is Backed by Chief of Civil Service." New York Times, 26 June 1977, p. 38.

956. "Fund and Appointment Woes Slow Agency to Protect 'Whistleblowers'." New York Times, 3 November 1980, p. 10.

957. Gaines, Richard. "Whistleblowing." Minneapolis Tribune, 18 April 1978.

958. Garde, Billie Pirner. "Whistleblowers' Arena-Carpers to Cynics." The Federal Times, 8 June 1981.

959. Gerth, Jeff. "U.S. Expanding Use of 1970 Crime Statute." New York Times, 8 December 1978, p. D1.

960. Gest, Ted. "Blowing the Whistle: A Thankless Job." U.S. News and World Report, 29 June 1981, pp. 50-51. See item 242.

961. Gibb, Francis. "Man who Exposed Malpractices By Drug Company Plans To Sue Swiss Government and EEC." Times of London, 29 January 1981.

962. Gibb, Francis. "Lord Soames Is Asked to Intervene for Scientist Who Defied Role in Criticizing Atom Centre Secrecy." Times of London, 1 November 1980.

963. Glaser, Vera. "The Executive Who Protects Whistle-Blowers." San Francisco Chronicle, 19 August 1979.

964. "Going Overboard." Wall Street Journal, 2 June 1977.

965. Gold, Bill. "VIP Pressure Awaits Every Whistle Blower." Washington Post, 6 April 1978.

966. Goldstein, Tom. "Civil Liberties for Employees." New York Times, 28 July 1978, p. 3.

967. "Goldwater Blows the Whistle on His Mates." U.S. News and World Report, 16 February 1976, p. 22.

968. Gordon, Max. "Can Business Fire at Will?" Nation, 14 July 1979, p. 42.

969. Graham, Sandy. "States Move to Catch Incompetent Doctors, But Progress Is Uneven." Wall Street Journal, 1 May 1981.

970. Greenfield, Meg. "Blowing the Whistle." Newsweek, 25 September 1978, p. 112. See item 246.

971. Greenhouse, Linda. "Revised Code of Ethics for Bar Still Faces Debate." New York Times, 10 August 1981, p. 10.

972. Greenhouse, Linda. "In Corporate Law, Who's the Client?" New York Times, 15 February 1981, p. 20.

973. Greer, Philip. "Good Guy Loses in Movie Scandal." Chicago Tribune, 21 January 1980.

974. Greer, Phillip and Myron Kanel. "It Doesn't Pay to Blow the Whistle on Hollywood Crime." Los Angeles Daily Journal, 31 January 1980.

975. "'Halt' Blowing the Whistle on Illegal Acts Should Not Be Punished." Detroit Free Press, 24 September 1980.

976. Harley, William. "Behind U.S.'s Tough New Line at the U.N. Washington Is Blowing the Whistle on a Favorite Sport of Underdeveloped Countries--Kicking Uncle Sam Around." U.S. News and World Report, 9 November 1981, pp. 36-37.

977. Hayes, John P. "The Men Who Blow the Whistle." Saga Magazine, May 1979, pp. 28-29. See item 247.

978. Hersh, Seymour. "C.I.A. Analyst Forced Out for Giving Senator Secret Data." New York Times, 13 November 1978, p. 3.

979. Hershow, Sheila. "Boat Rocker Nailed: Justice or Persecution?" Federal Times, 18 May 1981.

980. Hershow, Sheila. "DOE Staffer Claims Article Led to Transfer." Federal Times, 9 March 1981.

981. Hershow, Sheila. "Ex-Nixon Aide Now Reagan's Ethics Chief." Federal Times, 4 May 1981.

982. Hershow, Sheila. "Fitzgerald Seeks Contempt Ruling for Air Force Chief." Federal Times, 20 April 1981.

983. Hershow, Sheila. "Fraud: Feds, Private Citizens Bilk U.S. of More Than $150 Million." Federal Times, 1 June 1981.

984. Hershow, Sheila. "High Court to Rule on Immunity." Federal Times, 6 July 1981.

985. Hershow, Sheila. "Hill Aide's Suite Against FBI Dismissed." Federal Times, 1 June 1981.

986. Hershow, Sheila. "Interview with Bernard." Federal Times, 31 July 1978.

987. Hershow, Sheila. "MSPB Kills 4 Charges: Fired Labor IG Wins Job Fight." Federal Times, 25 May 1981.

988. Hershow, Sheila. "MSPB Tells Donovan to Air Report of Probe Sabotage." Federal Times, 16 March 1981.

989. Hershow, Sheila. "The Melody Lingers On." Federal Times, 1 June 1981.

990. Hershow, Sheila. "NRC Dissident Plan Gets Poor Reviews." Federal Times, 18 February 1980.

991. Hershow, Sheila. "Nuclear Knavery." Federal Times, 16 March 1981.

992. Hershow, Sheila. "On Raked Research: Cancer Institute Chief Didn't Sound Alarm." Federal Times, 15 June 1981.

993. Hershow, Sheila. "Sex and Politics in Census Shop." Federal Times, 23 March 1981.

994. Hershow, Sheila. "Theft Through the Mails." Federal Times, 1 June 1981. See item 424.

995. Hershow, Sheila. "Top Counsel Pick Refuses to Answer Senate Questions." Federal Times, 5 May 1980.

996. Hershow, Sheila. "Two Muted Whistleblowers Get Louder Voices at GSA." Federal Times, 29 June 1981.

997. Hershow, Sheila. "Whistleblowers: Promises, Promises on Hill." Federal Times, 4 July 1977.

998. "The High Cost of Whistling." Newsweek, 14 February 1977, pp. 75-77. See item 249.

999. Hinckle, Warren. "Mismanaging the Muni in the Military Way." San Francisco Chronicle, 12 May 1978.

1000. von Hipple, Frank. "Professional Freedom and Responsibility." Science, Technology and Human Values, January 1978, pp. 37-42. See item 530.

1001. von Hipple, Frank. "Protecting the Whistle Blowers." Physics Today, October 1977, pp. 9-13. See item 460.

1002. von Hoffman, Nicholas. "Alone at High Noon." Nation, 27 December 1980, pp. 709-710. See item 20.

1003. Holden, Constance. "Police Seize Primates at NIH Funded Lab." Science, 2 October 1981, p. 32. See item 461.

1004. Holden, Constance. "Scientist with Unpopular Data Loses Job." Science 14 November 1980, p. 749. See item 462.

1005. "House Blows Whistle on Pastore Blackout Pronouncement." Broadcasting, 3 May 1976, pp. 24-25.

1006. "H.U.D. Fights a Job Order on Whistleblower in Boston." New York Times, 4 January 1979, p. 16.

1007. Huddleston, Bob. "Don't Toot The Whistle." Federal Times, 25 May 1981.

1008. "Ice Cream Gate." Time, 18 August 1975, p. 67.

1009. "Inspectors Blow the Whistle on Federal Waste." U.S. News and World Report, 14 December 1981, p. 6.

1010. "ILEA Finds Cheating By Workers." Times of London, 17 January 1981.

1011. Irvine, Reed. "On Spying and Whistleblowing." New York Times, 24 may 1978, p. 22.

1012. "'I Thought I Heard a Whistle Blowing.'" Christian Science Monitor, 3 March 1980.

1013. Ivins, Molly. "In Albuquerque, N.M., Promises of Anonymity and Reward, Turn Informers into 'Crime Stoppers'." New York Times, 16 January 1978, p. 16.

1014. Jacobs, Bruce A. "Blowing the Whistle on Company Misdeeds." Industry Week, 31 March 1980, pp. 23-24. See item 23.

1015. Jacobs, Paul. "VA's Transfer of Two 'Whistle Blowers' Barred." Los Angeles Times, 26 October 1979.

1016. Jaroslovsky, Rich. "Blowing the Whistle Begins a Nightmare for Lawyer Joe Rose." Wall Street Journal, 9 November 1977.

1017. Jensen, Michael C. "Arco Urges Whistleblowing." New York Times, 19 May 1978, p. 1.

1018. "Judge Says Lawyer Needn't Disclose Fraud After Merger." Wall Street Journal, 1 September 1978.

1019. "Kerr-McGee Plan Is Called 'Pig-Pen' by a Witness." New York Times, 13 March 1979.

1020. Kessler, Ronald. "Administration is Paying 'Lip Service' to Ending GSA Abuses, Senate Told." Washington Post, 30 January 1980.

1021. Kessler, Ronald. "Solomon Reinstates Two GSA 'Whistleblowers'." Washington Post, 30 August 1978.

1022. Kohn, Howard. "The Government's Quiet War on Scientists Who Know Too Much." Rolling Stone, 28 March 1978, pp. 42-44.

1023. Kovler, Peter. "Blowing the Whistle: Can Conscientious Federal Employees be Protected?" Commonwealth, 15 September 1978, pp. 591-593. See item 258.

1024. Lenhart, Harry A. "The Tough New Faces on Company Boards: Critics Once Called Them 'Financial Gigolos,' But No More: Directors in Firm After Firm Are Firing Presidents, Blowing the Whistle on Dubious Decisions." U.S. News and World Report, 6 October 1980, pp. 83-86.

1025. Lerner, Max. "The Shame of the Professions." Saturday Review, 1 November 1975, pp. 10-12.

1026. Lewis, Anthony. "An Official Secrets Act?" New York Times, 30 March 1978, p. 33.

1027. Lockard, Duane. "The 'Great Tradition' of American Corruption." New Society, 31 May 1973, pp. 486-488. See item 442.

1028. Lubin, Joann S. "Spilling the Beans: Disclosing Misdeeds of Corporations Can Backfire on Tatlers." Wall Street Journal, May 1976, p. 1.

1029. Lubin, Joann S. "Watchdog Has Hard Time Hearing Whistles." Wall Street Journal, 17 October 1980.

1030. Lyons, Richard D. "Protection Doubted by Whistle-Blower." New York Times, 4 March 1978, p. 8.

1031. Lyons, Richard. "Carter Plans Proposal to Protect 'Whistle-Blowers' in Government." New York Times, 16 February 1978, p. 12.

1032. McCombs, Phil. "CIA 'Traitor'--Former Spy Victor Mannetti: 11 Years of Truth and Fantasy." Washington Post, 15 December 1980.

1033. MacClean, John. "Blow The Whistle and Lose Your Job." Chicago Tribune, 26 November 1980.

1034. Mansfield, Stephanie. "A Profile in Courage." Chicago Sun Times, 26 March 1978.

1035. "Many U.S. Workers Seeing Waste, Fraud Don't Blow Whistle." Wall Street Journal, 16 April 1981.

1036. Marks, Laurence. "Silencing the Whistleblowers." Atlas, 25 September 1978, p. 48. See item 265.

1037. "MSPB Cites Speedup in Handling Appeals." Federal Times, 29 June 1981.

1038. Marro, Anthony. "Fraud in Federal Aid May Exceed $12 Billion Annual, Experts Say." New York Times, 16 April 1978, p. 1.

1039. Marro, Anthony. "F.B.I. Needs Some Home Improvements, Honestly." New York Times, 15 January 1978, p. C5.

1040. Martin, Susan Taylor. "Whistle Blowers Beware." Detroit News, 5 June 1980.

1041. McAden, Fitz. "Pilot Lands $275, 000 Verdict in EAL Libel Suit." Miami Herald, 12 November 1980.

1042. McPherson, Myra. "The Making of the Whistle Blower: Robert Lowry's GSA Scandal Stories." Washington Post, 20 September 1978.

1043. Meyer, Priscilla S. "Blowing the Whistle Ends in Book, Movie and $500,000 a Year." Wall Street Journal, 15 February 1978.

1044. Miller, Herbert J. and R. Stan Mortenson. "Non-Whistle-Blowing Lawyers Risk Criminal Charges." Legal Times Washington, 10 March 1980.

1045. Miller, James Nathan. "What Happens When Bureaucrats Blow Whistles?" Reader's Digest, July 1978, pp. 197-204. See item 266.

1046. Miller, Judith. "Hamar Case: Did Bank Regulators Fail in Their Duties?" New York Times, 10 April 1978, p. 1. See item 266.

1047. Mintz, Morton. "Workers Unwarned of Asbestos Peril, Lawmakers Learn." Washington Post, 16 November 1979.

1048. Mitchell, Greg. "The Woman Who Blew The Whistle On Agent Orange." Family Circle, 26 August 1980.

1049. Mitchell, Greg. "Blowing the Whistle: For People Who Whistle While They Work, The Government Is Playing A New Tune." Washington Post, 12 August 1979, pp. 12-19. See item 268.

1050. "More Facts About Citibank Dissident." New York Times, 31 July 1978, p. 2.

1051. Nader, Ralph. "No Protection for Outspoken Scientists." Physics Today, July 1973, pp. 77-78. See item 466.

1052. "Newsman Loses Contempt Appeal." Los Angeles Times, 9 September 1981.

1053. "Nixon Attorneys Urge High Court To Give Him Immunity From Suit." New York Times, 1 December 1981, p. 3.

1054. Novak, Michael. "Peter Bourne and New Left: Is There a Connection?" New York Post, 29 October 1978, p. 13.

1055. "Nuclear Weapons Lab Assailed by Audit and a Radiation Expert." New York Times, 26 June 1979, p. 16.

1056. Oakes, John B. "'Whistle-blowing' on Staten Island," New York Times, 8 January 1980, p. A-19.

1057. Porterfield, Bob. "Why Investigative Reporting Is Dying." Editor and Publisher, 14 March 1981, p. 60. See item 690.

1058. Powers, Thomas. "The Good Soldier System." Commonwealth, 9 May 1980, p. 261.

1059. Press, Robert M. "Test Case for Whistle Blowers." Christian Science Monitor, 5 July 1979.

1060. "Prokop Quits MSPB Post." Federal Times, 25 May 1981.

1061. "Proposed Rules for Special Counsel Assailed." Federal Times, 12 November 1979.

1062. "Public Directors: A Possible Answer to Corporate Misconduct." Wall Street Journal, 23 March 1976.

1063. Purnick, Joyce. "Carey Asks Reform in the Civil Service." New York Times, 10 February 1980, p. 31.

1064. Raab, Selwyn. "Whistleblowers Accuse State Units of Harassment." New York Times, 19 May 1979, p. 1.

1065. Randolph, Eleanor. "They Called It As They Saw It, Lost Jobs?" Chicago Tribune, 25 May 1978.

1066. Rankin, Deborah. "Resignation of 2 Aides Disclosed by Citibank." New York Times, 3 August 1978, p. D-1.

1067. Rankin, Deborah. "Taxes and Accounting: Blowing the Whistle for the I.R.S." New York Times, 4 April 1978, p. 43.

1068. Reeves, Richard. "The Last Angry Men." Esquire, 1 March 1978, pp. 41-48. See item 32.

1069. Rodweder, Ralph. "Education of a Whistle Blower." Washington Star, 24 April 1978.

1070. Rozhon, L. "For Shipyard Safety Critic, Idealism Has a High Price." New York Times, 6 July 1980, p. 1.

1071. Rowan, Roy. "Rekindling Corporate Loyalty." Fortune, 9 February 1981, p. 54.

1072. Rubin, James. "Justice Department Orders U.S. Attorneys Not to Prosecute 'Whistleblowers' On Charges of Stealing Government Information." New York Times, 8 September 1978, p. 167.

1073. "The San Jose Three." Time, 16 February 1976, p. 78. See item 471.

1074. Santini, Maureen. "President Carter Signs Bill to Place Inspector Generals in 12 Federal Departments." New York Times, 13 October 1978, p. 15.

1075. Sawhill, John C. "A Question of Ethics." Newsweek, 29 October 1979, p. 27. See item 184.

1076. Schorr, Burt and Gerald F. Seib. "Texas Cover-Up: Why Did OKC Chief Conceal His Oil Deals to Friendly Brokers? Shareholders Are Not Told of Board's Investigation: SEC Probe Is Rebuffed: Woes of a Whistle-blower." Wall Street Journal, 13 May 1980.

1077. "SEC Rejects Bid to Force Firms' Lawyers To Tell Boards of Employer Wrongdoing." Wall Street Journal, 1 May 1980.

1078. "Senate Panel Hears Testimony by Two G.S.A. Whistleblowers." New York Times, 24 June 1978, p. 1.

1079. "Senators Planning Hearings on Shift of G.S.A Official." New York Times, 11 January 1980, p. 10.

1080. "Settlement of Attorney 'Whistleblower' Suit Set." Los Angeles Daily Journal, 29 January 1980.

1081. Shandler, Philip. "President Promises to Pursue Cases of Fraud and Waste in Government." Washington Star, 17 April 1981.

1082. Shandler, Philip. "Involving Employee in Appraisal of His Work Has Its Problems." Washington Star, 5 November 1980.

1083. Shandler, Philip. "Two Groups Assail 'Attacks' A-
       gainst Merit Office." Washington Star, 14 Octo-
       ber 1980.

1084. Shandler, Philip. "Union Says Merit Board Head Vio-
       lated Personnel Reform Act." Washington Star, 10
       October 1980.

1085. Shapley, Deborah. "Don't Swallow the Whistle, Blow
       It." Science, 27 April 1979, p. 389. See item
       472.

1086. Sheler, Jeffrey L. "When Employees Squeal on Fellow
       Workers." U.S. News and World Report, 16 Novem-
       ber 1981, p. 81. See item 34.

1087. Shipler, David K. "Soviet Workers Tell of Hazards of
       Complaining." New York Times, 2 December 1977,
       p. 1.

1088. Shonerd, Terri F. "MSPB Survey Finds: Sexual Harass-
       ment Costs U.S. $90 Million Annually." Federal
       Times, 11 May 1981.

1089. Siler, Tom. "College Grid Coaches Vow to Blow the
       Whistle on Cheaters." Sporting News, 2 February
       1980, p. 22. See item 694.

1090. Silver, Isidore. "Protecting Corporate Whistle Blow-
       ers." Newsday, 11 January 1979, p. 69.

1091. Sinzinger, Keith. "AFGE and GAP President: Help
       Special Counsel." Federal Times, 27 October
       1980.

1092. Sinzinger, Keith. "Agencies Given Broad Powers For
       Dismissals." Federal Times, 8 December 1980.

1093. Sinzinger, Keith. "Barking IGs Don't Bite." Federal
       Times, 15 June 1981.

1094. Sinzinger, Keith. "By Special Counsel: More Money,
       Staff Sought." Federal Times, 30 March 1981.

1095. Sinzinger, Keith. "Detective Charges NRC Ignored Safe-
       ty Defects." Federal Times, 22 December 1980.

1096. Sinzinger, Keith. "Elusive 'Frontier'." Federal
       Times, 30 June 1980.

1097. Sinzinger, Keith. "Feds Say: Reporting Waste Is Fruitless." Federal Times, 27 April 1981.

1098. Sinzinger, Keith. "Less Than Free Speech." Federal Times, 27 April 1981.

1099. Sinzinger, Keith. "MSPB Cites Penalty Power." Federal Times, 27 April 1981.

1100. Sinzinger, Keith. "MSPB Curbed On Complaints By Outsiders." Federal Times, 25 May 1981.

1101. Sinzinger, Keith. "Special Counsel Choice: A Political Insider." Federal Times, 20 April 1981.

1102. Sinzinger, Keith. "Special Counsel Pulls a Switch." Federal Times, 10 November 1980.

1103. Sinzinger, Keith. "The Sting Takes Toll." Federal Times, 1 June 1981.

1104. Sinzinger, Keith A. "Union GAP Enters Fight Over Special Counsel." Federal Times, 20 October 1980.

1105. Sinzinger, Keith. "Whistleblower Says GSA Sets Fresh Reprisal." Federal Times, 9 March 1981.

1106. Sinzinger, Keith. "Whistleblower Still Fighting 1977 Dismissal." Federal Times, 6 April 1981.

1107. Sinzinger, Keith. "Whistleblowers' 'Horror Stories' Stun Schroeder." Federal Times, 17 March 1980.

1108. Sinzinger, Keith A. "White House, Hill Respond To Whistleblower Survey," Federal Times, 4 May 1981.

1109. Snepp, Frank. "On C.I.A.-Secrecy, News Leaks and Censorship." New York Times, 3 March 1978, p. 25.

1110. Spiegel, Claire. "He Has 'Nothing to Do' County Employee Says." Los Angeles Times, 4 December 1978.

1111. Stertz, Brad. "34,000 Calls: Hot Line for U.S. Tipsters Finds Fraud." Los Angeles Times, 17 December 1981.

1112. Stessin, Lawrence. "Employees Don't Take Anti-Theft Moves Lightly." New York Times, 10 June 1979, p. 19.

1113. Stevens, Charles W. "The Whistle Blower Chooses Hard Path, Utility Story Shows." Wall Street Journal, 8 November 1978.

1114. Stieber, Jack. "Speak Up, Get Fired." New York Times, 10 June 1979, p. 19.

1115. Strobel, Lee. "He's Fired For Reporting Theft Suspect." Chicago Tribune, 19 March 1981.

1116. "Suffolk County Legislature Passes Whistle Blowers Law: Result of County Employee Spoke Out Publicly on a Sewer Scandal and Was Fired." New York Times, 13 September 1979, p. 13.

1117. "Suffolk Law Passed on Employee Rights." New York Times, 13 September 1979, p. 2.

1118. Sulzberger, A. O. "Study Finds Apathy Among Federal Whistle Blowers." New York Times, 16 April 1981, p. A-22.

1119. "Tape Said to Implicate Nixon in a Dismissal." New York Times, 7 March 1979, p. 19.

1120. "A Tempest at the SEC." Business Week, 4 May 1981, p. 58. See item 648.

1121. Thackray, John. "The Corporate Individual." Management Today, November 1980, pp. 74-77. See item 41.

1122. Thomas, Jo. "Iacocca Says Ford Ousted Three." New York Times, 12 February 1979, p. 1.

1123. Thornton, May. "Reagan Tightening the Rules on Leaking." Washington Post, 17 September 1981.

1124. Trausch, Susan. "Minister/Manager Works Both Sides of the Street." Boston Globe, 28 April 1981, p. 10.

1125. Trausch, Susan. "Heading Off Crises with Ethics." Boston Globe, 27 April 1981.

1126. Trausch, Susan. "Business Tries New Venture: Modest Investment in Ethics." Boston Sunday Globe, 26 April 1981.

1127. Treatster, Joseph. "The Hushing of America." Gallery, August 1979, pp. 40-43, 100-104. See item 42.

1128. "A Tug-Of-War Over Confidentiality." Business Week, 23 June 1980, pp. 34-37. See item 649.

1129. "Two AID Officials Quit in Dispute Over Formula." Federal Times, 1 June 1981.

1130. "Two Whistle Blowers Appeal to President." New York Times, 18 March 1978, p. 26.

1131. "Uncle Sam's Fraud Hotline." U.S. News and World Report, 20 August 1979, p. 38.

1132. "U.S. Slow to Shield Critical Employees: Fund Cuts and Appointment Woes Hamper Office Aimed to Aid Federal 'Whistleblowers'." New York Times, November 1980, p. 38.

1133. Vandivier, Kermit. "The Aircraft Brake Scandal." Harpers' Magazine, April 1972, pp. 45-52. See item 1391.

1134. Wade, Nicholas. "Protection Sought for Satirists and Whistle-Blowers." Science, 7 December 1973, pp. 1002-1003.

1135. "Watchdogs of Corporate Ethics." New York Times, 5 March 1981, p. 1.

1136. Weaver, Warren. "White House Studies Curb On Profits to Ex-Officials." New York Times, 16 May 1977, p. 1.

1137. Westin, Alan F. "Faculty Research and Whistle Blowers." New York Times, 10 January 1982, p. 61.

1138. Westin, Alan F. "Michigan's Law to Protect the Whistle Blowers." Wall Street Journal, 13 April 1981.

1139. "When Audit Rules Clash With Legal Ethics." Business Week, 14 April 1975, p. 72. See item 701.

1140. "When Must a Lawyer Blow the Whistle." _Business Week_, 21 May 1979, p. 17. See item 652.

1141. "A Whistle-blower Is Acquitted." _Newsweek_, 29 December 1980, p. 17.

1142. "The Whistle Blower." _Newsweek_, 30 August 1976, p. 9.

1143. "'Whistle-Blower' Bill Introduced in Council." _New York Times_, 4 August 1978, p. 3.

1144. "Whistleblower Loses Claim for Interest on Back Pay." _Washington Post_, 5 December 1978.

1145. "Whistle-Blower Protection Reported Planned for Bill." _New York Times_, 29 May 1978, p. 8.

1146. "Whistleblower Reinstated at HEW." _Science_, 3 August 1979, p. 1. See item 298.

1147. "The Whistleblowers." _Time_, 17 April 1972, pp. 85-86. See item 50.

1148. "Whistleblowers Due to Get $20,000 Bonus." _Federal Times_, 3 August 1981.

1149. "Whistleblowers Protected." _Legal Times Washington_, 21 January 1980.

1150. "Whistling Dixie." _Los Angeles Times_, 27 April 1981.

1151. Whitten, Les. "The Whistle Blowers." _Harpers' Bazaar_, September 1972, pp. 168-169. See item 300.

1152. Wicker, Tom. "To Hear the Whistle." _New York Times_, 2 May 1978, p. 35.

1153. Wilford, John Noble. "Scientists Discuss Divided Loyalty on Job." _New York Times_, 22 February 1976, p. 34.

1154. "Will Foreign Bankers Blow the Whistle on Brazil?" _Business Week_, 19 November 1979, p. 56.

1155. Willis, Ken. "Year Has Been Rough for Cheat Informant." _Atlanta Constitution_, 10 April 1979.

1156. Witkin, Richard. "F.A.A. Worker Says Safety Change Led to Reprisal." <u>New York Times</u>, 31 October 1980, p. 14.

1157. Wright, Connie. "When Will We Whip Whistle Blowers?" <u>Nation's Cities Weekly</u>, 9 June 1980, p. 3. See item 301.

1158. Wright M. D. Lewis and C. R. Herron. "Bad News Bearers Get Some Bad News." <u>New York Times</u>, 20 January 1980, p. 2.

1159. Young, David. "Hotline Nets 60 'Solid' Tips for Problems of GSA Waste." <u>Chicago Tribune</u>, 13 June 1979.

1160. Young, Joseph. "Question of Protection for Whistle Blowers." <u>Washington Star</u>, 1, April 1980.

1161. Young, Joseph. "Whistle Blowers Law Working Backwards?" <u>Washington Star</u>, 5 March 1980.

1162. Zimmerman, Mark D. "Whistle-Blowing: The Perils of Professional Dissent." <u>Machine Design</u>, 12 March 1981, pp. 83-86. See item 480.

Section IX

Congress, Courts, and Laws

A. Congressional Documents

1163. U.S. Congress. Ethics in Government Act of 1978-Public Law 95-521. Washington: U.S. Government Printing Office, 1978.

This act regulates financial disclosure statements for government personnel and establishes the Office of Government Ethics, a special prosecutor, and a Senate Legal Counsel. Regulations concerning these reports are detailed, including blind trust requirements, filing procedures, and civil penalties. Rules governing the copying, destruction, and use of such reports are described. Definitions of terms used in the legislation are provided.

1164. U.S. Congress. House. Commission on Administrative Review. Financial Ethics. Hearings and Meetings. 95th Congress, 1st Sess., 1977.

1165. U.S. Congress. House. Committee on Interstate and Foreign Commerce. Subcommittee on Transportation and Commerce. Hazardous Waste Disposal Problems at Federal Facilities. Hearing. 96th Congress, 2nd Sess., 1980.

Focuses on practices at the Naval Air Engineering Center, Lakehurst, N.J., and allegations that an employee was removed for disability because he publicly voiced concerns over conditions.

1166. U.S. Congress. House. Committee on the Judiciary. Ethics in Government Act of 1978 as Amended by Public Laws 96-19 and 96-28. Washington: U.S. Government Printing Office, 1979.

Booklet presenting the full text of the amended 1978 Ethics in Government Act, which requires financial disclosure for certain federal employees and limits post-employment conflicts of interest. It also establishes an Office of Government Ethics, with a description of the Office's authority, functions, administrative provisions, and authorization of appropriations procedures. It provides for appointment of a special prosecutor to investigate and prosecute suspected violations. Finally, it provides for the establishment of an Office of Senate legal Counsel.

1167. U.S. Congress. House. Committee on Post Office and Civil Service. Civil Service Reform Act of 1978. Reprint. 95th Cong., 2nd Sess., 1978.

Summarizes the major changes proposed for the federal civil service, the Committee's analysis of each title of the bill, and separate and dissenting views.

1168. U.S. Congress. House. Committee on Post Office and Civil Service. Civil Service Reform Hearings, on H.R. 11280. 95th Cong., 2nd Sess., 1978.

Report of 1,025 pages that includes testimony and statements from numerous officials and private citizens on President Carter's civil service reform proposal. Contains several documents of direct relevance to whistle-blowing issues.

1169. U.S. Congress. House. Committee on Post Office and Civil Service. Final Report on Violations and Abuses of Merit Principles in Federal Employment Together with Minority Views. Committee Print. 94th Cong., 2nd Sess., 1976.

1170. U.S. Congress. House. Committee on Post Office and Civil Service. Subcommittee on the Civil Service. Civil Service Reform Oversight,Whistle-blower. 96th Cong., 2nd Sess., 1980.

Statements and testimony received from elected officials, government agencies, public interest groups, professional associations, and whistle-blowers. At one point during the proceedings, the subcommittee chair characterized the hearings as "blowing the whistle on whistle-blowing protections."

1171. Entry deleted.

1172. U.S. Congress. House. Committee on Post Office and Civil Service. Subcommittee on the Civil Service. Federal Productivity and Performance Appraisal. Hearings. 96th Cong., 1st Sess., 1979.

Treats huge governmental expenditures as a two-sided problem: (1) fraud, waste and abuse, and (2) poor employee performance and poor management. These hearings address the latter by receiving statements from governmental and non-governmental experts. Some witnesses argue that new civil service laws make it easier to fire whistle-blowers. Suggestion is made

that performance appraisals should include evaluations of employee initiative in pursuing the government code of ethics.

1173. U.S. Congress. House. Committee on Post Office and
Civil Service. Subcommittee on Retirement and Employee Benefits. Right to Privacy of Federal Employee. Hearings on H.R. 1281 and related
bills. 93rd Cong., 1st and 2nd Sess., 1974.

1174. U.S. Congress. House. Committee on Standards of Official Conduct. Code of Official Conduct. 96th
Cong., 1st Sess., 1979.

1175. U.S. Congress. House. Committee on Standards of Official Conduct. Ethics Manual for Members and Employees of the U.S. House of Representatives.
96th Cong., 1st Sess., 1979.

1176. U.S. Congress. Joint Economic Committee. Acquisition of Weapons Systems. Hearings. 92nd Cong.,
2nd Sess. and 93rd Cong., 1st Sess., Part 6, 1973.

Includes testimony, statements, and submissions for
the record on defense contracting and whistle-blower
Gordon Rule.

1177. U.S. Congress. Joint Economic Committee. The Dismissal of A. Ernest Fitzgerald by the Department of Defense. Hearings. 91st Cong., 1st Sess., 1969.

Contains 216 pages of testimony, submissions, and
appendices on the firing of whistle-blower Fitzgerald.

1178. U.S. Congress. Senate. Committee on Appropriations.
Fraud in Government. Hearings. 95th Cong.,
2nd Sess., 1978.

Examines the establishment of a General Accounting
Office Special Task Force on Prevention of
Fraud, and problems in monitoring anti-fraud efforts
in various agencies.

1179. U.S. Congress. Senate. Committee on Governmental Affairs. Civil Service Reform Act of 1978 and Reorganization Plan No. 2 of 1978. Hearings, on S.
2640, S. 2707, and S. 2830. 2 Vols. 95th Cong.,
2nd Sess., 1978.

A 905-page appendix that contains letters, re-
prints of articles, excerpts from field hearings, and
statements from public officials, attorneys, scholars, and several whistle-blowers on the proposed Civil Service Reform Act of 1978, the Federal Disclosure and Accountability Act of 1977, and the Federal
Employee Protection Act of 1978.

1180. U.S. Congress. Senate. Committee on Governmental Affairs. Civil Service Reform Act of 1978. Conference Report. 95th Cong., 2nd Sess., 1978.

Conference Committee submits its 160-page report
and explanatory statement on the Act.

1181. U.S. Congress. Senate. Committee on Governmental Affairs. Civil Service Reform Act of 1978. Report. 95th Cong., 2nd Sess., 1978.

Analyzes major provisions, legislative history, and
additional and minority views of the Civil Service Reform Act.

1182. U.S. Congress. Senate. Committee on Governmental Affairs. Public Officials Integrity Act of 1977; Report to accompany S. 555. 95th Cong., 1st Sess.,
1977.

Discusses the need for revised legislation governing the accountability and integrity of public officials using historical examples of alleged criminal or
civil offenses committed by high officials. Inadequa-
cies in existing legislation are also detailed. The
1977 bill contains five principal sections. The report provides a section-by-section analysis of the
bill, individual provisions, and includes the actual
text. Changes which the legislation makes in the existing United States Code are detailed, and estimated
costs are given for implementing each provision.

*1183. U.S. Congress. Senate. Committee on Governmental Af-
fairs. The Whistleblowers: A Report on Federal
Employees Who Disclose Acts of Governmental Waste,
Abuse, and Corruption. 95th Cong., 2nd Sess.,
1978.

Thorough examination of the phenomenon of whistle-
blowing in government. Chapters include "The Whistle

blower's Dilemma," "Central Issues," "Communication," "Management's Recourse," "Civil Service Commission," "The Courts' Role," "Remedies," and "Appendices" (comprised of case studies).

1184. U.S. Congress. Senate. Committee on Government Operations. Watergate Reorganization and Reform Act of 1975. Hearings. 2 parts. 94th Cong., 1st Sess., 1975, 1976.

Addresses the effort to provide a series of mechanisms to safeguard against the kind of abuses that occurred during Watergate. Proposals examined include the establishment of an independent Public Attorney, creation of a Congressional Legal Service, formulation of new rules of conduct for executive branch personnel provision of judicial enforcement of Congressional subpoenas, and establishment of new criminal penalties for illegal campaign practices.

1185. U.S. Congress. Senate. Committee on the Judiciary. Nomination of Otto F. Otepka. Hearings. 2 parts. 91st Cong.1, 1st Sess., 1969.

Statements from Senator Everett Dirksen and Otto Otepka, accompanied by letters, legal briefs, memoranda and press reports tracing proceedings against Otepka, a State Department whistle-blower.

1186. U.S. Congress. Senate. Committee on the Judiciary. Subcommittee on Administrative Practice and Procedure. Federal Employee Disclosure Act of 1975. S. 1210. Hearings. 95th Cong., 1st Sess., 1976.

Includes extensive testimony by government whistle-blowers who describe the pressures they were under to remain silent and the personal consequences of speaking out.

1187. U.S. Congress. Senate. Committee on the Judiciary. Protecting Privacy and the Rights of Federal Employees. Report. 93rd Cong., 2nd Sess., 1974.

To accompany a bill to prohibit indiscriminate requirements that employees and applicants (a) disclose their race or religion; (b) attend meetings unrelated to employment; (c) report on their activities unrelated to their work; and (d) submit to questioning about personal relations and finances, this report examines each of these issues, provides a section-by-section analysis of the bill, and discusses its legislative history.

1188. U.S. Congress. Senate. Committee on the Judiciary. Subcommittee on Administrative Practice and Procedure. Federal Employee Disclosure Act of 1975, S. 1210. Hearings, on S. 1210. 94th Cong., 1st Sess., 1975.

Testimony by federal employees, members of the press, Congressmen, academicians, and employee unions on whistle-blowing issues. Bill designed to protect employees who give information to Congress from retaliation on the part of their agencies.

1189. U.S. Congress. Senate. Committee on the Judiciary. Subcommittee on Constitutional Rights. Military Surveillance. Hearings, on S. 2318. 93rd Cong., 1st Sess., 1974.

Two days of hearings on a bill providing that military personnel shall not be used to conduct surveillance of political activities of civilians except in unusual circumstances. In the words of the committee chair, "it is a piece of privacy legislation." Includes testimony, statement submitted for the record, correspondence from public officials, and evidentiary materials.

1190. U.S. Congress. Senate. Committee on the Judiciary. Subcommittee on Separation of Powers. Removing Politics from the Administration of Justice. Hearings. 93rd Cong., 2nd Sess., 1974.

1191. U.S. Congress. Senate. Committee on Labor and Public Welfare. Subcommittee on Health, and Committee on the Judiciary. Subcommittee on Administrative Practice and Procedure. Examination of the Phamaceutical Industry, 1973-74. Hearings. Part 7. 93rd Cong., 2nd Sess., 1974.

1192. U.S. Congress. Senate. Ethics in Government Act of 1978. Hearings. 95th Cong., 2nd Sess., 1978.

Proposed amendments and joint explanatory statements about the Ethics in Government Act of 1978, given by Conference Committee. The joint explanatory statement recounts the areas of disagreement between the two houses and sets forth the conforming changes and agreements.

1193. U.S. Congress. Senate. Special Committee on Official Conduct. Senate Code of Conduct. Hearings. 5th Cong., 1st Sess. on S. Res. 36, 1977.

Section IX

Congress, Courts, and Laws

B. Courts

1. Cases

1194. <u>Arnett v. Kennedy</u>, 413 U.S. 134 (1974).

Action brought by a non-probationary civil service employee dismissed from a position in the Office of Economic Opportunity (OEO) after accusing the OEO Regional Director and a co-worker of attempting to bribe a potential OEO grantee. Action dismissed.

1195. <u>Bernasconi v. Tempe Elementary School District</u>, 548 F. 2d 857 (9th Cir. 1977), cert. den. 434 U.S. 825.

Public school teacher and counselor who brought civil rights action against school district and others, alleging she was illegally transferred from her counseling position because of her national origin, and because she had engaged in constitutionally protected free speech. Appellant became concerned that children were being placed in classes for the mentally retarded because they were tested in English rather than their native tongue. She attempted to correct this problem internally but, frustrated by lack of action, advised parents of affected children to consult the local legal aid society. Court dismissed the claim of national origin discrimination but held that the school district had transferred plaintiff in retaliation for exercise of free speech.

1196. <u>Bottcher v. Florida Department of Agriculture and Consumer Services</u>, 361 F. Supp. 1123 (N.D. Fla. 1973).

Chemist given a conditional rating (indicating poor or substandard performance) by her superiors, allegedly in retaliation for disclosures she had made concerning inadequate testing methods used by her agency. Since the rating constituted an impediment to Bottcher's professional reputation and future advancement, the district court said it could not be imposed without the procedure guaranteed by the due process change.

1196a. <u>Clifford W. Richter v. Ellis Fischel State Cancer Hospital</u> U.S. Department of Labor. Office of Administrative Law Judges. (Case No. 79-ERA-1). July 6, 1979.

1197. <u>Donahue v. Staunton</u>, 471 F. 2d 475 (7th Cir. 1972).

Action under Civil Rights Act by former chaplain at state mental hospital against his superiors for wrongful discharge in violation of chaplain's right to freedom of speech. Plaintiff had publicly criticized the hospital's operations. Plaintiff was awarded punitive damages.

1198. Donovan v. Reinbold, 433 F. 2d 738 (9th Cir. 1970).

Civil rights action alleging that defendants, acting under cover of state law, caused plaintiff's loss of public employment as a lifeguard in retaliation for exercising his First Amendment rights. He had authorized newspaper articles about activities on city beaches. Court ruled plaintiff be reinstated and awarded $5,000 damages.

1199. Edwards v. Citibank, 418 N.Y.S. 2d 269 (1979).

Plaintiff, a former employee of defendant bank, brought action for breach of contract and wrongful discharge allegedly in reprisal for plaintiff's uncovering evidence of illegal foreign currency manipulation. Citibank's motion for summary dismissal granted and complaint dismissed.

1200. Geary v. U.S. Steel Corp., 319 A. 2d 174 (1974).

An employee contended a pipe designed and manufactured by defendant employer was unsafe and should not be marketed. When his immediate supervisors took no action, he took his complaint to their superiors. The complaint alleged that although the company ultimately withdrew the product, his firing was in retaliation for his complaints about the safety of the product. Court refused to permit the action.

1201. Gellert v. Eastern Air Lines, Inc., 370 S. 2d 802 (1979).

Pilot sued airline, his former employer, for defamation of character, breach of employment contract and intentional infliction of mental distress. He sought mandatory injunction requiring airline to institute aircraft safety and training safeguards. Principal question presented by this appeal is whether one may recover damages for intentional infliction of severe mental distress which is without physical contact. Court ruled one may not recover damages on the ground that, under Florida law, intentional infliction of mental distress is not actionable when not incident to or connected with an independent tort.

1202. <u>Givhan v. Western Line Consolidated School District</u>, 439 U.S. 410 (1979).

School teacher alleged that her dismissal infringed her right of free speech secured by First and 14th Amendments. On certiorari, U.S. Supreme Court found that the teacher's criticism of the school was subject to the protection of the First Amendment.

1203. <u>Harless v. First National Bank in Fairmont</u>, 246 S.E. 2d 210 (1978).

Former employee filed complaint against bank and its vice presidents, alleging that his discharge was in retaliation for his efforts to require his employer to operate in compliance with consumer credit and protection laws. Case before Court concerned only the issue of whether a cause of action existed. Court ruled that the complaint did have a valid cause of action.

1204. <u>Haurilak v. Kelley</u>, 425 f. Supp. 626 (D. Conn. 1977).

Action brought under Civil Rights Act seeking declaratory and injunctive relief and damages on ground that the plaintiff was suspended from employment as a police officer in violation of his First and Fourth Amendment guarantees. Plaintiff wrote letters to the mayor and sent copies to other public officials, alleging that the town's merit system for promotion was disciplinary action be taken against plaintiff and that no monetary damages be awarded.

1205. <u>Hostrop v. Bd. of Junior College</u>, 471 F. 2d 488 (1972).

Civil rights action by discharged college president against school board and its members. Court found that a confidential memo which was leaked to the public could not be grounds for dismissal.

1206. <u>Lewis v. Southeastern Pennsylvania Transportation Authority</u>, 440 F. Supp. 887 (E.D. Pa. 1977).

Plaintiff, a black woman, instituted action against her former employer charging she was dismissed in relation to having previously filed a complaint with the Pennsylvania Human Relations Commission, and because she openly opposed defendant's discriminatory practices. Case was dismissed.

1207. Magri v. Giarrusso, 379 F. Supp. 353 (E.D. La. 1974).

Police sergeant filed suit against superintendent of police and mayor seeking reinstatement due to alleged infringments of constitutional rights. Letter of dismissal made clear that this action was taken because of Magri's public criticism of the superintendent, police practices and policies. Reinstatement was denied.

1208. Martin v. Platt, 386 N.E. 2d 1026 (1979).

Action brought against former employer claiming retaliatorial discharge. The employees were executives with Magnavox. In 1974, they reported to the president of Magnavox that a vice-president was solicting and receiving "kickback" payments from Magnavox suppliers. After an investigation, no action was taken against the officers. However, the executives were discharged. Court ruled that employees, who were employees at will, could not maintain an action for retaliatory discharge.

1209. O'Sullivan v. Mallon 390 A. 2d 149 (1978).

Suit by discharged X-ray technician for break of employment contract. Complaint alleged that termination of employment at will of X-ray technician was in retaliation for her refusal to perform illegal acts (catheterizations). Court ruled that an employment at will may not be terminated by an employer in retaliation for an employee's refusal to perform an illegal act. Defendant's motion for dismissal denied.

1210. Perdue v. J.C. Penney, 470 Supp. 1234 (1979).

Action instituted on complaint that plaintiffs were wrongfully discharged from employment and that discharge constituted a prima-facie tort. Plaintiffs, in their capacity as internal auditors, were part of an investigative team to look into an illegal bribery and kickback scheme discovered between an J.C. Penney employee and a general contractor. Plaintiffs claim that when they discovered this wrongdoing, a cover-up was undertaken by defendants and that their termination was solely to perpetuate the alleged coverup. Defendant's motion to dismiss the complaint granted.

1211. Percivel v. General Motors Corp. 539 F. 2d 1126. (8th Cir. 1976).

Automobile executive brought complaint against employer seeking damages for alleged wrongful discharge. Plaintiff contended that he was discharged as a result of a conspiracy among his fellow executives to force him out of employment because he had complained about certain allegedly deceptive practices, had refused to give the government false information, and had, on the contrary, undertaken to correct alleged misrepresentations made to the government by the defendant. The action was dismissed.

1212. Petermann v. International Brotherhood, Etc., 344 P. 2d 25 (1959).

A complaint alleging that plaintiff had been employed by the union as business agent, that the secretary-treasurer of union had instructed him to testify falsely before a legislative committee, and that upon his failure to do so he had been discharged. Court stated that plaintiff alleged sufficient facts to show his discharge was improper and he was entitled to civil relief.

1213. Pickering v. Board of Education, 391 U.S. 563 (1968).

A high school teacher, who had written a letter to a local newspaper criticizing the school board and the superintendent for their handling of bond issues, was dismissed by the school board for conduct detrimental to the efficient operation of the schools. The Suppreme Court held that the board's action had violated Pickering's right to free speech and concluded that public employment did not necessitate the relinquishment of First Amendment rights.

1214. Pierce v. Ortho Pharmaceuticals, 166 N.J. Super. 335, 339 A. 2d 1023 (1979).

Action brought against former employer by research director of a pharmaceutical firm, who alleged she was driven out of her job because she would not approve a dangerous drug-testing and marketing plan. Cause of action established and remanded for trial.

1215. Pierce v. Ortho Pharmaceuticals, 84 N.J. 58, 417; A. 2d 505 (1980).

Supreme Court of New Jersey reversed Appellate Division's decision to remand for trial and reinstated summary judgment granted originally. Judgment in favor of defendant, Ortho Pharmaceuticals.

1216. Pilarowski v. Brown, 257 N.W. 2d 211 (1971).

Discharged county health department employee brought action against various county officials seeking writ of mandamus, damages and other relief for his discharge following writing of letters which were critical of elected county officials. Relief was granted to plaintiff requiring that trial judge issue a temporary injunction ordering plaintiff should receive his salary until a decision could be reached.

1217. Rafferty v. Philadelphia Psychiatric Center, 356 F. Supp. 500 (E.D. Pa. 1973).

Suit brought by nurse against psychiatric center. She alleged deprivation of her constitutional rights in connection with the termination of employment following publication of a news article in which she was quoted as being critical of patient care. Court ruled plaintiff be reinstated and awarded over $3,000 in back pay.

1218. Simpson v. Weeks, 570 F. 2d 240 (8th Cir. 1978).

Police officer brought a civil rights action against his former police chief and others, claiming they had conspired to deprive his of his constitutional right of free speech. Simpson was alleged to have discussed a pending case against Weeks (Weeks and other police officers were charged in a federal court with violating the civil rights of city prisoners) with the attorney representing the prisoners. After he was identified as having conferred with the attorney, Weeks transferred Simpson to the city jail and dramatically lowered Simpson's evaluation ratings.

Court granted mandatory injunction requiring Simpson to be reinstated in the position he had held prior to the transfer. In addition, nominal and punitive damages were awarded.

1219. Swaaley v. United States, 376 F. 2d 857 (Ct. Cl. 1967).

Court of Claims held that a navy shipyard mechanic who was dismissed for having complained to the Secretary of Labor about improper promotion procedures was entitled to damages.

1220. Tarasoff v. Regents of the University of California, 131 Cal. Rptr. 14 (1976).

Action brought against university regents, psychotherapists employed by university hospital, and campus police to recover damages for murder of plaintiff's daughter by psychiatrist's patient. Supreme Court of California held plaintiffs had a valid cause of action against defendant therapists and remanded for further proceedings.

1221. Trombetta v. Detroit, Toledo and Trenton R. Co., 265 N.W. 2s 385 (1978).

Former railroad employee brought action against railroad, alleging it had wrongfully discharged him from employment because of his refusal to alter pollution control reports. Court granted summary judgment to the railroad.

1222. Turner v. Kennedy, 332 F. 2d 304 (D.C. Cir) (mem.), cert, denied, 379 U.S. 901 (1964).

District of Columbia Circuit Court affirmed the discharge of a civil service employee who had made "false, irresponsible and unjustified" statements in letters he had written to Congressmen which were found by the Civil Service Commission to have demonstrated his unsuitability for employment and to have impaired the efficiency of his agency.

1223. United States v. Marchetti, 466 F. 2d 1309 (4th Cir.), cert. denied, 409 U.S. 1063 (1972).

Central Intelligence Agency sought to restrain a former employee from publishing a book about the agency. The Fourth Circuit affirmed an injunction against him, acknowledging that the government had met its heavy burden of showing potential harm.

1224. Watts v. Seward School Board, 454 P. 2d 732 (Alas. 1969), cert, denied, 397 U.S. 921 (1970).

Alaska Supreme Court upheld the dismissal of several teachers for their allegedly disruptive public charges of maladministration and improper practices by the school superintendent. Court viewed the state's interest in regulating this type of disclosure as significantly different from that involved in the regulation of the speech of citizens in general. Ruled that the disclosure was detrimental to harmony among the discharged teachers and their co-workers and to efficient operation of the schools.

Section IX

Congress, Courts, and Laws

B. Courts

2. Discussion

1225. Baran, Andrew. "Federal Employment--The Civil Service Reform Act of 1978--Roving Incompetents and Protecting Whistle Blowers." Wayne Law Review, 26 (November 1979), 97-118. See item 222.

*1226. Blades, Lawrence. "Employment at Will vs. Individual Freedom: On Limiting the Abusive Exercise of Employer Power." Columbia Law Review, 67 (December 1967), 1404-1435.

Argues that "many of the rights and privileges which are considered so important . . . that they are constitutionally protected. . . are vulnerable to abuse through an employer's power" (p. 1407). Focuses on the employer's traditional absolute right of discharge. Examines the legal underpinnings of the doctrine which do not adequately limit that power. Proposes adoption of remedies through the courts for abusively discharged employees.

*1227. Blumberg, Phillip I "Corporate Responsibility and the Employee's Duty of Loyalty and Obedience: A Preliminary Inquiry." Oklahoma Law Review, 24 (August 1971), 279-318.

Illustrates the changing nature of the corporate world by Ralph Nader's call for employees of both government and private organizations to disclose information about harmful or illegal practices. Examines statutes in both the United States and England regarding an employee's right to freely give opinions and information. Several alternatives to Nader's proposal are offered: (1) traditional agency law; (2) statutory and administrative requirements of social responsibility disclosure; and (3) social audit of corporation activities in area of social responsibility.

1228. Caplan, Arthur L. and Daniel Callahan, eds. Ethics in Hard Times. New York: Plenum Publishing, 1982. See item 736.

1229. Christiansen, Jon P. "A Remedy for the Discharged of Professional Employees Who Refuse to Perform Unethical or Illegal Acts: A Proposal in Aid of Professional Ethics." Vanderbilt Law Review, 28 (May 1975), 805-840. See item 606.

1230. Committee on Labor and Employment Law, The Association of the Bar of the City of New York. "At-Will Employment and the Problem of Unjust Dismissal." The Record, 36 (April 1981), 170-216.

1231. Conway, John. "Protecting the Private Sector At-Will Employee Who 'Blows the Whistle': A Cause of Action Based Upon Determinations of Public Policy." Wisconsin Law Review, 77 (1977), 777-812.

Discussion of the developing right of private sector employees to bring suit against the employer for a retaliatory discharge. First, "at-will employment" is discussed. Second, the developing public policy exceptions to the termination at-will doctrine are analyzed. Finally, the application of these exceptions to more specific problems of whistle-blowers are addressed. Concludes that the present state of public policy exceptions affords a proper means of protecting the whistle-blowing employee. However, judicial attitudes respecting the personal interests of the at-ill employment relationship must be recast in the public interest.

1232. Coven, Mark. "The First Amendment Rights of Policymaking Public Employees." Harvard Civil Rights--Civil Liberties Law Review, 12 (Summer 1977), 559584. See item 236.

1233. "The Defense of Liberty: The Constitutional Guarantees Are Not Self-Executing." Center Magazine, 12 (November/December 1979), 41.

1234. "Dismissals of Public Employees for Petitioning Congress: Administering Discipline and 5 U.S.C. Section 652(d). Yale Law Journal, 74 (1965), 1156-1170.

1235. D. M. R. "The Right of Government Employees to Furnish Information to Congress: Statutory and Constitutional Aspects." Virginia Law Review, 57 (June 1971), 885-919. See item 237.

1236. Dwoskin, Robert P. Rights of the Public Employee. Chicago: American Library Association, 1978.

Examines three areas: the concept of public employment, including its historical development and current status; the employee and the First Amendment, as related to the issues of free speech, political activities and the loyalty oath; and non-judicial remedies for public employees, such as hearings with employer before job action and unionization.

1237. Edwards, Charles A. "Protection of the Complaining Employee: How Much Is Too Much?" Employee Relations Law Journal, 6 (Autumn 1980), 207-227.

Statutory and regulatory protections are available to the employee complaining to a federal agency about work place conditions. Such protections include the 1964 Civil Rights Act, the National Labor Relations Act, the Fair Labor Standards Act, the Equal Pay Act, the Age Discrimination in Employment Act, and the 1970 Occupational Safety and Health Act.

1238. Feliu, Alfred G. "Discharge of Professional Employees: Protecting Against Dismissal for Acts Within a Professional Code of Ethics." Columbia Human Rights Law Review, 11 (Fall-Winter 1979-1980), 149187.

Comment examines the employment-at-will doctrine which has given employers power to discharge an employee for good cause, for no cause, or even cause morally wrong. Considers recent inroads made into this bulwark of employer control by Congress, the state legislatures, and the courts.

1239. Flores, Albert. "Engineering Ethics in Organizational Contexts: A Case Study." Unpublished paper, Center for the Study of Science and Technology, Rensselaer Polytechnic Institute, Troy, New York, 1981.

Discusses the Monsanto Company and its formal organizational mechanisms for insuring that its engineering staff designs appropriate safety features into all its manufacturing operations and chemical processes. Aims at determining how these mechanisms encourage engineers to regard safety as an integral part of their design engineering responsibilities, and to describe how engineers perceive these mechanisms as influencing their design practices. Argues that Monsanto supports its engineers in fulfilling professional and moral responsibilities for safety.

1240. Jackson, Dudley. Unfair Dismissal. London and New York: Cambridge University Press, 1975.

"Recent legislation on unfair dismissal, and its enforcement through a system of tribunals, has created
not only many new rights for workers, but also a distinct body of law . . . [D]escribes and analyses how
the law works" (p. 1).

*1241. Lindauer, Mitchell J. "Government Employee Disclo-
sures of Agency Wrongdoing: Protecting the Right
to Blow the Whistle." University of Chicago Law
Review, 42 (Spring 1975). 530-561.

Examines the disclosure rights of federal and state
government employees by first identifying each of the
various substantive constitutional and statutory
grounds. Attempts to provide a comprehensive survey
of the protections available to a whistle-blower by
discussing the overlapping applications of the separate substantive ground as they have been interpreted
by the courts. Final section address the procedural
protections that must be adhered to when the government seeks to sanction an employee who has harmed his
/her agency's interests. Suggests that "in both procedural and substantive areas, the courts have reached
an uneasy balance between public interest in favor of
and in opposition to the expansive protection of government employee disclosures" (p. 531).

1242. Lockhart, Paula K. "Professional Dissent: A Legal
Analysis." See item 716.

Begins with a review of the employment at will doctrine and the disclosure rights of public employees.
Other sections examine reform legislation: the Merit
Systems Protection Board, the Office of Special Counsel, and the Office of Inspector General.

1243. Lowy, Joan Bertin. "Constitutional Limitations on the
Dismissal of Public Employees." Brooklyn Law Review, 43 (Summer 1976), 1-30. See item 263.

1244. Malin, Martin. "Current Status of Legal Protection
for Whistleblowers." Paper read at Second National Conference on Ethics in Engineering, 5-6 March
1982, at Illinois Institute of Technology, Chicago,
Illinois. See item 722b.

1245. Nickel, Henry V. "The First Amendment and Public Em-
ployees--an Emerging Constitutional Right to be a

Policeman?" <u>George Washington Law Review</u>, 37 (December 1968), 409-424.

Examines the scope of legal protection under the First Amendment for dismissals based on the nature of the employe's communication which gave cause for firing. Calls for increased protection for government employees, but cautions against a blind application of that protection.

1246. Olsen, Theodore A. "Wrongful Discharge Claims Raised by At-Will Employees: A New Legal Concern for Employers." <u>Labor Law Journal</u>, 32 (May 1981), 265-297.

Discusses the traditional legal rules applicable to at-will employees, analyzes recent developments in this area, and considers legal positions that may be taken by employers in litigation in defense of their disciplinary actions.

*1247. Peck, Cornelius J. "Unjust Discharges from Employment: A Necessary Change in the Law." <u>Ohio State Law Journal</u>, 40 (1979), 1-49.

Argues that important constitutional guarantees are violated by continued adherence to the rule that a contract of employment for an indefinite term is a contract terminable at will by either party. Contends that the constitutionally protected interest in continued employment cannot be destroyed without observance of procedural due process guarantees. Also argues that discharge without cause constitutes a deprivation of equal protection of the law to the unorganized employees of private employers. A change to a rule requiring that employers show just cause to terminate employment will give rise to a number of problems, both substantive and procedural, which are reviewed in the final section.

1248. "Protecting At-Will Employees Against Wrongful Discharge: The Duty To Terminate Only in Good Faith." <u>Harvard Law Review</u>, 93 (1980), 1816-1844.

1249. Sanders, Wayne. "Constitutional Protection for Whistle Blowers: Has the First Amendment Called In Sick?" Paper presented at the Eleventh Annual Convention of the Popular Culture Association combined with the Third Annual Convention of the American Culture Association. 29 March 1981, the Netherland Hilton, Cincinnati, OH.

Explores the uses and limitations of the First and Fourteenth Amendments in protecting free speech in organizations, the private-public sector distinction, and criteria used to distinguish protected versus generally not protected speech with three broad categories: (1) cooperation with supervisors, e.g., showing an inability to handle criticism; (2) speech which threatens harmony among workers; and (3) where the employee demonstrates a lack of personal loyalty to his /her supervisors and/or organization. Concluding section discusses the special problems employees face when pressing free speech claims.

1250. Schneier, Mark. "Public Policy Limitations on the Retaliatory Discharge of At-Will Employees in the Private Sector." University of California (Davis) Law Review, 14 (1981), 811-837.

1251. Solomon, Lewis and Terry Garcia. "Protecting the Corporate Whistle Blower Under Federal Anti-Retaliation Statutes." The Journal of Corporation Law, 5 (Winter 1980), 275-297.

The common law approach to the rights of corporate whistle-blowers is discussed through the cases where courts upheld the employer's right to fire for any or no reason. This dismissal-at-will pattern is limited when the employee's statutory rights are violated. Examines the Occupational Safety and Health Act as an attempt to protect whistle-blowers from employer retaliation--a major change from the common law practice that could be strengthened.

1252. Stevens, George E. "The Legality of Discharging Employees for Insubordination." American Business Law Journal, 18 (Fall 1980), 371-389.

The employer's right to discharge an insubordinate employee is not absolute. To determine the present status of the law in this area, an up-to-date survey of cases is presented. This is supplemented with a discussion of public policy exceptions to the employer's right of dismissal and the impact of the National Labor Relations Act.

1253. "Substantive Due Process: The Extent of Public Employees' Protection From Arbitrary Dismissal." University of Pennsylvania Law Review, 122 (1974), 1647-1663.

Argues that a strong case can be made that the due process clause of the Fourteenth Amendment should protect government employees from arbitrary dismissal.

1254. Summers, Clyde W. "Individual Protection Against Unjust Dismissal: Time for a Statute." Virginia Law Review, 62 (April 1976), 481-532.

Contends that the anachronistic legal rule that employees can be discharged for any or no reason should be abandoned, and the protection now given under collective agreements should be extended to employees not so covered. Describes the unsatisfactory way that courts have responded to this problem and defends the comprehensiveness and importance of the body of law of unjust discipline developed under collective bargaining agreements.

1255. Summers, Clyde W. "Protecting All Employees Against Unjust Dismissal." Harvard Business Review, 58 (January-February 1980), 132-139. See item 39.

1256. Vaughn, Robert G. "Public Employees and the Right to Disobey." Hastings Law Journal, 29 (November 1977), 261-295. See item 291.

Examines the protections available to an employee who refuses to obey an order believed to be illegal. Evaluates arguments for and against judicial recognition of a right to disobey under those circumstances, explores the proper scope of the right if recognized, and analyzes the effect of recognition.

1257. Vaughn, Robert G. "Whistleblowing and the Character of Public Employment." The Bureaucrat, 6 (Winter 1977), 29-34. See item 299.

1258. Youngblood, Stuart A. and Gary Tidwell. "Termination at Will: Some Changes in the Wind." Personnel, 58 (May/June 1981), pp. 22-33.

Section IX

Congress, Courts, and Laws

C. Federal and State Anti-Reprisal Statues

Federal and State Statutes

Employee Protection Sections

1259. Age Discrimination Act of 1967, Pub. L. 90-202, Sec. 4.

1260. Asbestos School Hazard Detection and Control Act, 20 U.S.C., Sec. 3608.

1260a. California Assembly Bill No. 98. An act to amend sections 1101, 1103 and 1105 of the Labor Code. Introduced December 4, 1980; amended April 21, 1981, March 30, 1981.

1261. Civil Rights Act of 1964, Title VII, Pub. L. 88-352, Sec. 704.

1262. Civil Rights of Institutionalized Persons Act, 42 U.S.C., Sec. 1997 (d).

1263. Civil Service Reform Act of 1978, 5 U.S.C., Secs. 2301, 2302, 7102, 7116.

1264. Clean Air Act Amendments of 1977, Pub. L. 95-95, Sec. 312.

1265. Comprehensive Environmental Response, Compensation and Liability Act of 1980, 42 U.S.C., Sec. 9610.

1266. Connecticut Labor Code: Workmen's Compensation, Title 31, Sec. 379, "Discrimination Against Employee Filling Complaint."

1267. Connecticut General Statutes Annotated, Chap. 48, Sec. 4-61DD(a), "Whistle-Blowing by State Employees."

1268. Conspiracy to Obstruct Justice Act, 15 U.S.C., Sec. 1985 (2).

1269. Consumer Credit Protection Act of 1968, Pub. L. 90-321, Sec. 304.

1270. Employee Retirement Income Security Act of 1974, Pub. L. 93-406, Sec. 410.

1271. Energy Reorganization Act Amendment of 1978, 42 U.S.C., Sec. 5851.

1272. Fair Labor Standards Act, 29 U.S.C., Sec. 215.

1273. Farm Labor Contractor Registration Act Amendments of 1972, Pub. L. 92-500, Sec. 507.

1274. Federal Mine Safety and Health Act of 1977, Pub. L. 164, Sec. 105 (c).

1275. Federal Railroad Safety Act Amendment, 45 U.S.C., Sec. 441.

1276. Federal Water Pollution Control Act Amendments of 1972, Pub. L. 92-500, Sec. 507.

1277. Illinois Employment Code: Workmen's Compensation, Chap. 48, Sec. 138, 4(h), "Provision to Insure Payment of Compensation."

1278. Indiana Code: State Employees' Bill of Rights, Chap. 10, Sec. 4, "Violations for misuse reported by employees--Reprisals prohibited--furnishing false information."

1279. International Safe Container Act of 1977, 46 U.S.C., Sec. 1506.

1280. Jury Duty Act, 28 U.S.C., Sec. 1875.

1281. Longshoremen's and Harbor Act of 1972, 33 U.S.C., Sec. 948 (a).

1282. Louisiana State Labor Laws, Chap. 28, Sec. 1074.1(2), "Whistleblowers' Protection."

1283. Maryland Annotated Code, Chap. 850, Sec. 1, "Classified Employees--Disclosure and Confidentiality Protection."

1284. Michigan Compiled Laws Annotated, Sec. 15.361, "Whistleblowers' Protection Act."

1285. Missouri Workmen's Compensation, Sec. 287, 780, "Discrimination Against Employee for Exercise of Rights."

1286. National Labor Management Relations Act, 29 U.S.C., Sec. 158.

1287. New Jersey Labor and Workmen's Compensation Code, Title 34:15, Sec. 31-9.1, "Unlawful Discharge Of, Or Discrimination Against, Employee Claiming Compensation Benefits, Penalty."

1287b. New Jersey. "The Whistleblowers' Protection Act." An Act to provide protection to employees in certain cases and supplementing Title 34 of the Revised Statutes. Introduced June 8, 1981.

1288. Nuclear Regulatory Commission Authorization of 1978, Pub. L. 94-601, Sec. 10.

1289. Occupational Safety and Health Act of 1970, Pub. L. 91596, Sec. 11 (c).

1290. Oregon Labor and Industrial Relations Code: Workmen's Compensation, Chap. 659, Sec. 410, "Discrimination Against Workmen Applying for Workmen's Compensation Benefits Prohibited."

1291. Railroad Employers Act of 1908, 45 U.S.C., Sec. 60.

1292. Resource Conservation and Recovery Act of 1976, Pub. L. 94-580, Sec. 7001.

1293. Safe Drinking Water Act of 1974, Pub. L. 93-523, Sec. 1450.

1294. Solid Waste Disposal Act of 1976, 42 U.S.C., Sec. 6972.

1295. Surface Mining Control and Reclamation Act of 1977, 30 U.S.C., Secs. 1201, 1293.

1296. Texas Workmen's Compensation Law, Vol 22, Art. 8307C, "Protection of Claimants from Discrimination by Employers; Remedies, Jurisdiction."

1297. Toxic Substances Control Act of 1976, Pub. L. 94-469, Sec. 23.

1298. U.S. Nuclear Regulatory Commission. "Final Rule: Protection of Employees Who Provide Information." Federal Register 47 (July 14, 1982): 30452-30458.

1299. U.S. Nuclear Regulatory Commission. NRC Manual. Chapter 4125. "Differing Professional Opinions." Washington, DC: GPO, 1980.

1300. U.S. Nuclear Regulatory Commission. Office of Management and Program Analysis. A Survey of Policies

270

     and Procedures Applicable to the Expression of Dif-
fering Professional Opinions. Washington, DC:
GPO.

Section X

Bibliography of Bibliographies

1298. Bank of America. Bibliography: Corporate Responsibility for Social Problems. Vols. I-VI. San Francisco, CA: Bank of America, 1971-1977.

1299. Ben-David, Joseph. "Bibliography on the Sociology of Professions." Current Sociology, 12 (1963-64), 299-330.

1300. Bibliography of Society, Ethics and Life Sciences. Hastings-on-Hudson, NY: Hastings Institute, 1975.

1301. Business and Professional Ethics, selected issues 1977-.

1302. Caldwell, Lynton K., ed. Science, Technology, and Public Policy. A Selected and Annotated Bibliography. 3 Vol. Bloomington, IN: Indiana University, 1968-1972.

1303. Center for Business Ethics. "A Bibliography of Business Ethics Articles." Waltham, MA : Bentley College Center for Business Ethics, 1977 (mimeographed); updated, 1981.

1304. Center for Business Ethics. "A Bibliography of Business Ethics Books." Ibid.

1305. Christian, Portia. Ethics in Business Conduct: Selected References from the Record. Detroit, MI: Gale Research Company, 1970.

1306. Cohen, Robert S. "Bibliography of Recent Soviet Studies on the Ethical and Human Implications of Science and Technology." Harvard University Newsletter #16, (June 1976), 19-37.

1307. Comptroller General. Civil Service Reform: An Annotated Bibliography. Washington, DC: Office of Information Systems and Services, General Accounting Office, 1981, pp. 33-38.

1308. Dill, David E. et al. Syllabi for the Teaching of Management Ethics. New Haven, CT: Society for Values in Higher Education, 1979.

1309. Durbin, Paul T. and Carl Mitcham, eds. Research in Philosophy and Technology. An Annual Compilation of Research. Vol. 1. Greenwich, CT: JAI Press, 1978.

1310. Dwivedi, O. P. Public Service Ethics. Brussels: International Institute of Administrative Sciences, 1978. Appendix B.

1311. Eberwein, Wolf-Dieter and Peter Weingart. "Science and Ethics from the German Perspective: An Annotated Bibliography, 1965-1976." Newsletter on Science, Technology and Human Values, 20 (1977), 25-38.

1312. Education Fund for Individual Rights. "Bibliography." New York: The Fund, 1981. Unpublished mimeograph.

1313. Fleishman, Joel and Bruce Payne. "Bibliography." Durham, NC: Duke University, n.d. Unpublished mimeograph.

1314. Flores, Albert and Denise Tabor. "Annotated Bibliography on Professional Ethics of Scientists: New Ethical and Social Issues Posed by Recent Advances in Science and Technology." Research in Philosophy and Technology. Winter 1982.

1315. Flores, Albert and Denise Tabor. "A Selected Bibliography on Ethics and the Professions." The Society for the Study of Professional Ethics Newsletter, Autumn 1980.

1316. Flores, Albert. "A Concise Selected Bibliography on Professional Ethics-With Annotations." Science, Technology and Human Values, 26 (Winter 1979), 2936.

1317. Flores, Albert and Robert Baum. "Bibliography on Engineering Ethics." Business and Professional Ethics, 1 (1977), 3-7.

1318. Freedman, Richard. "An Annotated, Selective Checklist of Imaginative Literature Concerning the Relationship between Science, Technology and Human Values." Newsletter of the Program on Public Conceptions of Science, 10 (January 1975).

1319. Gothie, Daniel. A Selected Bibliography of Applied Ethics in the Professions: A Working Sourcebook. Charlottersville, VA: University Press of Virginia, 1973.

275

1320. Greer, P., ed. "Business Ethics Bibliography." Cambridge, MA: Harvard Business school, 1979. Mimeographed.

1321. Gunn, Elizabeth M. "Ethics and the Public Service: An Annotated Bibliography and Overview Essay." Public Personnel Management, 10 (1981), 172-199.

1322. Hansen, Kirk. "Selected Course Outlines on Business and Ethics." Stanford University, 1981. Mimeographed).

1323. Harvard University Program on Technology and Society. Technology and the Individual. Research Review No. 6. Cambridge, MA: Harvard University Press, 1970.

1324. Harvard University Program on Technology and Society. Technology and the Polity. Research Review No. 4. Cambridge, MA: Harvard University Press, 1969.

1325. Harvard University Program on Technology nd Society. Technology and Values. Research Review No. 3. Cambridge, MA: Harvard University Press, 1969.

1326. Hennigan, Patrick J. "Case Materials and Selected Bibliography." New York: Columbia University, n.d. Unpublished mimeograph.

1327. Hurley, C. C. "Civil Service Reform: An Annotated Bibliography." Review of Public Personnel Administration, 2 (Summer, 1982), 59-90.

1328. Johansen, Elaine. "Case Study Models of Political Corruption to Assist Teaching Ethics in Administration: A Bibliographic Essay." Proceedings of the Annual Meeting, Fourth National Conference on Teaching Public Administration, 29-30 May 1981, Lexington, KY.

1329. Jones, Donald G. A Bibliography of Business Ethics, 1971-1975. Charlottesville, VA: University of Virginia Press, 1977.

1330. Jones, Donald G. A Bibliography of Business Ethics, 1976-1980. Charlottesville, VA: University of Virginia Press, 1982.

1331. Karakida, K., Y. Ishihara, T. Sato, and K. Nakamura.
       "Bibliography of Important Works on Science and
       Ethics in Japan." Harvard University Newslet-
       ter, 16 (June 1976), 38-51.

1332. Ladenson, Robert F. A Selected Annotated Bibliogra-
       phy of Professional Ethics and Social Responsibili-
       ty in Engineering. Chicago, IL: Illinois Insti-
       tute of Technology, 1980.

1333. La Follette, Marcel Chotkowski. The Citizen and Sci-
       ence Almanac and Annotated Bibliography. Bloom-
       ington, IN: The Poynter Center, Indiana Univer-
       sity, 1977.

1334. Mitcham, Carl and Robert Mackey. Bibliography of
       the Philosophy of Technology. Chicago: Univer-
       sity of Chicago Press, 1973.

1335. National Academy of Public Administration. Ethics
       in the Public Service: Materials Prepared for a
       Pilot Training Session. Washington, DC: The
       Academy, 1979. Part VIII.

1336. Parris, Judith. "'Whistle Blowers in the Executive
       Branch." Issues Brief No. IB78006. Washington,
       DC: Congressional Research Service, 1979.

1337. Piattelli-Palmarini, M. "Selected Bibliography of
       Works on Science and Ethics in Italy." Harvard
       University Newsletter, 16 (June 1976), 52-67.

1338. "Selected Bibliography on Professional Ethics." Sci-
       ence, Technology and Human Values, 22 (January
       1978), 52.

1339. Stanford Research Institute. Analysis and Bibliogra-
       phy of Literature on Corruption. Washington, DC:
       National Institute of Law Enforcement and Criminal
       Justice, 1978.

1340. Stupak, Ronald J. "Curricula Material on Values, Eth-
       ics, and Morals in Public Administration: A Mod-
       ule." Washington, DC: New York Institute of Tech-
       nology, 1982.

1341. U.S. Civil Service Commission. Ethics, Values, and
       Administrative Responsibility: A Training Manual

for Government Managers--Part IV: Annotated
<u>Bibliography</u>. Washington, DC: The Commission,
1976.

1342. U.S. Department of Housing and Urban Development.
<u>Training and Development Sources: Compendium for
Offices of Inspector General</u>. Washington, DC:
The Department, 1981.

1343. Vogel, David. "A Bibliography of Materials for Teaching Business Ethics." Berkeley, CA: Graduate
School of Business Administration, 1979. Mimeographed.

1344. Walter, LeRoy, ed. <u>Bibliography of Bioethics</u>. Detroit, MI: Gale Research, 1977.

1345. West, F. E. <u>Science for Society: A Bibliography</u>.
Washington, DC: American Association for the Advancement of Science, 1974.

1346. White, Anthony D. <u>Ethics in Local Government</u>.
Monticello, IL: Council of Planning Librarians,
1977.

1347. Woodstrom, Roy. <u>Impact of Technology on Society: A
Selective Bibliography</u>. Minneapolis: University
of Minnesota Library, 1973.

Section XI

Guide to Resources

A. Journals and Series

A. Journals and Series

Administration and Society. Sage Publications Inc. 275 South Beverly Drive, Beverly Hills, CA 90212.

America: National Catholic Weekly Review. 1909 America Press, 106 W. 56th St., New York, NY 10019.

The Bureaucrat. P.O. Box 347, Arlington, VA 22210.

Business and Professional Ethics. Human Dimensions Center, Rensselaer Polytechnic Institute, Troy, NY 12181.

Business and Society. Walter E. Heller College of Business Administration, 430 South Michigan Avenue, Chicago, IL 60605.

Federal Times. Army Times Publishing Co., 475 School St., S.W., Washington, DC 20024.

HBS Case Services(formerly Intercollegiate Case Clearinghouse). Soldier's Field. Boston, MA 02163.

Harvard Business Review. Harvard University Graduate School of Business Administration, Soldiers Field. Boston, MA 02163.

Hastings Center Report. Hastings Center, 360 Broadway, Hastings-on-Hudson, NY 10706.

Journal of Business Ethics. Kluwer Academic Publishers Group, Distribution Center, Box 322, 3300 Alt Dordrecht, Netherlands.

Occasional Monographs, Values in Business Management Program, C. W. Post Center, Long Island University. Greenvale, NY 11548.

Occasional Papers Series, Center for the Study of Ethics in the Professions. Illinois Institute of Technology, Chicago, IL 60616.

Perspectives on the Professions: Ethical and Policy Issues. Center for the Study of Ethics in the Professions, Illinois Institute of Technology, Chicago IL 60616.

Public Administration Review. Bi-monthly, American
    Society For Public Administration, 1120 G Street,
    N.W. Washington, DC 20005.

National Civic Review. National Municipal League 47
    East 68th Street, New York, NY 10021.

B. Periodical Guides

Business Periodicals. H. W. Wilson Co., 950 Univer-
    sity Avenue, Bronx, NY 10452.

Joint Reference Library: Publications on Governmental
    Problems

Management Research. (Bi-Monthly) University of Mass-
    achusetts, School of Business Administration, Bus-
    iness Publication Services Room 357, Amherst, MA
    01003.

Public Affairs Information Service. 11 West 40th
    Street, New York, NY 10018.

Personnel Literature. U.S. Office of Personnel Man-
    agement Library, Washington, DC 20415.

Personnel Management Abstracts. University of Michi-
    gan, Graduate School of Business Administration,
    Ann Arbor, MI 48109.

Sage Public Administration Abstracts. Sage Publica-
    tions Inc., 275 South Beverly Drive, Beverly
    Hills, CA 90212.

Reader's Guide to Periodical Literature. H. W. Wil-
    son Co., 950 University Avenue, Bronx, NY 10452.

C. Directories

Career Guide to Professional Associations: A Directory
    of Organizations by Occupational Field. Cranston,
    RI: Carroll Press, 1976.

Clapp, Jane. Professional Ethics and Insignia. Metu-
    chen, NJ: Scarecrow Press, 1974.

Directory of Research Persons in Applied Ethics. Newark, DE: Center for the Study of Values, 1979.

EVIST: Ethics and Values in Science and Technology Resource Directory. Washington, DC: American Association for the Advancement of Science, 1978.

Jones, Donald G. Directory of Centers and Institutes Concerned with Business Ethics. Drew University, 1980. Mimeographed.

Merit Systems Protection Board. Index to Decisions of the United States Merit Systems Board. Washington DC: U.S. Government Printing Office, 1980.

Society for the Study of Professional Ethics, Directory. Villanova, PA: The Society, 1981.

D. Audio-Visual Resources

The CIA Case Officer. Washington, DC: Institute for Policy Studies, 1978. 30 min.

Portrayal of John Stockwell, who served the Central Intelligence Agency (CIA) for 12 years, mostly in Africa and Vietnam. Soon after his last assignment as chief of the Angolan Task Force during 1975 and early 1976, he resigned from the CIA. Reveals previously unknown information about CIA practices and policies.

Focus on Ethics: A Multimedia Seminar. Santa Monica, CA: Salenger Educational Media, 1977.

Readings, films, workbooks. "The main objective of this program is to facilitate and encourage thought about matters of business ethics" (p. 7).

Protecting the Whistle-Blowers. Pacific Tape Library Los Angeles, n.d. 38 min.

Roundtable discussion including columnist Jack Anderson, whistle-blower Ernest Fitzgerald and others.

Steiner, John F. Ethical Principles of Business Executives. Los Angeles Area Chamber of Commerce and the Center for the Study of Business in Society, n.d. 14 min. videotape.

Twelve executives discuss the question "Do you have an ethical principle or code of ethics that you follow in making decisions in everyday business life and if so, what is it?"

The Swine Flu Caper. Washington, DC: Institute for Policy Studies, 1978. 22 min.

A documentary on Dr. Anthony Morris, a leading virologist with the National Institutes of Health and the Food and Drug Administration. He was fired after he objected to the mass inoculation program for swine flu. The program led to the deaths of approximately 100 people, and more than $2 billion in claims because of adverse reactions to the shots. It shows Dr. Morris as a whistle-blower who believes that the government employee must be responsible primarily to the public and follow his own conscience despite risks to himself.

Robert Wall: Ex-FBI Agent. Washington, DC: Institute for Policy Studies, 1971. 29 min.

Former FBI Special Agent Robert Wall describes how he spied on the Institute for Policy Studies, on black activist Stokley Carmichael, and others, and why he finally decided to leave the FBI.

Section XII

Personal Guidance and Accounts

A. Personal Guidance Books and Articles

1348. Broida, Peter B. "How to Whistle." The Government Standard, 37 (August 1979), 14.

Reviews the process of registering a complaint under the Civil Service Reform Act, which is designed to protect whistle-blowers.

1349. Chermiss, Cary. Staff Burnout: Job Stress in the Human Services. Beverly Hills, CA: Sage, 1980.

Significance of and preventive measures for job stress are analyzed.

1350. Cowle, Jerry. How to Survive Getting Fired--And Win. Chicago, IL: Follett Publishing Co., 1979.

An empathic treatment of dismissal including "the day the roof fell in," why it's better to be fired than to resign, and the new job search.

1351. Culbert, Samuel A. The Organization Trap and How to Get Out of It. New York: Basic Books, 1974.

1352. Feinman, Jeffery. The Purple Pages. New York: Hawthorn Books, 1979.

A consumer action-oriented guide to complaining and getting results including a directory of more than 1,700 government and corporate organizations.

*1353. Government Accountability Project. A Whistle-blower's Guide to the Federal Bureaucracy. Washington, DC: Institute for Policy Studies, 1977.

Gives examples of whistle-blowers who acted to gain accountability in government. Addresses the timing, method, and probability of success for whistle-blowing; how not to blow the whistle; and pathways through the bureaucracy such as agency appellate systems, the Civil Service Commission, Congress, and unions. Examines proposals to reform the Civil Service Commission as one way to protect employees.

1354. Maiken, Peter T. Ripoff: How To Spot It, How to Avoid It. Mission, KS: Andrews and McMeel, 1979.

Methods used by persons in a wide variety of occupations to "rip off" various types of victims are described.

1355. Nader, Ralph, Peter, J. Petkas, and Kate Blackwell, eds. Whistle-Blowing: The Report of the Conference on Professional Responsibility. New York: Grossman Publishers, 1972. See item 1382.

1356. Maurer, Harry. Not Working: An Oral History of the Unemployed. New York: Holt, Rinehart, and Winston, 1980.

1357. Mertins, Herman, Jr., ed. Professional Standards and and Ethics: A Workbook for Public Administrators. Washington, DC: American Society for Public Administration, 1979. See item 387.

1358. Perry, Tekla. "Knowing How to Blow the Whistle." IEEE Spectrum, 18 (September 1981), 56-61. See item 469.

1359. Peskin, Dean B. Sacked: What to Do When You Lose Your Job. New York: AMACON, 1979.

    Since 10 to 12 million people lose their jobs every year, this "survival kit" provides practical advice on how to weather the initial shock, followed by the psychological preparation necessary for successful re-entry into the work force.

1360. Raven-Hansen, Peter. "Do's and Don'ts for Whistleblowers: Planning for Trouble." See item 470.

1361. Schwimmer, Lawrence D. How to Ask for A Raise Without Getting Fired: And 24 Other Assertiveness Techniques for the Office. New York: Harper and Row, 1980.

    "Whether you are a clerk or an executive, an assertive style produces greater effectiveness with your co-workers and customers. Just as important, it immeasurably increases their respect for you as a capable, assured professional" (p. 1).

1362. Sweet, Donald H. Decruitment: A Guide for Managers. Reading, MA: Addison-Wesley, 1975.

    Written for the executive as well as the personnel administrator, the individual being fired or "decruited," and the employees who remain in the organization. This book explores a wide variety of problems associated with terminating employees.

1363. Troisi, Angelo M. "Softening the Blow of 'You're Fired.'" Supervisory Management, 25 (June 1980), 14-19.

Recommendations for the manager on how to fire employees properly including a discussion of settlements and outplacement.

1364. Uris, Auren. Executive Dissent: How to Say No and Win. New York: AMACON, 1978.

Sees dissent as beneficial since it highlights organizational and individual values. Uris explores possible resolutions to protesters' concerns and offers advice to both employees and executives in the management of non-conformity.

1365. "Warning From a Whistle Blower." Planning, 47 (December 1981), 20-21.

A whistle-blower relates his personal experiences in an area-wide planning agency. He was not able to protect himself from retribution and believes it important that a whistle-blower know what to expect.

Section XII

Personal Guidance and Accounts

B. Personal Accounts

291

1366. Agee, Philip. Inside the Company: CIA Diary. San Francisco, CA: Straight Arrow, 1975.

1367. Boulton, David. The Grease Machine: The Inside Story of Lockheed and Dollar Diplomacy. New York: Harper and Row, 1979.

Documents the Lockheed bribery scandal from 1970 to 1975.

1368. Boyd, James and Jack Anderson. Confessions of a Muckracker: The Inside Story of Life in Washington during the Truman, Eisenhower, Kennedy, and Johnson Years. New York: Random House, 1979.

1369. Boyd, James. "The Indispensable Informer." Nation, 5 May 1979, p. 495.

Discusses the author's informing on Senator Thomas Dodd's illegal behavior. Boyd sees informants as necessary when organizations evade laws and defraud the public.

1370. Brown, Rhonda and Paul Matteucci. "The High Cost of Whistle-Blowing." Inquiry, 1 September 1981, pp. 14-19.

Account of a government employee who spent eight years trying to convince people that the American missile warning system is dangerously inadequate.

1371. Byrd, Carol. "Whistleblowing: The Adversary Within." The Graduate, (1982), 40-43.

Describes experiences of three whistle-blowers: Clifford Richter, a chief radiation officer at Ellis-Fischel State Cancer Hospital in Columbia, Missouri, who reported radioactive seeds erroneously left in a discharged patient; Beth Harris, a social worker in a New Jersey school, who complained about over sedation of a physically handicapped boy; and Anthony Morris who charged the swine flu vaccine program was both ineffective and dangerous. Includes comments by several researchers--DeGeorge, Elliston, James and Westin.

1372. Eddy, Paul, Elaine Potter and Bruce Page. Destination Disaster: From the Tri-Motor to the DC-10. New York: Quadrangle, 1976.

Offers a provocative look at the aviation business and its race to build the fastest and biggest airplanes at the expense of safety. Claims are documented and substantiated by case reports and statistical evidence.

1373. Fitzgerald, Ernest A. The High Priests of Waste. New York: W. W. Norton, 1972.

Autobiographical account of the man who revealed to Congress the $2 billion cost overrun on the C-5A transport plane. Well documented study of mismanagement and inefficiency in the federal bureaucracy.

1374. Gibbs, Lois. Love Canal: My Story. Albany, NY: State University of New York Press, 1982.

Lois Gibbs recounts from the early days to the present her involvement in the Love Canal crisis. The Love Canal story -- its history, effects, impact on human lives, and her struggle for a remedy are discussed.

1375. Green, Robert. The Sting Man: Inside ABSCAM. New York: E. P. Dutton, 1981.

An investigative reporter discusses how a confidence man and the Federal Bureau of Investigation set up a sting operation that unexpectedly penetrated the underworld of government.

1376. Gulley, Bill with Mary Ellen Reese. Breaking Cover. New York: Simon and Schuster, 1980.

Described as an "alumnus whistle-blower," a retired military officer reveals the "secretive White House" as it existed during the Johnson, Nixon, Ford, and Carter administrations.

1377. Hayes, John. The Lonely Fighter. New York: Lyle Stuart Publishers, 1978.

Account of Andrew Susce, an Internal Revenue Service (IRS) employee. In 1944, he investigated a Mafia boss who defrauded the government of millions in tax money. The IRS ignored Susce's report and fired him when he went public. The federal government has continually refused to deal with the case.

1378. Herbert, Anthony B. with James T. Wooten. <u>Soldier</u>. New York: Holt, Rinehart, and Winston, 1973.

An autobiographical account of a highly decorated military officer who reported Vietnam atrocities and was subsequently relieved of his command.

1379. Levine, Adeline G. <u>Love Canal: Science, Politics, and People</u>. Lexington, MA: Lexington Books, 1982.

A sociological study which chronicles the efforts of citizens living in the Love Canal area of Niagara Falls to secure the resources they needed to escape their homes poisoned by chemical wastes.

1380. Maas, Peter. <u>Serpico</u>. New York: Basic Books, 1973.

Describes what happened to Serpico, the New York City patrolman who blew the whistle on the City Police Department.

*1381. Mitchell, Greg. <u>Truth ... And Consequences: Seven Who Would Not Be Silenced</u>. New York: Dembner Books, 1982.

Based on numerous interviews, Mitchell describes the fate of seven whistleblowers: Maude DeVictor, the Veterans Administration counselor who uncovered the effects of Agent Orange; Jim Maslinski, an inmate who testified against jailhouse rapists; Michael Bayliss, an engineer who revealed the dangerous conditions at Hooker Chemical: Sheriff Ron Donell, who went undercover to gather evidence against a corrupt prosecutor; Lois Gibbs, a housewife who led the residents of Love Canal in their fight for evacuation; Bill Kuykendall, a control room operator trainee who exposed safety and security hazards at a nuclear power plant; and Hugh Kaufman, a middle-level official in Washington who helped force the federal government to finally defuse "toxic time bombs."

*1382. Nader, Ralph, Peter J. Petkas, and Kate Blackwell, eds. <u>Whistle-Blowing: The Report of the Conference on Professional Responsibility</u>. New York: Grossman Publishers, 1972.

Divided into four main sections, this book begins with four keynote speeches by Ralph Nader, Senator William Proxmire, Robert Townsend, and Arthur Miller. Then, presentations by eleven whistle-blowers, which describe the nature of their actions, the pressures that led them to act, and the retaliation most of them faced, form the basis for the second part of this book. Parts III and IV evolved out of their suggestions, as well as from the conference and further research into whistle-blowing.

1383. Nathan, Robert S. "Corporate Criminals Who Kept Their Jobs." Business and Social Review, 33 (Spring 1980), 19-21.

1384. Paigen, Beverly. "Controversy at Love Canal." The Hastings Center Report, 12 (June 1982), 29-37.

Reviews the history and elements of controversy at Love Canal, and identifies six factors that impeded a swift resolution. Concludes with several steps that can be taken by communities and scientists to ease future controversies.

1385. Powers, Thomas. "The Good Soldier System." Commonwealth, 9 May 1980, p. 261.

1386. Proxmire, William. The Fleecing of America. Boston: Houghton-Mifflin Co., 1980. See item 275.

1387. Rashke, Richard. The Killing of Karen Silkwood: The Story Behind the Kerr-McGee Plutonium Case. Boston, MA: Houghton Mifflin Co., 1981.

Report of an inconclusive investigation into the mysterious death of Ms. Silkwood, the would-be whistle-blower.

1388. "The San Jose Three." Time, 16 February 1976, p. 78.

1389. Snepp, Frank. Decent Interval: An Insider's Account of Saigon's Indecent End Told by the CIA's Chief Strategy Analyst in Vietnam. New York: Random House, 1977.

Taking care not to use information that would endanger national security, Snapp revealed the cover-up by the Central Intelligence Agency (CIA) and the State Department during America's final days in Vietnam. This book sparked a secrecy suit.

1390. Stern, Gerald. <u>The Buffalo Creek Disaster</u>. New York: Random House, 1977.

An account of one of the largest lawsuits in American history written by the lawyer who represented the survivors of the devastating 1972 coal mine disaster.

1391. Vandivier, Kermit. "The Aircraft Brake Scandal." <u>Harpers' Magazine</u>, April 1972, pp. 45-52.

Personal account of whistle-blowing by an employee of the B.F. Goodrich Company who blew the whistle on the intentional sale of faulty and dangerous aircraft brakes.

*1392. Westin, Alan F., ed. <u>Whistle-Blowing! Loyalty and Dissent in the Corporation</u>. New York: McGraw-Hill, 1980.

Ten autobiographical accounts of whistle-blowers. Westin provides an introduction explaining why whistle-blowing is on the rise and a conclusion recommending what can and should be done.

1393. Winter-Berger, Robert N. <u>The Washington Pay-off</u>. New York: Dell, 1972.

An insider's view of corruption in government. Discusses the wheeling and dealing, influence peddling, kickbacks, pay-offs, and bribes as seen first-hand during Winter-Berger's time as a lobbyist (1964-1969).

Section XIII

Organizations and Telephone Hotline Numbers

Organizations

American Assembly of Collegiate Schools of
Business
760 Office Parkway, Suite 50
St. Louis, MO 63141
(314) 872-8484

American Association for the Advancement of
Science
Committee on Scientific Freedom and Responsibility
1515 Massachusetts Avenue, N.W.
Washington, DC 20005
(202) 467-4400

American Civil Liberties Union
22 E. 40th Street
New York, NY 10016
(212) 725-1222

American Ethical Union
2 West 64th Street
New York, NY 10023
(212) 873-6500

American Federation of Government Employees
1325 Massachusetts Avenue, N.W.
Washington, DC 20005
(202) 737-8700

American Society for Public Administration
1120 G. Street, N.W.
Washington, DC 20005
(202) 393-7878

Bentley College
Center for Business Ethics
Waltham, MA 02154
(617) 891-2000

Center for Science in the Public Interest
1757 S Street, N.W.
Washington, DC 20009
(202) 322-4250

Clearinghouse on Fraud and Abuse of Public Funds
National Criminal Justice Reference Service
Box 6000
Rockville, MD 20850
(301) 251-5500

Dobrovir, Oakes, and Gerhardt
2005 L Street, N.W.
Washington, DC 20036
(202) 785-8919

Duke University
Institute of Policy Sciences and Public Affairs
4875 Duke Station
Durham, NC 27706
(919) 684-6612

Ethics Resource Center
1730 Rhode Island Avenue, N.W.
Washington, DC 20036
(202) 223-3411

The Federal Times
475 School Street, S.W.
Washington, DC
(202) 554-7131

Fund for Constitutional Government
121 Constitution Avenue, N.W.
Washington, DC 20002
(202) 544-5189

General Accounting Office
Federal Personnel and Compensation Division
441 G Street, N.W.
Washington, DC 20548
(202) 234-9382

Government Accountability Project
1901 Q Street, N.W.
Washington, DC   20009
(202) 234-9382

The Hastings Center
360 Broadway
Hastings-on-Hudson, NY   10706
(914) 478-0500

Illinois Institute of Technology
Center for the Study of Ethics in the Professions
Chicago, IL   60616
(312) 567-3017

National Academy of Public Administration
1120 G. Street, N.W.
Washington, DC   20005
(202) 393-7878

National Association of Schools of Public Affairs
    and Administration
1120 G. Street, N.W.
Washington, DC   20005
(202) 393-7878

National Municipal League
47 East 68th Street
New York, NY   10021

National Referral Center
Library of Congress
Washington, DC   20540
(202) 287-5670

National Science Foundation
Office of Science and Society
1800 G Street, N.W.
Washington, DC   20550
(202) 655-4000

Office of Government Ethics
1120 Vermont Avenue, N.W.
Washington, DC 20419
(202) 653-9000

Office of the Special Counsel
1120 Vermont Avenue, N.W.
Washington, DC 20419
(202) 653-9000

Program in Business Ethics
University of Southern California
University Park
Los Angeles, CA 90007
(213) 743-5578

Public Citizen, Inc.
c/o Ralph Nader
P.O. Box 19404
Washington, DC 20036
(202) 293-9142

Society for Business Ethics
Loyola University
Chicago, IL 60611
(312) 670-3140

Society for the Study of Professional Ethics
Rhode Island College
Providence, RI 02808
(401) 456-8000

Society for Values in Higher Education
University of Delaware
Newark, DE
(302) 738-8146

Task Force for the Prevention of Fraud
General Accounting Office
441 G Street, N.W.
Washington, DC 20548
(202) 633-6987

U.S. House of Representatives
Post Office and Civil Service Committee
The Capitol
Washington, DC   20515
(202) 224-4054

U.S. Senate
Committee on Governmental Affairs
The Capital
Washington, DC   20510
(202) 224-4751

Union of Concerned Scientists
1208 Massachusetts Avenue
Cambridge, MA   02138
(617) 547-5552

Washington Ethical Society
7750 16th Street, N.W.
Washington, DC   20012
(202) 882-6650

The Washington Post
ATTN: Mike Causey
1150 15th Street, N.W.
Washington, DC   10071
(202) 223-6000

Telephone Hotline Numbers

Government Wide

General Accounting Office - (800) 424-5454
In Washington, DC call   633-6987

Federal Information Center - (202) 755-8660

Agencies

ACTION - (202) 254-7523; (800) 424-8580

Agriculture - (202) 546-1441; (800) 424-9098

Coast Guard - (202) 275-7252; (800) 424-3912

Commerce - (202) 724-3519; (800) 424-5197

Community Services Administration - (202) 643-5430

Consumer Product Safety Hotline - (800) 538-2666

Department of Labor - (202) 633-7374

Department of Defense - (800) 424-9098

Energy - (202) 252-4073; (800) 424-9246

Environmental Protection Agency - (202) 245-3090

Federal Election Bureau - (202) 523-4066; (800) 424-9530

General Services Administration - (202) 566-1780; (800) 424-5210

Health and Human Services - (202) 472-4222

Housing and Urban Development - (202) 472-4200; (800) 424-8590

Interior - (202) 343-2424; (800) 424-5081

Interstate Commerce Commission - (202) 275-7252; (800) 424-9530

National Aeronautics and Space Administration (NASA) - (202) 755-8304

Small Business Administration - (202) 635-7557

Transportation - (202) 426-0123; (800) 424-9393

Veterans Administration - (202) 389-5394

XIV. Author Index

Behrman, J. 64, 731

Bell, C. 490a

Ben-David, J. 1299

Ben-Horin, D. 879

Benjamin, J. 658

Benjamin, M. 732

Bennetts, L. 880

Benson, G. 309, 435

Bequai, A. 67, 312

Berg, I. 65

Berg. L. 310

Berebeim, R. 66

Bernstein, M. 311

Blades, L. 4, 223, 1226

Blumberg, P. 5, 6, 1227

Blumenthal, R. 883

Blumenthal, W. 68

Bogen, K. 7, 448, 449

Boffey, P. 491, 884

Bok, S. 224, 225, 491a,
492, 703, 704

Boland, R. 492a, 492b,
810

Boling, T. 69, 70, 313,
314, 811

Bollens, J. 315

Boulton, D. 1367

Bowie, N. 316, 705,
733

Bowman, J. 71, 72, 228,
317, 318, 319, 320

Bossy, M. 659

Boyan, A. 227

Boyd, J. 436, 885,
1368, 1369

Boyle, C. 660

Bradley, D. 812

Bradshaw, T. 73

Branch, T. 229

Bredemier, K. 886

Brenner, S. 74

Brill, S. 603, 887

Brodt, B. 889

Broida, P. 1348

Brooks, H. 493

Brooks, R. 437

Broome, T. 494

Brown, D. 813

Brown, J. 661

Brown, R. 1370

Burke, M. 604

Burck, G. 75

310

Ford, D. 527

Foster, G. 360

Foundation of the South-
west Graduate School of
Banking 117

Fox, C. 458, 953

Frankel, C. 613

Frankel, G. 954

Franklin, B. 955

Frederick, W. 118

Freedman, B. 753

Freedman, M. 614

Freedman, R. 1318

French, P. 371a, 754,
755, 756

Fried, C. 615

Friedlander, G. 459

Friedrich, C. 362

Frome, M. 241

Fulmer, R. 119

Gaines, R. 957

Galbraith, J. 817

Garde, B. 958

Gardiner, J. 120

Garson, G. 121, 818

Gavin, J. 122

Geis, G. 123

Geraghty, J. 616

Gerth, J. 959

Gest, T. 242, 960

Gewirth, A. 757

Gibb, F. 961, 962

Gibbs, L. 1374

Glaser, V. 963

Glass, H. 124

Gillespie, N. 125

Gold, B. 965

Goldman, A. 758, 759

Goldman, I. 126, 778

Goldstein, T. 966

Golembiewski, R. 363

Goodman, C. 127

Gordon, M. 128, 968

Gorovitz, S. 667

Gothie, D. 1319

Government Accountabil-
ity Project 243, 244,
245, 1353

Grady, J. 760

Graham, G. 364

Graham, J. 249a

318